T0340044

A ZEN LIFE

A Zen Life:
D. T. Suzuki
Remembered

photographs by Francis Haar
edited by Masao Abe

WEATHERHILL · *Boulder*

Weatherhill
An imprint of Shambhala Publications, Inc.
2129 13th Street
Boulder, Colorado 80302
www.shambhala.com

© 1986

The calligraphy appearing on the title page, representing the Chinese character for *satori*, is by Tsunemori Kaminoda.

Printed in the United States of America

Shambhala Publications makes every effort to print on acid-free, recycled paper.

Weatherhill is distributed worldwide by Penguin Random House, Inc., and its subsidiaries.

Library of Congress Cataloging-in-Publication Data
A Zen life. / Bibliography
p.
Includes index.
1. Suzuki, Daisetz Teitaro, 1870–1966.   2. Zen Buddhists—Japan—Biography. / 3. Scholars, Buddhist—Japan—Biography.
I. Haar, Francis, 1908–1997. / II. Abe, Masao, 1915–2006
BQ 988. U887Z46   1986
294.3'927'0924   [B]   86-11132 /

ISBN 978-0-8348-0213-1

BVG 01

Contents

v

Part Three

Francis Haar's photographs
follow pages 12 and 172.

Francis Haar

Preface

I T WAS 1939, in Paris, that I first heard the name of D.T. Suzuki
from my French and Hungarian artist friends who were interested
in Zen Buddhism. The subject intrigued me because I felt that
somehow it seemed to relate to art. The following year I moved to Japan
where I met again the French artist, Mrs. Lebovitch, whom I had known
in Paris. She had moved to Kyoto and started to practice Zen meditation
with Mrs. Ruth Sasaki, an American lady married to a Japanese Zen master. Her Japanese husband subsequently passed away and she took over
his position, becoming the first Occidental to reach the position of a Zen
Buddhist bishop. Mrs. Lebovitch recommended some books by D.T.
Suzuki for me to read. The first book I read was *Living by Zen,* which
I found fascinating but rather difficult to understand in the beginning.
Since I was living in Kamakura at that time and D.T. Suzuki lived in
Kita Kamakura, I was hoping that someday I would have a chance to
meet him in person.

My first encounter with Dr. Suzuki came about in 1950 as a result of
knowing Mr. Owen Zurhellen, who was then the American vice-consul
in Yokohama. We used to meet every Sunday at the Catholic church in
Kamakura and on the way home we used to discuss different questions.
On one of these occasions Dr. Suzuki's name came up, and I found out
he was also an admirer of Suzuki's writings. I told him I would be very
interested to meet Dr. Suzuki personally. Then one day he called and

said that he had successfully arranged an appointment for us to visit Dr. Suzuki at his residence in Kita Kamakura.

A week later, as we were walking up the old moss-covered steps to Engakuji monastery, we envisioned meeting someone with a large impressive stature. But instead we found a small, fragile man sitting and working in front of a typewriter at a low table.

He accepted us very warmly despite the fact that we could only speak in generalities about Zen. We were impressed by his patience and humility, even though he was such a renowned scholar.

Some weeks later, I called to ask if I could visit him again, this time with my camera. He generously agreed and I was able to visit him a few more times to take pictures of him. These occasions were unique experiences for me. In front of the camera most of us become self-conscious, or at least we try to present our best self. Not so Dr. Suzuki. He left me to observe him with my camera, while he continued his work, completely unaware of my presence. This was a lesson in the "ego-less" personality of Zen Buddhist teaching, and the result speaks for itself in my portrait studies.

A year later Dr. Suzuki was invited to teach some courses at Columbia University. In 1957, when I visited New York, I heard that he was lecturing there. I found out the time and went to hear one of his lectures. I was surprised to find the classroom overflowing, not even standing room left. I also noticed that in the audience there were not only students but also middle-aged specialists from other fields.

The following year I met Dr. Suzuki in Boston, where he was then teaching. After I took some pictures of him he said he wished introduce me to another Zen Buddhist scholar, Dr. Shin'ichi Hisamatsu, who was also an expert on Japanese art. When, at a later date, I visited Dr. Hisamatsu in Japan and showed him Dr. Suzuki's pictures, he picked up the one which was also my favorite and asked if he could have it. I discovered afterwards he liked it so much that he published the picture in a Japanese art magazine, along with an article about it.

My last occasion to meet Dr. Suzuki was when I was working in Chicago. Some of my friends at the time, also interested in Zen, heard that Dr. Suzuki was comming for a short visit. We called him and succeeded in inviting him to attend a private party. We were all sitting informally on the carpet in a large living room when Dr. Suzuki arrived. As I knew him personally, I greeted him first but before I could explain the reason for this get-together, he looked around and asked me, "What do all these people want from me?" "I think they want to ask you some questions about Zen," I answered. "This will be alright," he said. Then the first question was posed: "Why does the Occidental mentality emphasize the objective, while the Orientals are involved in the subjective?" His response came in the form of a question: "But is there any objective without the subjective?"

Acknowledgments

W E WOULD LIKE TO THANK *The Eastern Buddhist* for permission to reprint the following articles from *The Eastern Buddhist D.T. Suzuki Memorial Issue* 2, no. 1, (August 1967): "D.T. Suzuki: The Man and His Work" (Merton); "Memories of Dr. D.T. Suzuki" (Fromm); "In Memoriam" (Benz)—originally in German, we thank Jim King for his translation; "A Sower of Seeds" (Gundert); "Mondo: At the Death of a 'Great Death-Man'" (Hisamatsu); "The Stone Bridge of Joshu" (Kondo); "The 'Mind-less' Scholar" (Watts); and "On My First Coming to Meet Dr. D.T. Suzuki" (which Mr. DeMartino slightly revised and enlarged for this volume). We thank *The Eastern Buddhist* for permission to reproduce sections of the Chronology and Bibliography that also appeared in the same issue. "D.T. Suzuki" by Shokin Furuta is reprinted by permission of the *Japan Quarterly* 14, no. 1 (Jan.-Mar., 1967). Shunjūsha in Tokyo is gratefully acknowledged for permission to use Suzuki's "Autobiography" (translated by Mami Chida and Steve Antinoff) and "D.T. Suzuki's Position in the History of Thought (Shimomura) (translated by Jeff Shore) that both originally appeared in *Suzuki Daisetz no Hito to Gakumon* (Personality and Learning of Suzuki Daisetz) (1961), and "Remembering Dr. Daisetz Suzuki" (Nishitani) as well as "Memories of Suzuki Sensei" (Abe) that originally appeared in *Kaiso Suzuki Daisetz* (Memories of Suzuki Daisetz) (1975). Mr. Nishitani's article was also translated by Jeff Shore. Mr. Howard

Curtis translated Masao Abe's piece. We extend our thanks to Sanseido, Tokyo, for permission to use "Satori," from *Living by Zen* (1949). Professor Abe's "The Influence of D.T. Suzuki in the West" has been expanded and revised for this volume, but we thank Iwanami publishers in Tokyo for permission to use their original 1971 version *Suzuki Daisetz—Hito to Shisō* (Suzuki Daisetz—The Man and His Philosopy) for the translation by Howard Curtis that appears here. "Early Memories" by Suzuki originally appeared in *The Field of Zen* (1969) and we thank the Buddhist Society, London, for its use. "D.T. Suzuki and Zen Buddhism in Europe" (Humphreys) appears courtesy of Suzuki Daisetz Hakushi Shōju Kinen Kai (The Publication Committee to Honor D.T. Suzuki and his Life Achievement); it appeared in their publication *Bukkyō to Bunka* (Buddhism and Culture). And finally, many thanks to Mrs. Mihoko Bekku, formerly Miss Okamura, for permitting us to translate her articles that appear in Chapter 15. "Wondrous Activity," parts 1 and 2, originally appeared in *Tosho* (Books) in 1971, and part 3 appeared in *Daihōren* (The Great Dharma Wheel) in September, 1966 (both publications edited by *The Eastern Buddhist*). Part 4, "Daisetz the Death Man" originally appeared in *Suzuki Daisetz—Hito to Shisō*. Our thanks for the translation go to Mr. Jeffrey Hunter.

The articles in this book that are reprinted from other sources have been edited for consistency of style only. Except for the titles of published works, the Pinyin system of Chinese romanization is preferred throughout. The Wade-Giles system of romanization appears on its first occurrence in each chapter only to indicate that it was used in the original publication.

Masao Abe

Editor's Introduction

D R. D. T. SUZUKI is widely known as an exponent of Zen in the West. Quite often, in Westerners' minds, Zen and Suzuki are associated with one another. It is undeniable that almost single-handedly D.T. Suzuki introduced Zen to the West and was responsible for making it penetrate into various aspects of Western learning and culture. The breadth of his unusual achievement, however, is not limited just by the introduction of Zen to the West. He also, for example, promoted studies of Mahayana Buddhism (including the *Lankavatara* and *Gandavyuha* sutras, and Pure Land Buddhism), Chinese thought, Japanese culture, and the comparative study of Buddhism and Christian mysticism. His studies may not be strictly objective and historical in the sheer academic sense, but are full of profound insights and vivid interpretations. Until now, no Western or Japanese scholar has attempted to make a comprehensive and integrated study of the whole body of Suzuki's writings—comprising nearly ninety titles in Japanese and over thrity volumes in English—which he published during his long and productive lifetime spanning ninety-five years. The deepest significance of Suzuki's achievement, however, does not lie in his extensive research into Buddhist-related fields and the resultant voluminous publications. It lies precisely in the fact that his research, writing, and lecturing sparked a radical change in Western ways of thinking, and promoted a fresh reevaluation of traditional spirituality for his fellow Japanese country-men.

Throughout his life, especially in his mature period, Suzuki was ex-plicitly critical of the dualistic, conceptual, and analytical way of thinking so predominant in the Western tradition, and he repeatedly emphasized the importance of returning to the basic experience prior to the dichot-omy between subject and object, being and nonbeing, life and death, good and evil—in order to awaken to the most concrete basis for life and the world. Suzuki tirelessly expounded Zen simply because he be-lieved that Zen is nothing but this basic nondualistic Awakening. In 1959, in *Zen and Japanese Culture* he wrote:

> If the Greeks taught us how to reason, and Christianity what to believe, it is Zen that teaches us to go beyond logic and not to tarry even when we come up against "the things which are not seen." For the Zen point of view is to find an absolute point where no dualism in whatever form obtains. Logic starts from the division of subject and object, and belief distinguishes between what is seen and what is not seen. The Western mode of thinking can never do away with this eternal dilemma, this or that, reason or faith, man or God, etc. With Zen, all these are swept aside as something veiling our insight into the nature of life and reality. [pp. 360–61]

Thus, Suzuki repeatedly emphasized the necessity of awakening to the non-discriminative wisdom or *prajna*-intuition which is realized prior to the separation between self and other, subject and object, man and God. To Suzuki, however, this *prajna*-intuition does not exclude dis-crimination or analytic thinking. Instead, it gives the proper foundation to them and makes them alive and energetic. He thus emphasizes the "discrimination of non-discrimination" as the most concrete funda-mental wisdom in which knowing, being, and loving (compassion) are united.

This is a challenge to the Western way of thinking, a challenge which Suzuki put forth throughout his many writings. His basic intention, however, is not to exalt an Oriental principle over an Occidental one, but to advance a nondualistic, intuitive awakening as the most funda-mental realization for human existence, East and West. In this way, he also intended to free the genuine spirit of Zen from the stereotyped interpretation prevailing in the traditional forms of Zen. Suzuki was therefore beyond "Zen" and tried to open the most authentic way of thinking and living for the future of humanity.

A few years ago, Francis Haar, a Hungarian-born photographer, asked me to collaborate with him to publish his photographs of D.T. Suzuki in book form. He had lived in Japan for almost twenty years and was personally acquainted with Suzuki during his last several years. Haar showed me about ten photographs of Suzuki that he had taken in Kamakura, Tokyo, New York, and Boston. I found them to be excellent, touching photographs, which vividly expressed the Zen personality of Suzuki. The number of photographs were too few, however, to be published by themselves as a book, so, in combination with Haar's photographs we decided to publish a collection of essays and memories of D.T. Suzuki, written by intimate friends and students of Suzuki and some essays by scholars who are especially interested in Suzuki's works. As the editor, I invited a number of people to contribute an essay or reminiscences, and also collected several essays from Japanese publications which are included here in translation. *The Eastern Buddhist*, a journal founded in 1921 by D.T. Suzuki and his wife Beatrice Lane Suzuki, published a special issue on D.T. Suzuki in 1967, shortly after Suzuki died. It included invaluable contributions from an international array of Suzuki's colleagues and students, but the circulation of this precious historical memorial issue was limited to those scholars familiar with the journal. Thus, with the permission of *The Eastern Buddhist* and the original authors, I have included here eight essays and reminiscences from this memorial issue of *The Eastern Buddhist* (volume 2, number 1, new series) because they deserve the wider audience I hope the present volume will afford them.

The book is divided into four parts. Part One presents the personality of D.T. Suzuki. Chapter 1, "Early Memories," was originally written for the fortieth anniversary of the Buddhist Society in London. It emphasizes Suzuki's personal struggle in the early years of his religious quest, culminating in his spiritual breakthrough at Engakuji temple compound in the winter of 1899, just before he embarked on his trip to the United States. In contrast, chapter 2, "An Autobiographical Account," covers almost the whole span of his life until the date of the interview (1961), which served as the occasion for this piece; it is more factual, and gives more information concerning Suzuki's activities and aquaintances. As Suzuki himself states in the beginning of chapter 2, he had "an aversion" to anything like an autobiography and as a rule never offered "anything like an autobiography or a reminiscence." Consequently, these two pieces provide rare glimpses into Suzuki's life and times, and serve to complement each other wonderfully. Part One also includes a chapter entitled "Satori" from Suzuki's book *Living by Zen.* This book was written in English in 1948, three years after the end of the Pacific War, but was published in Japan. In the Preface Suzuki wrote:

> Since the end of the War the author had frequent occasion to meet several young American and English inquirers concerning the teaching of Zen. Their approach was more or less characterized by the modern scientific spirit. This made him go over anew the ground which he had been accustomed to cover in a rather old-fashioned traditional way. Besides, he has come to feel the necessity of revising to a certain extent his understanding of Zen in accordance with his later experience and reflections. The present booklet is a partial result of these reconsiderations.

Satori is one of the most favored and important themes of Zen for Suzuki. I included "Satori" in this commemorative volume because it expresses Suzuki's newly interpreted view of satori shortly after the end of the Pacific War. Given a limited circulation when it was published, I include it here because I believe that it will be of great significance to modern readers.

I selected essays which mainly discuss Suzuki's works and significance in Part Two, and selections in Part Three represent personal memories and reminiscences of Suzuki from among the many people who knew him. Part IV includes a chronology of significant events in Suzuki's life and a bibliography of his works intended to help guide the reader toward a further understanding of Suzuki.

The present volume is not by any means intended to be a comprehensive and systematic study of D.T. Suzuki in an academic sense—an urgently necessary project—but rather a handy, readable document which conveys the personal nature of this great man. We hope it will afford readers the opportunity to reconsider the broad significance of Suzuki's works—especially in terms of the intellectual history of the East and the West. In this respect, I believe Francis Haar's photographs provide a unique and insightful compliment to the text—a visual encounter with this special personality, Daisetz T. Suzuki, who throughout his life so ardently emphasized going beyond letters and words.

PART ONE

1

Early Memories

MY FAMILY HAD BEEN PHYSICIANS for several generations in the town of Kanazawa.[1] My father, grandfather and great-grand-father were all physicians and strangely enough they all died young. Of course, it was no very unusual thing in those days to die young, but in the case of a physician under the old feudal regime it was doubly unfortunate, since the stipend his family received from his feudal lord was cut down. So my family, although of samurai rank, was already poverty-stricken by my father's time, and after his death when I was only six years old we became even poorer owing to all the economic troubles which befell the samurai class after the abolition of the feudal system.

To lose one's father in those days was perhaps an even greater loss than it is now, for so much depended on him as head of the family—all the important steps in life such as education and finding a position in life afterwards. All this I lost, and by the time I was about seventeen or eighteen these misfortunes made me start thinking about my karma. Why should I have these disadvantages at the very start of life?

My thoughts then started to turn to philosophy and religion, and as my family belonged to the Rinzai sect of Zen it was natural that I should look to Zen for some of the answers to my problems. I remember going to the Rinzai temple where my family was registered—it was the smallest Rinzai temple in Kanazawa—and asking the priest there about Zen.

Like many Zen priests in country temples in those days he did not know very much. In fact he had never even read the *Hekigan Roku*,[2] so that my interview with him did not last very long.

I often used to discuss questions of philosophy and religion with the other students of my own age, and I remember that something which always puzzled me was, what makes it rain? Why was it necessary for rain to fall? When I look back now I realize that there may have been in my mind something similar to the Christian teaching of the rain falling on both the just and the unjust. Incidentally, I had several contacts with Christian missionaries about this time. When I was about fifteen there was a missionary from the Orthodox Church[3] in Kanazawa, and I remember him giving me a copy of the Japanese translation of Genesis in a Japanese-style binding, and telling me to take it home and read it. I read it, but it seemed to make no sense at all. In the beginning there was God—but why should God create the world? That puzzled me very much.

The same year a friend of mine was converted to Protestant Christianity. He wanted me to become a Christian, too, and was urging me to be baptized, but I told him that I could not be baptized unless I was convinced of the truth of Christianity, and I was still puzzled by the question of why God should have created the world. I went to another missionary, a Protestant this time, and asked him this same question. He told me that everything must have a creator in order to come into existence, and hence the world must have a creator, too. Then who created God, I asked. God created himself, he replied. He is not a creature. This was not at all a satisfactory answer to me, and always this same question has remained a stumbling block to my becoming a Christian.

I remember, too, that this missionary always carried a big bunch of keys about with him, and this struck me as very strange. In those days no one in Japan ever locked anything, so when I saw him with so many keys I wondered why he needed to lock so many things.

About that time a new teacher came to my school. He taught mathematics, and taught it so well that I began to take an interest in the subject under his guidance. But he was also very interested in Zen, and had been a pupil of Kosen Roshi,[4] one of the great Zen masters of that time. He did his best to make his students interested in Zen, too, and distributed printed copies of Hakuin Zenshi's work *Orategama*[5] among them. I could not understand much of it, but somehow it interested me so much that in order to find out more about it I decided to visit a Zen master, Setsumon Roshi, who lived in a temple called Kokutaiji near Takaoka in the province of Etchu. I set off from home not really knowing how to get to the temple at all, except that it was somewhere near Takaoka. I remember traveling in an old horse-drawn omnibus, only big enough to hold five or six people, over the Kurikara Pass through the mountains. Both the road and the carriage were terrible, and my head was always bumping against the ceiling. From Takaoka I suppose I must have walked the rest of the way to the temple.

I arrived without any introduction, but the monks were quite willing to take me in. They told me the *roshi*[6] was away, but that I could do *zazen* in a room in the temple if I liked. They told me how to sit and how to breathe and then left me alone in a little room telling me to go on like that. After a day or two of this the *roshi* came back and I was taken to see him. Of course at that time I really knew nothing of Zen and had no idea of the correct etiquette in *sanzen*. I was just told to come and see the *roshi*, so I went, holding my copy of the *Orategama*.

Most of the *Orategama* is written in fairly easy language, but there are some difficult Zen terms in it which I could not understand, so I asked the *roshi* the meaning of these words. He turned on me angrily and said, "Why do you ask me a stupid question like that?" I was sent back to my room without any instruction and told simply to go on sitting cross-legged. I was left quite alone. No one told me anything. Even the monks who brought me my meals never spoke to me. It was the first time I had ever been away from home and soon I grew very lonely and home-sick, and missed my mother very much. So after four or five days I left the temple and went back to my mother again. I remember nothing about my leave-taking with the *roshi*, but I do remember how glad I was to be home again. A most ignoble retreat.

Then I started teaching English in a little village called Takojima on the Noto peninsula—that peninsula protruding into the Japan Sea. There was a Shin temple there with a learned priest who showed me a text-book of the Yuishiki school called *Hyappo Mondo*. "Questions and Answers about the Hundred Dharmas." But it was so remote and ab-struse that, though I was eager to learn, I could not understand it at all well.

Then I got another position, teaching in Mikawa, a town about five *ri* (fifteen miles) from our home in Kanazawa. Again I missed my mother very much and every weekend I used to walk all the way back to see her. It took about five hours and it meant my leaving the house at about 1 A.M. on Monday morning in order to be at the school on time. But I always stayed at home until the last minute as I wanted to see my mother as much as possible.

I might add, by the way, that the English I taught in those days was very strange—so strange that later when I first went to America nobody understood anything I said. We always translated everything absolutely literally, and I remember being very puzzled by the way one says in English "a dog *has* four legs," "a cat *has* a tail." In Japanese the verb to have is not used in this way. If you said "I *have* two hands" it would sound as though you were holding two extra hands in your own. Sometime afterwards I developed the idea that this stress in Western thought on possession means a stress on power, dualism, rivalry which is lacking in Eastern thought.

During the six months I spent in Mikawa my Zen study stopped. But then I moved to Kobe, where my brother was working as a lawyer, and soon afterwards he sent me to Tokyo to study, with an allowance of six yen a month. In those days a student's board and lodging for a month cost about three yen fifty sen. The university I chose to study at was Waseda, but one of the first things I did on arriving in Tokyo was to walk down to Kamakura to study Zen under Kosen Roshi, who was Abbot of Engakuji at that time. I remember that I walked all the way from Tokyo to Kamakura, leaving Tokyo in the evening and arriving in Kamakura early the next morning.[7]

The *shika* monk, the guestmaster, took me to have my first introduction to the *roshi* with ten sen "incense money" wrapped in paper and offered to him on a tray. The guestmaster impressed me very much. He looked just like the pictures of Daruma[8] I had seen, and had very much a Zen air. The *roshi* was seventy-six years old when I first met him. He was a very big man, both in stature and personality, but owing to a recent stroke he had difficulty in walking. He asked me where I came from, and when I told him that I was born in Kanazawa he was pleased and encouraged me to go on with my Zen practice. This was probably because people from the Hokuriku district around Kanazawa were supposed to be particularly patient and steady.

The second time I met him, in a special interview, he gave me the koan[9] *Sekishu*, "the sound of one hand." I was not at all prepared to receive a koan at that time. In fact as regards Zen my mind was like a piece of blank paper. Anything could be written on it. Each time I went to *sanzen* he just put out his left hand toward me without speaking, which puzzled me very much. I remember trying to find reasonable answers to the koan of the sound of one hand, but all these Kosen Roshi naturally rejected, and after going to *sanzen* a few times I got into a kind of blind alley.

One interview with him impressed me particularly. He was having breakfast on a veranda overlooking a pond, sitting at a table on a rather rough little chair and eating rice gruel which he kept ladling out of an earthenware pot into his bowl. After I had made my three bows to him he told me to sit opposite him on another chair. I remember nothing that was said at that time, but every movement he made—the way he motioned me to sit on the chair, and the way he helped himself to the rice gruel from the pot—struck me with great force. Yes, that is exactly the way a Zen monk must behave, I thought. Everything about him had a directness and simplicity and sincerity and, of course, something more which cannot be specifically described.

The first time I attended his *teisho* lecture was also unforgettable. It was a solemn business, starting with the monks reciting the *Heart Sutra* and Muso Kokushi's last words[10]—"I have three kinds of disciples" and so on—while the *roshi* prostrated himself in front of the statue of the Buddha, and then got up on his chair facing the altar, as though he were addressing the Buddha himself rather than the audience. His attendant brought him the reading stand, and by the time the chanting was finished he was about ready to start his lecture.

It was on the forty-second chapter of the *Hekigan Roku*, the one where Hokoji visits Yakusan, and after the interview Yakusan tells ten monks to see him off down the mountain to the temple gate. On the way the following conversation takes place: "Fine snow falling flake by flake. Each flake falls in its own proper place."

This struck me as a strange subject for Zen monks to talk about, but the *roshi* just read the passage without a word of explanation, reading as though he were entranced and absorbed by the words of the text. I was so impressed by this reading, even though I did not understand a word, that I can still see him sitting in his chair with the text in front of him reading "Fine snow falling flake by flake." All this happened in 1891, when he was seventy-six and I was twenty-one.

I remember that year, too, attending the ceremony of Toji at the winter solstice, when the monks all pound rice to make rice cakes and have a general carousal which goes on all night. The first of these rice cakes was always offered to the Buddha, and the second to the *roshi*. Kosen Roshi was very fond of rice cakes dipped in grated *daikon*[11] sauce, and in fact he would eat any amount of them. On that occasion he demanded a second helping, which his attendant monk refused to give him, saying that it was not good for him to eat so much. The *roshi* replied, "I shall be quite all right if I take some digestive medicine."

On January 16 of the following year, 1892, the *roshi* suddenly died and, as it happened, I was present at his death. I was in the anteroom next door to his with his attendant monks, when suddenly we heard the sound of something heavy falling in the *roshi's* room. The attendant monk rushed in and found him lying unconscious on the floor. Apparently just as he was coming out of the washroom he had a stroke, fell and hit his head on the chest of drawers. That large body falling on the floor made a big noise. A physician was immediately summoned, but when he arrived and felt the *roshi's* pulse he said it was too late. The *roshi* was already dead.

Kosen Roshi's successor as Abbot of Engakuji was Shaku Soen.[12] At the time when Kosen Roshi died he had just come back from a visit to Ceylon to study Theravada Buddhism and was already a rising personality. He was not only very brilliant intellectually, but had also received his *inka-shomei*, or certificate to become a *roshi*, while he was still quite young—an unusual thing in those days when it took about fifteen years to reach so advanced a stage. After receiving his *inka* he went to Keio University to study Western subjects, which was again an unusual thing for a Zen priest to do. Many people criticized him for this step, including Kosen Roshi, who told him that Western studies would be of no use to him at all. But Shaku Soen never took any notice of other people's criticisms, and just went on in his own way. So altogether he was a remarkable person, with rather unconventional tendencies.

At Kosen Roshi's funeral he was the chief mourner and performed all the ceremonies, and in the spring of 1892 he was installed as the new abbot and I started to go to *sanzen* with him.

He changed my koan to *mu*, as I was not getting on very well with 'the sound of one hand,' and he thought I might have my *kensho* quicker and earlier with *mu*. He gave me no help at all with the koan, and after a few *sanzen* with him I had nothing to say.

There followed for me four years of struggle, a struggle mental, physical, moral, and intellectual. I felt it must be ultimately quite simple to understand *mu*, but how was I to take hold of this simple thing? It might be in a book, so I read all the books on Zen that I could lay my hands on. The temple where I was living at the time, Butsunichi, had a shrine attached to it dedicated to Hojo Tokimune,[13] and in a room in that shrine all the books and documents belonging to the temple were kept. During the summer I spent nearly all my time in that room reading all the books I could find. My knowledge of Chinese was still limited, so many of the texts I could not understand, but I did my best to find out everything I could about *mu* intellectually.

One of the books which interested me particularly was the *Zenkan Sakushin*, "Whips to drive you through the Zen barrier," compiled by a Chinese master of the Ming dynasty called Shuko. It was a collection of writings on Zen discipline and of advice given by various masters on how to deal with the koan. One of the examples I found in this book I thought I must try to follow. It said, "When you have enough faith, then you have enough doubt. And when you have enough doubt, then you have enough satori. All the knowledge and experience and wonderful phrases and feelings of pride which you accumulated before your study of Zen—all these things you must throw out. Pour all your mental force on to solving the koan. Sit up straight regardless of day and night, concentrating your mind on the koan. When you have been doing this for some time you will find yourself in timelessness and spacelessness like a dead man. When you reach that state something starts up within yourself and suddenly it is as though your skull were broken in pieces. The experience that you gain then has not come from outside, but from within yourself."

Then in the way of moral effort I used to spend many nights in a cave at the back of the Shariden building[14] where the Buddha's tooth is enshrined. But there was always a weakness of willpower in me, so that often I failed to sit up all night in the cave, finding some excuse to leave, such as the mosquitoes.

I was busy during these four years with various writings, including translating Dr. Carus's *Gospel of Buddha* into Japanese, but all the time the koan was worrying at the back of my mind. It was, without any doubt, my chief preoccupation and I remember sitting in a field leaning against a rice stack and thinking that if I could not understand *mu* life had no meaning, for me. Nishida Kitaro[15] wrote somewhere in his diary that I often talked about committing suicide at this period, though I have no recollection of doing so myself. After finding that I had nothing more to say about *mu* I stopped going to *sanzen* with Shaku Soen, except for the *sosan* or compulsory *sanzen* during a *sesshin*.[16] And then all that usually happened was that the *roshi* hit me.

It often happens that some kind of crisis is necessary in one's life to make one put forth all one's strength in solving the koan. This is well illustrated by a story in the book *Keikyoku Soden*, "Stories of Brambles and Thistles," compiled by one of Hakuin Zenshi's disciples, telling of various prickly experiences in practicing Zen.

A monk came from Okinawa to study Zen under Suio, one of Hakuin's great disciples and a rough and strong-minded fellow. It was he who taught Hakuin how to paint. The monk stayed with Suio for three years working on the koan of the sound of one hand. Eventually, when the time for him to go back to Okinawa was fast approaching and he had still not solved his koan, he got very distressed and came to Suio in tears. The master consoled him saying, "Don't worry. Postpone your departure for another week and go on sitting with all your might." Seven days passed, but still the koan remained unsolved. Again the monk came to Suio, who counseled him to postpone his departure for yet another week. When that week was up and he still had not solved the koan, the master said, "There are many ancient examples of people who have attained satori after three weeks, so try a third week." But the third week passed and still the koan was not solved, so the master said, "Now try five more days." But the five days passed, and the monk was no nearer solving the koan, so finally the master said, "This time try three more days and if after three days you have still not solved the koan, then you must die."

Then, for the first time, the monk decided to devote the whole of whatever life was left to him to solving the koan. And after three days he solved it.

The moral of this story is that one must decide to throw absolutely everything one has into the effort. "Man's extremity is God's opportunity." It often happens that just as one reaches the depths of despair and decides to take one's life then and there that satori comes. I imagine that with many people satori may have come when it was just too late. They were already on their way to death.

Ordinarily there are so many choices one can make, or excuses one can make to oneself. To solve a koan one must be standing at an extremity, with no possibility of choice confronting one. There is just one thing which one must do.

This crisis or extremity came for me when it was finally settled that I should go to America to help Dr. Carus with his translation of the *Tao Te Ching*. I realized that the *rohatsu sesshin*[17] that winter[18] might be my last chance to go to *sesshin* and that if I did not solve my koan then I might never be able to do so. I must have put all my spiritual strength into that *sesshin*.

Up till then I had always been conscious that *mu* was in my mind. But so long as *I* was conscious of *mu* it meant that I was somehow separate from *mu*, and that is not a true *samadhi*. But toward the end of that *sesshin*, about the fifth day, I ceased to be conscious of *mu*. I was one with *mu*, identified with *mu*, so that there was no longer the separateness implied by being conscious of *mu*. This is the real state of *samadhi*.

But this *samadhi* alone is not enough. You must come out of that state, be awakened from it, and that awakening is *prajna*. That moment of coming out of the *samadhi* and seeing it for what it is—that is satori. When I came out of that state of *samadhi* during that *sesshin* I said, "I see. This is it."

I have no idea how long I was in that state of *samadhi*, but I was awakened from it by the sound of the bell. I went to *sanzen* with the *roshi*, and he asked me some of the *sassho* or test questions about *Mu*. I answered all of them except one, which I hesitated over, and at once he sent me out. But the next morning early I went to *sanzen* again, and this time I could answer it. I remember that night as I walked back from the monastery to my quarters in the Kigen'in temple, seeing the trees in the moonlight. They looked transparent and I was transparent too.

I would like to stress the importance of becoming conscious of what it is that one has experienced. After *kensho*[19] I was still not fully conscious of my experience. I was still in a kind of dream. This greater depth of realization came later while I was in America, when suddenly the Zen phrase *hiji soto ni magarazu*, "the elbow does not bend outwards," became clear to me. "The elbow does not bend outwards" might seem to express a kind of necessity, but suddenly I saw that this restriction was really freedom, the true freedom, and I felt that the whole question of free will had been solved for me.

After that I did not find passing koans at all difficult. Of course other koans are needed to clarify *kensho,* the first experience, but it is the first experience which is the most important. The others simply serve to make it more complete and to enable one to understand it more deeply and clearly.

At the Engakuji temple compound in Kita Kamakura, 1954.

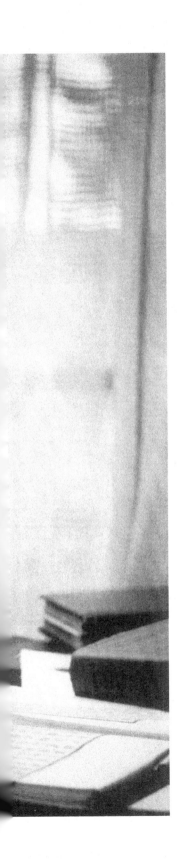

At Shoden'an, in the Engakuji compound, 1955.

Cambridge, Massachusetts, 1958.

With Mihoko Okamura in Cambridge.

At Matsugaoka Bunko (Pine Hill Library), inside the temple compound of Tokeiji. *From left to right:* D.T. Suzuki, Shin'ichi Hisamatsu, and Masao Abe, July 1961. (Photo taken by Mihoko Okamura.)

With Mihoko and Francis Haar in Cambridge.

2

An Autobiographical Account

I HAVE BEEN REQUESTED TO RECOUNT something like an autobiography. I really have an aversion to this kind of thing, and as a rule I do not offer anything like an autobiography or a reminiscence. In particular, I hardly ever give a chronological account of my life. Granted that man lives in time—and that living itself is time—past, present, and future naturally emerge. So it is an ordinary occurrence that in the course of the discussion, the past will come up. Therefore, without adhering to a strict chronological account of my past, I shall relate my reminiscences, as has been requested.

I was born [in 1870] in the city of Kanazawa in the province of Kaga. As the early generations of feudal lords in Kaga ruled over a rich domain, they had considerable power under the Tokugawa shogunate. They did not like being under the watchful eye of the shogunate, however, and so elected to conceal themselves as much as possible. They were enthusiastic about cultural undertakings but did not concern themselves with things political. Kanazawa thus naturally became a place where culture developed. Later, during Rennyo's[1] time, vigorous progress was made in the propagation of the Pure Land Shin Buddhist sect. Prior to that, due to the presence of Eiheiji Temple in the province of Echizen and Sojiji Temple[2] in the province of Noto, the Soto sect was powerful in the Kanazawa area. After Rennyo, however, there was a tremendous expansion of Pure Land Shin Buddhism. Pure Land Shin Buddhist temples have thrived in Hokuriku since that time and there are excellent branches of both the East and West Honganji[3] in the region. Perhaps because of this, it can be said that the people of Hokuriku naturally possessed a religious mind (though one cannot *really* speak of naturally possessing a religious mind). Moreover, people in Hokuriku were often said to be comparatively slow-witted; indeed, they had a disposition toward heaviness and slowness in action. On the other hand, they seem to have had a tendency not to tire, but to persevere to the end once they started something. In this regard, the distinctive characteristics of the people from Kaga became somewhat known throughout Japan.

The religion of my family was Zen, in particular the Rinzai sect, which was rare in Kaga, where the Soto sect predominated. Pure Land Shin Buddhism, as I said earlier, was also strong. My father was a doctor and a Confucian. My mother was not particularly a follower of either the Pure Land Shin or Zen sects, but had a deep interest in Buddhism, which I believe stemmed from the natural and social environment of the region. My father died early. In the northern area of Japan each household usually has a Buddhist altar. While family altars of the Pure Land Shin sect are elaborate, our altar was very simple and made of plain wood. Because my father was a Confucian, there was no posthumous Buddhist name written on the mortuary tablet. I forget exactly what was written on it, but it was a name in the Confucian style and I think I still have it somewhere. Nevertheless, this by no means meant that my parents abandoned Buddhism.

Furthermore, it appears that in Kaga the esoteric strain of Pure Land Shin Buddhism, which is usually called *hijibomon*[4], was quite popular. My father died when I was six, and although I have no recollection of my mother acting as a Pure Land Shin Buddhist follower, it seems to me that she was a member of this *hijibomon*. And when I was nine or ten, I had a kind of *hijibomon* "baptism." I still remember it now. As I grow older and I think about religious practices and their psychology, I have come to understand that the way *hijibomon* works can be interpreted in terms of a general religious psychology. Shinran excommunicated his own son for having had an inclination towards *hijibomon*. This kind of intolerance towards *hijibomon* is characteristic of Pure Land Shin Buddhism. However, it seems certain that even in Pure Land Shin Buddhism there is something that inevitably crops up in the form of *hijibomon*. This is a rather doctrinal matter and would perhaps be better dealt with at a later date; I will set it aside for now. In any event, I may have been influenced by my mother's involvement with *hijibomon*.

The year following my father's death my older brother died. It must have been a terrible experience for my mother to lose both her husband and one of her children within a two-year period. Because her eyes became weak, she went to Kurodani in Etchu Province, in order to receive the curative powers of the waterfall presided over by the guardian deity Fudo.[5] She also went to the hospital, of course, but I think the religious feeling within her moved her to visit the waterfall. I do not know if it was because of this influence or not, but I naturally came to be interested in the area of religion too.

Moreover, around that time I frequently heard that the young heir of the Honda family—my family had at one time served as their retainers—went to Kyoto and practiced Zen under the chief abbot of Daitokuji Temple,[6] though I do not know who the abbot was during that period. So in all these ways I came to hear about Pure Land Shin Buddhism and Zen, or, rather than saying that I heard about them, it would be better to say that there was a religious atmosphere in my family where the spirit of Pure Land Shin Buddhism and Zen was present. My mother did not especially talk about religion. She did have a priest come and chant a sutra every month, and she lit the candles in the family altar every morning. I never saw her personally chant sutras, although she did pray to Buddha every day. Thus in silence there can be an influence which affects children. When one observes the current practices of Catholics, it can be seen that every effort is made to strengthen education. And the fact that Catholics especially emphasize the education of women from early childhood may have resulted naturally from the importance of the mother's influence.

Regarding my education: I have not, in fact, formally graduated from a single school that I have attended. I moved on to the middle school attached to the Ishikawa Professional School, which is roughly equivalent to what we call junior high school today, without finishing primary school. A couple of years after I entered this school, the minister of education officially announced the establishment of a new system of education. Arinori Mori, the minister of education, and a man of genuine ability, established five or six upper middle schools—in those days we did not call them high schools—throughout the country. Kanazawa was selected as the site for what came to be called the "Fourth Upper Middle School," and I was admitted to that school.

The students discussed all kinds of things while I was in middle school. During that period Sakutaro Fujioka, Ryokichi Yamamoto (who in those days was still known as Ryokichi Kaneda), and some other students interested in writing, created a magazine called *Meiji Yoteki* which they put out not so regularly as once a month, but as often as they were able. Nishida[7] did not yet have any relationship with this group at that point. The articles for the magazine were all written in the classical Chinese style known as *kanbun*. I gave several issues of the magazine to a man I know, but I am not sure whether or not he still has them. Publishing that magazine was quite an experience. It was not a magazine for fiction, but contained, for example, an essay on Kusunoki Masashige[8] and some travel journals. We felt fiction was beneath us, something to be written by libertines. We therefore wrote in the difficult classical Chinese style. Our interest lay in discussing history.

When, at length, the Ishikawa Professional School became the Fourth Upper Middle School, Kitaro Nishida appeared. He had not been enrolled in the Ishikawa Professional School before; rather, he transferred from what was then known as a teachers' preparatory school. A man named Naomatsu Takebe had organized the Ishikawa Professional School, and he brought in three or four teachers who had graduated from universities in Tokyo. This was a year or two before the school was converted into the Fourth Upper Middle School. Among the teachers brought in from Tokyo was a teacher of mathematics named Jikei Hojo, who later became head of a teachers' college in Hiroshima, went on to become president of Tohoku University, and came finally to Gakushuin University, from which he retired. Jikei Hojo was a real educator. The mathematics he taught us was considerably different from anything we had learned hitherto, and I came to have a great interest in mathematics for the first time. This was entirely due to Hojo Sensei. At that time, Nishida frequently said that he wanted to become a specialist in mathematics, but he wound up becoming a philosopher instead.

Hojo Sensei, during his days in Tokyo, had practiced *zazen* under Kosen Imagita,[9] at Engakuji Temple. He thus came to Kanazawa a strong Zen advocate. Accordingly, even though he was a math teacher, he would gather the students around him and talk about Zen. In addition, a priest named Setsumon, who was a disciple of Dokuon Osino, was residing at Kokutaiji Temple in the province. This priest visited Kanazawa monthly, where he would lecture on Zen. Consequently, I traveled to Kokutaiji Temple to practice *zazen* and to find out what *zazen* was. Kokutaiji Temple in Etchu was a little beyond Takaoka. I crossed the Kurikara Pass to Takaoka in an old horse-drawn omnibus and walked from there. At Kokutaiji Temple I met Setsumon and listened to his lecture. This was the beginning of my relationship with Zen. Strictly speaking, I had an encounter with Zen on an earlier occasion, but I will omit that. I would have to say that the beginning of my karmic connection with Zen was my meeting with Setsumon.

I arrived in Tokyo in 1891, and shortly thereafter I was brought to Kosen Imagita's temple in Kamakura through the introduction of Senkichiro Hayakawa, a man who had become well-known as president of Mitsui Bank, and who also practiced *zazen*. From then on I frequently commuted between Tokyo and Kamakura. But the next year—I believe it was on January 16—Kosen Roshi died. This Kosen Imagita was truly a great man. Seen from the perspective of modern Zen, he was a great Zen master. But at that time I did not perceive this at all; I saw him simply as a Zen priest and for the first time began doing *sanzen*. Even today his Zen *teisho*[10] remain in my memory, though in those days I attended his *teisho* without understanding a thing.

Physically, Kosen Roshi was a big man, and he may even have been partially paralyzed, for I recall that when he tried to perform the three bows and similar acts, he could not move his legs easily, and even on tatami his knees would hit with a thud. He seemed a very simple Zen priest, yet in comparison with Zen monks of today there is a world of difference. I was twenty-one at the time, so it was almost seventy years ago. In those seventy years Zen monks have changed considerably, or rather I should say they have changed radically. At Engakuji Temple in 1891 I was twenty-one, and did not know anything. At twenty-one there are a good number of people who are rather clever, but I was from the countryside, and was quite ignorant and unsophisticated, knowing only that which pertained to my own small world.

Among those who practiced Zen at Engakuji Temple and who later became famous, there were, as mentioned previously, the educator Jikei Hojo and Senkichiro Hayakawa, later to become the president of

Mitsui Bank. Then there was Satoo Akizuki, who became the ambassador to Belgium and then retired; his younger brother Samaya Suzuki, who I believe also became president of a bank; and Yoshimasu Kawamura, who became a Supreme Court justice and, among other judges, gained great renown. There was also Tokuan Torio, a man of vigorous spirit. He was a great man, though it was said that Tesshu Yamaoka, as a human being, was of a more ripened and harmonious character and had cultivated himself more deeply. I believe Tesshu Yamaoka did *sanzen* at Mishima. Because there were no trains to Mishima in those days, Yamaoka would go there from Tokyo by horse. He also came to Engakuji Temple in Kamakura as well. He met Kosen Roshi, but whether he actually did *sanzen* with him or not I do not know.

At that time a man named Yujiro Motora was professor of psychology at Tokyo Imperial University. This man did *sanzen* and kept a *sanzen* diary in which he recorded his exchange with the *roshi*. In those days Tokyo Imperial University published a magazine—I do not recall whether it was called *Philosophy Magazine* or *Psychology Magazine*. Motora published something about his experiences during *sanzen* in this magazine. For a while this caused quite an uproar. It has been customary never to disclose to anyone what goes on in the *roshi*'s room during *sanzen*. That is probably best—not because it has to be a secret but because even if the content of the interview with the *roshi* is divulged, it does not do anyone any good; on the contrary, it can even obstruct the progress of the other practitioners. From this perspective, while it is not necessary that what goes on in *sanzen* be kept a secret, it is traditionally said to be better to hold one's tongue. Nevertheless, Motora published his article and it created quite a stir.

It was not until later that I met Soseki Natsume.[11] He came to Engakuji Temple after the death of Kosen Roshi, who had been succeeded by Shaku Soen. I do not know when Soseki Natsume graduated, but I do know it was with a major in English. At that time he would come to Kigen'in, a small temple within the Engakuji compound and which still exists today, in order to do *sanzen*. During that period I was being put up at the same temple. Shaku Soen, three other Buddhist priests, and a Shinto priest named Shibata had been invited to the World's Parliament of Religions convened as part of the 1893 World's Fair in Chicago. Barely able to read English himself, Shaku Soen was nevertheless obligated to deliver a five- to ten-minute address in English. I translated the draft of his speech and had Natsume check the translation. That was the sum total of my dealings with Soseki Natsume.

Shaku Soen was indeed a great man. He had been a novice under Ekkei of Myoshinji Temple in Kyoto and was recommended by Ekkei to Kosen Imagita, who took him on as a disciple. Shaku Soen was very brilliant, and it is said that even in the area of *sanzen* he had progressed rapidly. Consequently, he was very much loved by his teacher. Upon completion of his monastic training he entered Keio Gijuku University, where he studied under Yukichi Fukuzawa,[12] and then preceded on to Ceylon. This was unprecedented behavior for a Zen priest at that time. Having completed their Zen training in a general way, Zen monks are usually called *daiosho* (great priest) or *daizenji* (great Zen master), and then they go around behaving haughtily. Soen Roshi, by contrast, entered a secular school and then went as far as India and Ceylon in order to undergo further training. There still exists a record kept by Soen Roshi of those days entitled *Saiyu Diary*. If you consider the period ranging from the outset of Imagita Kosen's tenure as *roshi* up through the present, Soen Roshi's era marked the heyday of Engakuji Temple. True, Kosen Roshi was responsible for the construction of the present meditation hall. But while monks were attracted to Engakuji during Imagita Kosen's time, there were not many laymen who came. This may have been the result of the poor means of transportation, for in those days there were no trains. I was affiliated with the monastery at Engakuji for around five years before I left for America. The number of people, monk and layman alike, who came for *sanzen* with Soen Roshi during that time was amazing. The records of that period may still be existent; in any event, there were countless monks and a quite a variety of laymen.

Life in the monastery was exceedingly miserable. The food was so bad that it is not even worth talking about. I think it was surprising that we could survive. There were any number of stories about monks who were invited to a meal outside the monastery, ate excessively, and injured their stomachs. Indeed, there were probably those monks who, as a result of the strenuous exertions made during their monastery life, were unable to live long even when they finally returned to the secular world. But when you are twenty-seven or twenty-eight, to exert yourself a bit probably does not pose a problem.

As I alluded earlier, I became involved with the World's Parliament of

Religions by translating into English the draft of Soen Roshi's address. At this conference Soen Roshi met Dr. Paul Carus, who later wrote the book *The Gospel of Buddha*, and indeed was inspired to do so as a consequence of his discussions with Shaku Soen. I translated *The Gospel of Buddha* into Japanese. Carus wrote a number of books, but the one among them that sells well even today is *The Gospel of Buddha*. Having completed this work, Carus decided to translate Laozi's [Lao Tzu's] *Tao Te Ching* into English but could not find anyone in America able to assist him. He was searching for someone who could read the text well. Shaku Soen asked me if I would like to go to America for this purpose, and so, through this connection, I went to the United States. I went to America thinking it would afford me the opportunity to go to Ceylon as well. Looking back on it now, it was strange; I went to America, but far from making it to Ceylon, poverty forced me to remain at Carus's publishing company, helping out in various ways in the editorial department. One year grew into the next and I wound up staying in America for more than a decade. After that I traveled around Europe for a year before returning to Japan.

To my way of thinking, people must realize that it was the World's Parliament of Religions which introduced Buddhism to America, and that it was after this conference that American interest in Buddhism began to emerge. The fact that Soseki Natsume was involved precisely at this juncture, by checking my translation of Soen Roshi's address, shows that his contribution, though small, was rather significant. Shaku Soen went to the convocation together with another Buddhist named Doki, who later became chief abbot of the Shingon sect. An invitation was extended to Soen Roshi to visit La Salle, southeast of Chicago, where Carus and Hegeler[13] were residing. He stayed there for about a week, during which time a variety of exchanges about Buddhism occurred. This was the karmic connection that led Carus to write *The Gospel of Buddha*.

It was not only the appearance of Shaku Soen at the World's Parliament of Religions and Carus's writing of *The Gospel of Buddha* that gave rise to the birth of American interest in Buddhism. The celebrated Indian Vivekananda came to the World's Parliament of Religions as a representative of Hinduism. He spoke excellent English and on his way back to India lectured throughout America. In this way, American concern with the Orient began to ferment, and part and parcel with this,

American interest in Buddhism started to take hold. Generally speaking, however, because America is a Christian country, there was not all that much interest in Buddhism and the like.

I suppose it was my writing on Zen topics in English, after my return to Japan from Europe and America, that constituted the first step in the recent interest and popularity of Zen in the West. Prior to that there was hardly anyone who wrote specifically about Zen. Tenshin Okakura,[14] another great man, made reference to Zen from the perspective of painting and tea, and in his *Book of Tea* spoke of the relationship between Zen and the Way of Tea. It was probably the first book that made Zen known in Europe and America. However, I guess I was the first to make a special study of Zen in English.

Shortly after Okakura's book appeared, a man named Chikudo Ohazama put out, in German, a book entitled *Das Lebendige Buddhismus* (Living Buddhism). Then there was Kaiten Nukariya, a scholar of the Soto sect. It would have been wonderful if he could have lived longer, but unfortunately he died. Nukariya wrote *The Religion of the Samurai*, in which he deals with Zen. But again, there was no one who wrote about Zen, as such. As I have just now indicated, there were those who treated Zen tangentially under such titles as *The Religion of the Samurai* and *Living Buddhism*. However, with the exception of myself, there was probably no one who focused on Zen itself.

Upon my return to Japan from America and Europe, I took jobs teaching English, first at Gakushuin University and shortly thereafter at Tokyo Imperial University. I obtained these posts through the assistance of Sakutaro Fujioka. During my stint at Gakushuin University I did not do much of anything in particular, except continually go to Kamakura for *sanzen*. By this time the train had been introduced and the transportation facilities were good, so I would constantly come here to Kamakura. I do not think I wrote about Zen during that period, with the exception of several articles I authored during World War I for a magazine, started up by a man named Robertson Scott.[15] These were the articles that were later published as a book under the title *Introduction to Zen Buddhism*.

Soen Roshi died in 1919, so there was no reason to stay in Tokyo. Besides, a bit of a problem arose at Gakushuin University. After the president who succeeded Maresuke Nogi died, a celebrated military man became president. This man's views and mine—how shall I say it—came into collision. In all probability he enjoyed the support of the officials of the Imperial Household Agency connected to Gakushuin University at that time. Anyway, we had a kind of disagreement and I quit the university. With Soen Roshi dead and having quit my job, I saw no reason to remain in Tokyo. As I was reflecting upon all of this, Otani University, which now wanted to expand, invited me to teach. I got the job with the assistance of Nishida and Gessho Sasaki, a remarkable man who to my great distress died young.

Otani University gave me an unprecedented amount of money. For a university, this constituted an extraordinary commitment. The money enabled me to put out *The Eastern Buddhist*. I wrote something for every issue. In those days there was hardly anyone who wrote in English, so I thought, if I put out the magazine I would be forced to translate into English what others had written. But as translating the works of others cannot help but be time consuming and troublesome, I decided to do my own writing. Thus, my books on Zen came into being.

While I was working at Otani University, I went to China with a Buddhist named Sanji Muto. Indeed, it was through the good offices of Sanji Muto that I was able to make the trip. An event of considerable interest during my journey was my visit to the temple of the celebrated Tai Hsu [T'ai Hsu][16] who had as one of his devotees Chiang Kai-Shek. The temple was in a place called Haueh Tou in the vicinity of Ningpo. I went there together with priests of the Butsunichi [of Engakuji Temple] and Jukoin [of Daitokuji Temple]. I would like to go there again and meet with Tai Hsu one more time.

At that point of my life I felt I must see a Chinese monastery no matter what the cost. (Subsequently I have sought out monasteries wherever I have gone, even in America and Europe.) I stayed at several Chinese monasteries, trying to observe the life there. Reading the Zen records of the Tang dynasty, one comes across Zen monks who, descending from the meditation platform, did this and that. I wanted to see how they actually did such things and so I traveled about visiting various monasteries in China.

At that time there resided in China a famous priest of the Pure Land sect—I no longer remember his name[17]—who was undergoing the practice of what is called *heikan* (seclusion). This is a practice whereby one shuts oneself up in a room for, say, a year, during which time he does not meet anyone. The Pure Land priest was much discussed by his fellow priests. As a rule he would not meet anyone, but as I had come especially from Japan, I was able to see him. He was in a room and we talked through an opening similar to the kind of window through which money is passed in post offices and banks. What struck me as strangely out of place was that there was a clock hanging on a wall in the room. It was an old-fashioned clock with a pendulum, much like we used to have in Japan. I can still remember that clock hanging on the wall. We talked about Pure Land Buddhism; I have quite forgotten whatever else we discussed—it may have been recorded in my book *Impressions of Chinese Buddhism*. In addition to my encounter with this man, I also met and held various discussions with Buddhists and scholars in Shanghai and Beijing [Peking].

Among Chinese Buddhists of that period the vogue was to study Yosacara. Even in those monasteries, which were considered as belonging to the Zen sect, it seems there was no practice of *zazen* or any of the other practices which characterize monastic training as carried out in Japan. Furthermore, the monasteries were not very clean. They were large, but they were really filthy. It may be that if one went there today the situation would be different. In any event, the trip was instructive.

In 1935 or 1936 I again set out for London, having been invited to attend The World Congress of Faiths which was being held there. At the request of the Japanese Foreign Ministry I served as an exchange professor. Since no one else was in a position to go, I was asked if, in the course of my stay in London, I might give some lectures. Consequently, I lectured at three or four places around London. On these occasions, of course, I lectured on Zen, and specifically on the relationship between Zen and Japanese culture. On the way back to Japan I lectured in America as well.

It was about forty-five years ago that I actually began writing books on Zen, so I have been writing continuously on Zen in English for over forty years. After the Second World War a man named Christmas Humphreys of The Buddhist Society of London said he wanted to publish all of my books. He took copies of them back to England and published them there. At that juncture I had written five or six volumes. The publication in England of these books helped Zen to spread. Were it not for the publication of my books in England—had they been restricted to Japan where they were printed at best in quantities of five hundred or one thousand copies—my writings would never have reached a worldwide audience.

My decision to write in English originated as a result of my many conversations with Dr. Paul Carus, while we were translating Laozi's *Tao Te Ching* and my reflections while translating *The Gospel of Buddha* into Japanese. My conviction gradually emerged that Westerners did not understand Buddhism. Consequently, rather than writing on Zen from the outset, I first wrote in English my *Outlines of Mahayana Buddhism*. That book got me started, and from that, my translation of the *Discourse on the Awakening of Faith in the Mahayana* naturally followed.

After that I turned my attention to Zen. Because there were already quite a few people writing about Buddhism, or studying Pali or Sanskrit, I thought it better to write on Zen, for up to that point no one else had done so in English, and since, with regard to Zen, I considered myself to have had some attainment. Thus began my writings on Zen.

Above all, having spent eleven or twelve years abroad—over a decade in America and a year or so wandering about Europe—I discovered, upon my return, a great deal in Japan that I had never noticed before. Comparatively speaking, there was much in the West that was superior and which had to be introduced into Japan. Nevertheless, there was much that Japan—or the Orient—had to make known to the West, particularly in the areas of philosophy and religion. The necessity for this task to be undertaken has constituted the incentive that has motivated me up until now.

After World War II, I was invited to Hawaii again. This was my second visit there. The Pacific War was a ridiculous war for the Japanese to have initiated; it was probably completely without justification. Even so, seen in terms of the phases of history, it may have been inevitable. It is undeniable that while British interest in the East has existed for a long time, interest in the Orient on the part of Americans heightened as a consequence of their coming to Japan after the war, meeting the Japanese people, and coming into contact with various Japanese things. To come back to my trip to Hawaii, however; the East-West Philosophers' Conference convened in Honolulu was supposed to be a conference only for philosophers, but it involved religion as well. This kind of event served as an opportunity to arouse further interest in Oriental philosophy and religion.

The conference in Hawaii ended in August 1949. The following year, sponsored by the Rockefeller Foundation, I made a lecture tour of several renowned American universities. When, two or three years ago, I came to feel that I at last wanted to return to Japan and research a variety of things, I was repeatedly invited to speak at various universities on the east coast of the United States. In addition, my book *Zen and Japanese Culture*, which grew out of my lectures in England and America, was translated into German, as was my *Introduction to Zen Buddhism*, for which the celebrated psychologist C. G. Jung wrote an introductory essay. Moreover, during the war all my books were translated in France. All of these things probably contributed to the spread of Zen. The number of copies of my books, originally published in insignificant amounts, would never have been as great as it later became, even with the publication of my books in England. But with their translation into various languages, they came to be read extensively. The result was that Zen came to attract more and more interest among Europeans and Americans.

Technology and science are quite splendid, but they tend to create an attitude of indifference toward the value of the individual. Individuality is much talked about in the West, but it is in legal or political terms that it is prized. In terms of religion or faith, however, concern among Westerners with regard to individuality is extremely weak. Furthermore, with industrialization or mechanization, man comes to be used as a thing, and, as a result, the unbounded creativity of mankind is destroyed. Therefore, in order to emphasize the importance of true individuality and human creativity, I consider it necessary to write about Zen more and more. Those who are doing just that are gradually appearing, but to my way of thinking—as the chance of some of these writers causing misunderstanding is great—from here on in, it is crucial that Japanese, in particular, undertake the task of trying to clarify Zen for the West. I have my arguments for why I take this position, but I will defer their discussion to another day.

It is inconvenient that from now on we will not be able to write in Japanese, but there is no other recourse if Zen is to be made comprehensible to Westerners; as a "skillful means," it is probably all right to write, time and again, in Western languages. By doing so we may even be able to view Zen anew, from a different angle. Until now we have seen Zen solely through the medium of Chinese and Japanese texts, the latter possessing many of the peculiarities of Chinese. Allow me to conclude by saying that we must now begin to consider how to interpret Zen in the context of Western thinking and feeling.

3

Satori

1

TO UNDERSTAND ZEN, it is essential to have an experience known as *satori*, for without this one can have no insight into the truth of Zen, which, as we have already seen, is generally paradoxically expressed:

"When snow covers white all the mountains, why is one left uncovered (literally, not white)?"

"The ascetic, pure in heart, does not enter Nirvana (i.e. Paradise), the monk violating the precepts does not fall into Hell."

"What I know, you do not know; what you know, I know all."

"While the post is moving around all day, how is it that I do not know?"

"How is it that a man of great strength cannot lift his legs?"

All these statements defy being fitted into the frame of logical reasonableness. To make them intelligible satori is needed. They are in fact purposely set forth by Zen masters to confuse those minds whose field of operation cannot go beyond our everyday common sense experience. When satori is attained the irrationalities cease to be such, they fall back to the level of logic and common sense. The hunter is said not to know the mountains because he is right in them. He is to be up in the air if he wishes to see the whole range of the undulations. Satori achieves this feat, it detaches a man from the environment, and makes him survey the entire field. But this does not mean that satori keeps him always away from the field where it operates. This is a dualistic way of interpreting satori, for a genuine satori is at once transcendental and immanental. It becomes really operative at the point where subject is object and object is subject. Or we can say that unless this identity is effected there is no satori. In satori what is immanental is transcendental and what is transcendental is immanental. The hunter is at once out of the mountains and in them, for he has never gone one step away from them.

We must remember, however, that satori is not a mere intellectual discipline; nor is it a kind of dialectic whereby contradictoriness becomes logically tenable and turns into a reasonable proposition. Satori is existential and not dialectical, as Kierkegaard may say. It does not work with logical formulas and abstractions. It is a concrete fact in itself. When it states that the waters do not flow but the bridge does, it is, to men of satori, not a paradox but a direct statement of their living existential experience. Kierkegaard says that faith is an existential leap. So is satori. Faith has a Christian ring, while satori is specifically Zen. In my view both are experientially identifiable.

What is given us primarily, immediately, is a continuum which is not divisible into atoms; but as we "experience" it, it divides itself into an infinity of atoms. This is due to our sense limitations and to the construction of consciousness. We do not ordinarily reflect on this fact and go on with our daily life taking sensual-intellectual facts of experience for finalities. Those who reflect, however, build up a world of concepts and postulate a continuum. But as this is the result of intellectual deliberation, the continuum is not apprehended as such by most of us. To us therefore God is not an object of immediate experience. He is inferred by logical process. He is thought of, he is not seen. From thinking to seeing is not a continuous process, it is a leap. For however much we multiply our atomic experiences of parts, no continuum as a concrete whole will be experienced. The concrete whole is to be intuited as such. The whole is not to be prehended by accumulation; a whole thus arrived at is no more than parts added, and however far we may carry this addition it goes on *ad infinitum.* An all-embracing whole must be directly grasped as a whole complete in itself. But if it is grasped in the way in which parts, atomic parts, are grasped, it ceases to be a whole, it turns to be a part of the whole which, as an infinitely expansible totality, forever eludes our prehension, which is postulationally conditioned. Therefore, the continuum, undivided, undivisible, infinitely cumulative, and yet as a concrete object of prehension, cannot belong to the world of particulars. It belongs to another order of existence, it constitutes a world by itself, and it is attainable only by transcending our everyday experience of sense-intellect, that is, by an existential leap. This is satori.

It is thus seen that satori is the apprehending of the continuum as such, as not subject to differentiation and determination. But the continuum thus apprehended as the object, as it were, of satori, experience ought not to be judged as standing against particular objects of our daily experience. When this way of thinking is cherished, satori is no more satori, it turns to be one of sense-experiences, and creates a new continuum over the one we already have, and we shall have to repeat this process indefinitely.

Another important thing to remember is that satori takes in the continuum not only as undifferentiated and undeterminated but as infinitely divided and determinated. This means that satori is never in conflict with the world of sense-intellect, it never negates its experiences. When it declares that the spade is in my hands and yet I am empty-handed, it does not mean to contradict the fact of the spade's actually being in the hands, but it only means that each single fact of experience is to be related to the totality of things, for thereby it gains for the first time its meaning. The negating by satori of our everyday facts of experience is to make us thereby realize that God's hands are also holding the spade. When satori makes us conscious of the spade being held in God's hands and not in my hands which I imagine to be my own, each movement I perform becomes directly connected with the one who is more than myself and reflects his will. Hence the Christian saying, "Let thy will be done, not mine". Christians are more ethical and do not speak about negating our common-sense experience. Satori in this respect reflects the general characteristic of Buddhist teaching, especially that of *prajna* philosophy. The *prajna* begins its thinking with denying everything; the idea, however, is not to build up a system of philosophy, but to free us from all our egoistic impulses and the idea of permanency, for these are the source of human miseries and not at all intellectually tenable and spiritually altogether unsound. They are the outgrowth of Ignorance (*avidya*), declares the Buddha. Satori is enlightenment (*sambodhi*) just the opposite of ignorance and darkness. Enlightenment consists in spiritually elucidating facts of experience and not in denying or abnegating them. The light whereby satori illuminates the continuum also illuminates the world of divisions and multitudes. This is the meaning of the Buddhist diction: *shabetsu* (difference) and *byodo* (sameness) are identical.

That "a seed of mustard conceals Mount Sumeru," or that "in a handful of water scooped up in my palm the mermaids are seen dancing to their hearts' content," may sound too extravagant for serious consideration of philosophically-minded people. But when you have satori, these miracles will be what you are performing at every moment of life. What distinguishes Christianity from Buddhism in one respect at least, and in the deepest way, is in their way of interpreting miracles. With Buddhists, especially with Zen followers, their life is a series of miracles. They do not perform them at a certain specified place and in a certain specified time as Christ did. It was Jerusalem where he turned out a great number of fish and bread, it was in the country of the Gergesenes and other places that he cast out so many devils. Christians cannot go any further than these deeds of Christ, they cannot transform one's whole life into one grand miracle. When Shomatsu (1799–1871) of Sanuki was warned against Christianity's overriding Japan in no time, he said, "I am not worried about it. No religion could be better than the one that turns most ordinary sinful souls into Buddhas." Is this not the miraculous event —that we sinful mortals are all transformed just as we are into enlightened ones? Buddhism, especially Zen, prides itself on executing this miracle by means of satori. The miracle in Buddhist terminology is known as *acintya-moksha*, "unthinkable emancipation."

One may ask: "How could such a miracle be performed by one act of satori? How could we, limited as we are in every possible way, intellectually, physically, morally, and otherwise, ever expect to achieve such a wonder of wonders?" If satori were a special act to be carried out by a special faculty of mind, like seeing by the eye, or hearing by the ear, it can never manage to comprehend the continuum. The continuum thus comprehended will be an object among many other objects, one of the multitudes, one particularized by means of intellect, and will vanish into the body of the continuum itself. There will still be another continuum left which is to be prehended somehow. As for satori itself, it will turn into an act or a form of intuition. Zen does not propose this kind of miracle. In satori the continuum is not subjected to the process of intellection and differentiation, it is not a concept here, though we have to speak of it, as if it were. Satori is the continuum becoming conscious of itself. When it perceives itself as it is in itself there is a satori. Therefore, there is in satori no differentiation of subject and object. What is perceived is the percipient itself, and the percipient is no other body than the perceived; the two are in a perfect state of identification; even to speak of identification is apt to mislead us to the assumption of two objects which are identified by an act of intuition. Satori is not, therefore, to be confused with intuition. There has never been two from the very first. It was the human act of knowing that God divided himself and became to be conscious of himself as not God and yet God. Therefore, Zen starts with a negation, with denying knowledge, with contradicting human experience which is fundamentally conditioned in bifurcation. Zen has realized that this is the only way to reach the bottomless abyss of the Godhead where God remains God and no process of becoming not-God has yet begun. Here we cannot talk about intuition or identification, there is only an absolute state of self-identity. Silence is probably a most eloquent way of indicating or suggesting it. But silence from the human point of view lends itself most readily to all kind of misinterpretation, hence of falsification. It is for this reason that Zen resorts to such paradoxes as these:

"I am facing you all day long yet we have never met since eternity."

"I have been in a state of enlightenment even prior to the appearance of the first Buddha."

"Behold, the whole range of eastern hills is walking on the waters."

Someone asked the master, "How do we escape this intense heat of the midsummer day?" Said the master, "Why not leap into the midst of the boiling water, of the blazing furnace?" "How could one escape," the monk was persistent, "from the intensity of this heat?" The master immediately responded, "The cooling breeze blows over the quiet sea!"

These Zen expressions are not meant just to contradict our sense-intellect experiences. They are, on the contrary, the most natural utterances of satori. Or you can say that these are the Zen way of reaffirming our experience, not indeed from the partial and therefore inevitably distorted point of view as engendered by the intellect, but from the totalistic point of view in which reality is grasped not only in its atomic and disconnected aspects but also as the undifferentiated, undetermined continuum. In conformity with this view gained in satori, the Zen master is a most ordinary man with no mysteries, with no miracles about him, he is not at all distinguishable from a man in the street. He talks conventionally, acts like a sensible man, and eats and drinks as do ordinary human beings.

Chokei Ryo (長慶稜, 853–932) once produced his staff before the congregation, saying, "When you understand this, your disciplining in Zen comes to a finish." Is this not plain and simple enough? Zen is just a matter of a stick. When you know it, you know the undifferentiated continuum. There is no mystification about it.

When a monk came to Dogo Chi (道吾智, 779–835) and asked, "What is the deepest secret you have finally come to?" Dogo came down from his chair, bowed to the visitor and said, "You are welcome, indeed, coming from afar, but I am sorry I have not much to entertain you with." Is this not the most ordinary way of receiving visitors among us? And is this Dogo's deepest satori which he got before the light flashed from God's command, "Let there be light"?

Ryutan Shin stayed with Tenno Go (天皇悟, 748–807) for three years, but having no instructions in Zen as he expected, he asked, "It is some time since my arrival here, but I have yet had no words from you, O master, in the way of spiritual teaching." Said the master, "Ever since your arrival here I have been teaching you in matters of spiritual enlightenment." Ryutan did not understand this and asked again, "When were such matters ever imparted to me?" The master's reply was, "When you bring me tea to drink, do I not take it? When you bring my food to eat, do I not accept it? When you bow to me, do I not acknowledge it by nodding? When was I ever at fault in instructing you in matters spiritual?" Dogo stood still for a while thinking about it. The master said, "If you want to see into the matter, see it at once; deliberation makes you miss the point forever." This is said to have awakened the disciple to the truth of Zen.

A remarkable story, indeed. The most innocent and "unreligious" affairs of our routine life are turned into matters of deep spiritual significance. God in heaven is brought down on earth and made to talk with us and to us in a familiar way. While Zen makes the master's staff go through a supernatural transformation, and, turning it into a dragon, makes it swallow up the whole universe[1], it settles down on the other hand to most insignificant incidents of life and finds itself comfortably satisfied with them. Here God is found not as an august being inspiring awe and trepidation, but as one intimately familiar and approachable and lovable to the utmost. When satori is made to scale heaven and

earth and to plunge headlong into the midst of the chaotic undifferentiated continuum, we are apt to take it as something altogether beyond
our lackadaisical life. But when we come across such stories as exem-
plified by Ryutan and Tenno, satori faces us as a thing quite within our
hold, something even an illiterate plain-thinking peddler might be induced to grapple with.

Haku-un Tan (白雲端, 923–1072) composed the following verse on
Tenno's "spiritual" instruction given to Ryutan:

> Putting aside his layman's white dress,
> He comes to the Zen master and tastes bitter hardships:
> He takes the tea reverentially to the master;
> He looks after his well-being with love and devotion.
> One day, as if incidentally, he reviews
> Affairs of the past three years;
> Would not this evoke the street-vender's hearty laugh
> Who goes peddling pastry before the temple steps?

2

Satori obtains when eternity cuts into time or impinges upon time, or,
which is the same thing after all, when time merges itself into eternity.
Time means *shabetsu*, differentiation and determination, while eternity
is *byodo*, all that is not *shabetsu*. Eternity impinging upon time will then
mean that *byodo* and *shabetsu* interpenetrate each other, or, to use Kegon
terminology, the interfusion of *ri* (the universal) and *ji* (the individual).
But as Zen is not interested so much in conceptualization as in "existential thinking" so called, satori is said to take place when consciousness
realizes a state of "one thought." "One thought" (一念), *ichinen* in Japanese and probably *ekakshana* in Sanskrit, is the shortest possible unit of
time. Just as English-speaking people say "as quick as thought," thought
i.e., *nen* represents an instant, i.e., time reduced to an absolute point with
no durability whatever. The Sanskrit *kshana* means both thought and
instant. When time is reduced to a point with no durability, it is "absolute present" or "eternal now." From the point of view of existential
thinking, this "absolute present" is no abstraction, no logical nothingness, it is on the contrary alive with creative vitality. Satori is the experi-

ence of this fact. Buddhist scholars often define *ichinen*, "one thought" as a point of time which has neither the past nor the future, that is to say, *ichinen* is where eternity cuts into time, and when this momentous event takes place, it is known as satori.

It goes without saying that satori is no stopping the flow of consciousness as it is sometimes erroneously contended. This error comes from taking *samadhi* as preliminary to the experience of satori and then confusing *samadhi* with the suspension of thoughts—a psychological state of utter blankness, which is another word for death. Eternity has a death-aspect too as long as it remains in itself; that is, as long as it remains an abstraction like other generalized ideas. Eternity to be alive must come down into the order of time where it can work out all its possibilities, whereas time left to itself has no field of operation. Time must be merged into eternity when it gains its meaning. Time by itself is non-existent very much in the way eternity is impotent without time. It is in our actual living of eternity that the notion of time is possible. Each moment of living marks the steps of eternity. To take hold of eternity, therefore, consciousness much be awakened just at the very moment when eternity lifts its feet to step into time. This moment is what is known as the "absolute present" or "eternal now." It is an absolute point of time where there is no past left behind, no future waiting ahead. Satori stands at this point, where potentialities are about to actualize themselves. Satori does not come out of death, it is at the very moment of actualization, it is in fact the moment itself, which means that it is Life as it lives itself.

The bifurcation of reality is the work of the intellect, indeed it is the way we try to understand it in order to make use of it in our practical life. But this is not the way to understand reality to the satisfaction of our hearts. The bifurcation helps us to handle reality, to make it work for our physical and intellectual needs, but in truth it is never appealing to our inmost needs. For the latter purpose reality must be taken hold of as we immediately experience it. To set it up, for instance, in space and time, murders it. This is the fundamental mistake we have committed in the understanding of reality. At the beginning of the intellectual awakening we thought we achieved a grand feat in arranging reality within the frame of time and space. We never thought this was really preparing for a spiritual tragedy.

Things are made to expand in space and to rise and disappear in time; a world of multiples is now conceived. Spatially, we are unable to see the furthest limits; temporally, we desire to fix the beginning and end of things, which, however, defy the efforts of our scientists and philosophers. We are thus kept prisoners in the system of our own fabrications. And we are the most discontented prisoners, knocking furiously against the fates. We have systematized things by means of space and time, but space and time are terribly disturbing ideas. Space is not time, time is not space; infinite expansion cannot be made to harmonize with perpetual transformation; the spatial conception of the world tends to keep things stabilized in the Absolute, while the temporal interpretation of it keeps us in a most uncomfortably uneasy frame of mentality. We crave for something eternal and yet we are forever subjected to states of transience. A life of sixty or seventy years is not at all satisfying, and all the work we can accomplish during this short interval does not amount to much. Take the nations instead of individuals, their time-allowance may be longer, but what difference do they make in cycles of millenniums? Cultures are more enduring and seem to have some worth. But if we are encompassed in vastness of space and endlessness of time, what are they with all the philosophers, artists, and with all the generals and strategists? Are they not all too much like vanishing foam or shooting stars?

Men of satori are not, however, at all worried about all these things. For satori stands firmly on the Absolute Present, Eternal Now, where time and space are coalesced and yet begin to get differentiated. They lie there dormant as it were with all their futurities and possibilities; they are both there rolled up with all their achievements and unfoldments. It is the privilege of satori to be sitting in the Absolute Present quietly surveying the past and contemplating the future. How does the Zen master enjoy this privilege, we may ask? The following sermon given one day by Ummon (雲門) is eloquently illustrative of this point. Ummon, of the tenth century, is the founder of the school bearing his name and one of the most astute exponents of Zen. His sermon runs thus:

"I am not going to ask you anything about what has preceded this day the fifteenth of the month, but let me have a word about what is to follow this day the fifteenth."

So saying he gave his "word": "Every day is a fine day."

A few words of comment are needed. As we know, the original Chinese is very vague. Literally, it reads: "The fifteenth day before, I

do not ask; the fifteenth day after, bring me a word (or a sentence)."
But what is the subject about which Ummon requests "no asking"?
What is again the subject regarding which he wants to have "a word"?
Nothing is specified. But in reality no such specifications are needed here.
What Ummon wants is to make us grasp the absolute "fifteenth day of
the month." The absolute fifteenth is the Absolute Present completely
cut off from the past fifteen days as well as from the coming fifteen days.
One who has truly grasped the "Fifteenth" can give "a word" that
Ummon requests.

Ummon's own was, "Every day is a fine day," (literally, "Day [after]
day, this [a] fine day", 日日是好日). This corresponds singularly to Eckhart's beggar's greeting, "Every morning is a good morning," which
was given in answer to a conventional "Good morning." Ummon's
statement in itself seems simple and most ordinary, but we may not at
once see when and how this is connected with the absolute "fifteenth."
To trace this connection a rather rationalistic explanation may be
needed. Ummon's sermon or request is superficially innocent enough,
but really it is a terrific challenge to our rationalistic way of thinking.
Zen abhors this and desires not to have anything to do with logic and
abstraction. But, humanly speaking, we cannot very well escape it.
With all the limitations of human consciousness, we do our utmost to
express the inexpressible.

Ever since *avidya*, Ignorance, asserted itself, we take great pleasure in
dividing up reality into pieces; we divide time into years, months, days,
hours, seconds, and this second into millions of infinitesimal parts. But,
for all practical purposes, a year of twelve months and a month of thirty
days works well. Ummon and his disciples found themselves now standing on the line of time-division, the day being the fifteenth of the month.
The line does not belong to the preceding fifteen days, nor can it be
classed with the fifteen days to come. The past is past, and the future
is not yet here. The line is the absolute line of the Present, altogether
timeless, as a spatial, geometrical line has no width. But, existentially
speaking, the absolute "fifteenth day" is not empty and con entless; in
it indeed are hoarded up all the past deeds or achievements already taking
effect, and also all the possibilities that are to materialize in time to come.
How would the Zen master give expression to this fact? He is not a
dialectician, not a metaphysician, he is not used to subtleties of intellec-

tion. He is a most practical man in the sense of a radical empiricist, he does not conceptualize. Hence Ummon's utterance, "Every day is a fine day." This is his description of the Absolute Present seen from his viewpoint of a satori. And it is well to remember that this kind of description directly issuing out of experience and not at all elaborated by the intellect is permitted only to men of satori.

As far as satori itself is concerned, a reference to the past fifteen days of the month and also to another fifteen days to come is irrelevant. The reference here, however, supplies a background to Ummon's direct statement; it makes the latter stand out more intelligibly; it is further a kind of decoy whereby to catch the real thing. For this reason, Ummon's statement in regard to the fifteenth day of the month need not be made the special object of attention. The idea is to get the audience's mind centered in the "Absolute Present," not conditioned by the future or the past. This is the day dividing the month into two, with the fifteen days ahead and the fifteen days behind; if so, it cannot be called one of the past fifteen days, nor is it proper to take it for one of the coming fifteen days. What is past is no more here, and what is to come is not yet here; could Ummon's "fifteenth day" be merely chimerical? But he, including all his disciples, is decidedly living the fifteenth of the month as determined by the calendar then in prevalence. "A word" must be given to this real "existence," however dialectically it is non-existent. Engo (圜悟) of the Song [Sung] dynasty, who commented on Ummon in his *Hekiganshu* says in essence: "When he refers to the past fifteen days and to the fifteen days to follow, he is not restrained by a world of differentiation, he overrides all the ten thousand things of determination. If we are retained by words and try to interpret him accordingly, we shall be farthest away from him." Ummon, as master of Zen, is not to be reached by means of mere concepts and their manipulation.

Setcho (雪竇, 980–1052), a great literary genuis and one of the foremost Zen masters of the Song belonging to Ummon's school, composed a poem on "The Fifteenth Day" of his predecessor:

Put one aside,
Hold on to seven.
Heaven above and earth below and the four quarters,
Nowhere his equal is to be found. (1)

He walks quietly on the murmuring waters of the stream;
He surveys the sky and traces the shadow
   of the flying bird. (2)
The weeds grow rampant,
The clouds are densely overhanging. (3)
Around the cave the flowers are showered where
   Subhuti is lost in meditation;
The advocate of the Void deserves pity as much as
   contempt. (4)
No wavering here!
If you do, thirty blows! (5)

Setcho's verse is too cryptic and may require notes to make the sense accessible to the ordinary reader:

(1)   The numerals, one and seven, here have not much to do with the main theme except reminding us of Ummon's "fifteen" or "fifteenth." "To put one aside" and "to hold on to seven," therefore, convey no real meaning, they just purport to give a warning against attaching oneself to numbers, that is, concepts, and getting hopelessly entangled in the dialectical meshes. When, however, a man is freed from such attachments and entanglements, he is "the only honored one in heaven above and on earth below"—the utterance legendarily ascribed to Buddha at his birth.

(2)   When "the only honored one" makes his appearance, he works miracles all around. He walks quietly on the stream and its waters safely sustain him; he gazes at airy nothing and can chalk out the traces left by the flying bird. These are, however, only symbolic of the far greater and essentially characteristic miracle he performs, for he may live in a most prosaic and karma-bound way as we all do, and yet in his inner life he is not at all bound by karma, fettered by the laws, he is free and the master of himself in every sense of the word. He has grasped the Absolute Present, he lives in it though apparently his life is regulated like ours in time and by its limitations. He is dead in Adam (time and space) and lives in Christ (Absolute Present). He may be in the midst of a blazing fire, and is not hurt; he may be swallowed up by the waves of the ocean, and is not drowned. Why? Because he is now Life itself —Life out of which time and space are woven.

(3)   While satori has its own world, it is also discoverable in a world

of multitudes. Indeed, if it avoids the latter, it cannot be a genuine satori. It ought never to be identified with Emptiness (*sunyata*) inert and contentless. Hence the weeds are luxuriantly growing and clouds heavily overhanging. Satori is to thrive in differentiation. As it transcends time and space and their determinations, it is also in them. When thoroughly immersed in them and identified with them, satori becomes meaningful.

(4)   The gods and all other heavenly beings may have an unmixed feeling of reverence for the one who has detached himself from all worldly ties and passions and is living in the Void; they may shower heavenly flowers over Subhuti, the ascetic completely absorbed in a self-denying and world-forgetting *samadhi* (meditation), but satori is not there. It on the contrary looks down with pity, if not with disdain, on such one-sided transcendentalism or all-annihilating absolutism.

(5)   On this point we are not allowed to waver; no compromise is possible; the way of satori lies ahead of us clear of all dualistic complexities. If we cannot go straight forward with satori in the Absolute Present, we shall certainly deserve Setcho's thirty blows.

3

The following story will help get us acquainted with the Zen master's way whereby he contrives to lead his disciples to the lively content of the Absolute Present.

Baso (馬祖, –788) had one day a walk with Hyakujo (百丈, –814), one of his pupils. Seeing a flock of wild geese flying across the sky he said, "What are they?" Answered Hyakujo, "They are wild geese, master." Baso asked again, "Whither are they flying?" "They are all gone now." Baso turned toward Hyakujo and gave a twist to his nose. Feeling much pain Hyakujo gave a suppressed cry. Baso immediately pursued, "Are they really gone?"

This awakened Hyakujo to a state of satori, and the experience was demonstrated on the following day when the master mounted the platform to give his congregation a talk on Zen. Hyakujo came forward and began to roll up the matting which is generally spread before the master for his disciples to make their bowings to him. This rolling up as a rule means the end of the session. Baso came down from his seat and made for his room.

Hyakujo was called in, and Baso said, "When I had not said a word why did you roll up the matting?"

Hyakujo said, "Yesterday you were kind enough to give my nose a twist which pained me very much."

"Where is your mind wandering today?"

"The nose does not hurt me any more today."

"You have indeed a deep insight into the matter of 'this day' "—was Baso's testimony.

"This Day" here means the Absolute Present and corresponds to Ummon's "The Fifteenth Day." "This day" or "today" is 今日 *konnichi* in Japanese, for which more expressive term is often used by the Zen masters, that is, 即今 *sokkon*. 即 *soku* is a difficult term to translate, it means "just this," or abstractly, "self-identity;" *sokkon*, therefore, is "this very moment" and the master would often demand of you, 即今事作麼生, "What is the matter of this very moment?" When Baso twisted Hyakujo's nose, his idea was to make his disciple awake to the fact of the Absolute Present, and not just to be concerned with the flying birds. The birds are in space and fly in time: you look at them and you put yourself immediately in space-relations: you observe that they are flying, and this at once confines you in the frame of time. As soon as you are in the system of time and space, you step off the Absolute Present, which means that you are no more a free self-regulating spirit, but a mere man, karma-fettered and logically-minded. Satori never comes out of such existence. Hence Baso's boundless love which prompted him to give a twist to Hyakujo's nose. The pain itself had nothing to do with Hyakujo's satori. The incident afforded him an opportunity to break up the framework of consciousness, which vigorously and tyrannically places the mind under the rules of space and time and consequently of logical conceptualization. The master's business is to take these shackles away from the disciple's mind. He does this generally by means of negations or contradictions, proposing "to see a rainfall suspended," or "not to call a fan a fan, or a spade a spade." This may still have a trace of intellection, but the twisting of the nose, or the kicking in the chest, or the shaking by the collar is something utterly unheard of in the annals of spiritual discipline. But its effectiveness has repeatedly and fully been proved by the Zen masters.

It is interesting to cite the sequence of the Hyakujo incident, for it was quite dramatic. When he returned to his own quarters from his interview with Baso in regard to the rolling up of the matting, he was found to be crying aloud. A brother-monk anxiously enquired, saying what was the matter with him. But Hyakujo said, "You go to the master and find out by yourself what is the matter with me." The brother-monk went to Baso and asked about Hyakujo. Baso said, "You go back to him once more and find it out directly from him." The brother-monk came back to Hyakujo and asked him about it again. But Hyakujo instead of answering him burst into a roar of laughter. The monk was nonplused. "A while ago you were crying, and how is it that you are now laughing so?" Hyakujo was nonchalant and said, "I was crying before, but I am now laughing."

Undoubtedly, Hyakujo must have undergone a deep psychological change since his nose was pinched by his master Baso. He evidently realized that there was another life than that which is always under the enthrallment of the time-concept, that is, that which is generally found ruminating over the frustrations of the past and looking forward full of anguish to events yet to happen. The Hyakujo now crying, now laughing, does not lose sight of the Absolute Present. Before his satori his crying or laughing was not a pure act. It was always mixed with something else. His unconscious consciousness of time urged him to look forward, if not thinking of the past. As the result he was vexed with a feeling of tension, which is unnecessarily exhausting. His mind was never complete in itself, it was divided, torn to pieces, and could not be "one whole mind," 一心 (*isshin*) or 一念 (*ichinen*). It lost its rest-place, balance, stillness. Most modern minds are, therefore, neurotics, victims of logical confusion and psychological tension.

4

In "Our Sense of the Present," an article in *Hibbert Journal*, April number, 1946, the author, Ethel M. Rowell, refers to "a stillness which abides in the present, and which we can experience here and now." This stillness, this timeless time, is "the instant made eternity," that is, it is moment infinitely expanding—"one moment, one and infinite." The writer's characterization of the sense of the Present is very informing in its connection with satori as explained in this chapter. But she does not go very far beyond merely describing the sense itself. Ultimately a sense of the Present is perhaps a reflection in us of the presence of Him who is always present, who himself is the eternity at the heart of the present, "the still point of the turning world." And to learn to rest in the present is perhaps a first step toward the "practice of the presence of God." This is tentative enough, but does not open up to a satori. The mere feeling for the present is not enough to make one leap into the eternity and self-sufficiency of the Present.

The feeling still leaves something dualistic whereas satori is the Absolute Present itself. And because of this, the experience goes along with every other experience growing out of the serialistic conception of time. Hence Hyakujo's remarks: "It pained me yesterday but it does not today," "I am laughing now though I was crying a little while ago." Out of such daily experiences as pain and no-pain, crying and laughing, human consciousness weaves a time-continuum, and regards it as reality. When this is accomplished, the procedure is now reversed, and we begin to build up our experiences on the screen of time. Serialism comes first now, and we find our lives miserably bound up by it. The Absolute Present is pushed a way back, we are no more conscious of it. We regret the past and worry about the future. Our crying is not pure crying, nor is our laughing pure laughing. There is always something else mixed up with it, that is, the present has lost its innocence and absoluteness. The future and the past overlay the present and suffocate it. Life is now a suffocated one, maimed and crippled.

A vinaya[2] teacher once asked a Zen master, "How do you discipline your daily life?"

The master said, "When I am hungry I eat, when I feel tired I sleep."

TEACHER: "That is what everybody generally does. Could he be said to be disciplining himself as much as yourself?"

MASTER: "No, not in the same way."

TEACHER: "Why not the same?"

MASTER: "When they eat, they dare not eat, their minds are filled with all kinds of contrivances. Therefore, I say, not the same."

E.M. Rowell cites in her article the story of a London woman after an air raid during the war: "After a night of blitz a woman was seen to come repeatedly to the door of her battered little house, and to look anxiously up and down the street. An official approached her: "Can I do anything to help you?" She answered, "Well, have you seen the milkman anywhere about; my man always likes his early cup of tea." And the author adds: "The past was hostile, the future unreliable, but the companionable present was there with her. Life was precarious but, —her husband wanted his early cup of tea!'"

The only difference between the Zen master who ate and slept heartily and the London woman who wanted milk for her husband's early cup of tea is that the one had satori while the other was just an ordinary human; the one deeply looked into the secrets of the Absolute Present which is also "this present little instant" of everybody and of the whole world, while most of us, including the other, are experiencing it and have a feeling for it, but have not yet had any satori about it.

We read in the Bible (Matt. 6:34): "Take therefore no thought for the morrow; for the morrow shall take thought for the things of itself. Sufficient unto the day is the evil thereof." The idea expressed here by Jesus exactly corresponds to the Zen conception of the Absolute Present. Zen has its own way of presenting the idea, and its satori may seem remote from the Christian feeling. But when Christians stand all naked, shorn of their dualistic garments, they will discover that their God is no other than the Absolute Present itself. They generally think of him as putting on so many ethical and spiritual appendages, which in fact keep him from them; they somehow hesitate to appear before him also in their nakedness, that is, take hold of him in the Absolute Present. The Christian sense of the Absolute Present does not come to a focus and crystalize as it were into a satori; it is too diffused, or still contains a residue of time-serialism.

5

Zen has several names for satori as it is observed in its relationship with various fields of human experience. Some of them are "the mind that has no abode," "the mind that owns nothing," "the homeless mind," "the unattached mind," "mindlessness," "thoughtlessness," "the one mind." These designations all refer to the popular conception of "mind," and Zen strongly denies its existence as reality. But this denial is not the outcome of rationalization but based on actual experience. The dualistic notion of mind or thought and matter has been the bane of human consciousness, and we have been prevented from properly understanding ourselves. For this reason, Zen is most emphatic in its insistence on "mindlessness," and this not necessarily as proved syllogistically but as matter of fact. To clear consciousness of any trace of attachment to the mind-concept, Zen proposes various practical methods, one of which is according to Daishu Yekai (大珠慧海), a disciple of Baso, as follows:[3]

"If you wish to have a clear insight into the mind that has no abode, you have it at the very moment when you are sitting (in the right mood of meditation). Then you see that the mind is altogether devoid of thoughts, that it is not thinking of ideas good or evil. Things past are already past, and when you do not pursue them, the past mind disappears by itself, together with its contents. As to things that are to come, have no hankerings after them, do not have them conjured up in imagination. Then the future mind will disappear by itself with all its possible contents. Things that are at this moment before your mind are already here. What is important in regard to things generally, is not to get attached to them. When the mind is not attached, it raises no thoughts of love or hate, and the present mind will disappear by itself with all its contents.

"When your mind is thus not contained in the three divisions of time (past, future, and present), it can be said that mind is not in time (that is to say, it is a state of timelessness, or a timeless moment).

"If the mind should be stirred up, do not follow the stirrings, and the following-up mind will by itself disappear. When the mind abides with itself, do not hold on to this abiding, and the abiding mind will by itself disappear. Thus when the no-abiding mind obtains, this is abiding in no-abode.

"When you have a clear cognizance of this state of mind, your abiding mind is just abiding and yet not abiding at all in any particular abode. When it is not abiding it is not conscious of any particular abode to be known as no-abiding. When you have thus a clear insight into the state of consciousness not abiding anywhere, (that is, when it is not fixed at any particular object of thought) you are said to have a clear insight into the original mind. This is also known as seeing into one's own being. The mind indeed that has no abode anywhere, is no other than the Buddha-mind."

This no-abiding mind is the absolute present, for it has no abode anywhere in the past, or in the future, or in the present; the mind is not decidedly what it is commonly understood by those who are not yet awakened to satori.

Daishu says somewhere else in his book on "Abrupt Awakening" that "when the mind penetrates through This Instant, what is before and what is after are manifested at once to this mind; it is like the past Buddhas at once facing the future Buddhas; the ten-thousand things (concur) simultaneously; so says the sutra: Where all things are known in one thought, this is the spiritual field, for all-knowledge is attained here." All these things are possible only when one's mind is awakened to the absolute present, not as a logical conclusion, but as satori-consciousness.

Here is an interesting story of an old woman keeping a teahouse at the foot of the Ryutan monastery in Reishu. Tokusan (德山, 780–865) who later became noted for his staff, dropped in a teahouse by the roadside while pilgrimaging in search of a good Zen master. He was a scholar of the *Vajracchedika Sutra* (Diamond Sutra), but hearing of Zen which taught that the mind itself was Buddha, he could not accept it and wanted to interview a Zen student. Shouldering his precious commentary on the sutra, he left his abode in Sichuan [Szu-chuan].

He asked the old woman to serve him a *tenjin* (點心). *Tenjin* means refreshments but literally "mind-dotting." She asked what was in his rucksack. He said, "A commentary on the *Diamond Sutra*."

The old woman resumed, "I have a question to ask you. If your answer is satisfactory, I will serve you refreshments free. If otherwise, you will have to go somewhere else."

Tokusan said, "Well, I am ready."

The question was this: "According to the *Diamond Sutra*, we have, 'The past mind is unattainable, the present mind is unattainable, the future mind is unattainable.' Now, will you please let me know which mind it is you really want to dot?"

This baffled the *Diamond* scholar, and the old woman made him go somewhere else for his refreshments.

I do not know how *ten-jin*, literally "mind-dotting," came to mean refreshments, but the old woman made a very pungent use of the character, *jin* or *shin* (mind), to put the proud scholar's mind at an impasse.

Now, how should we understand the statement in the *Diamond Sutra*? What does the mind past, present, and future mean? What is the signification of "unattainable"?

When satori obtains in the Absolute Present, all these questions solve themselves. The mind or consciousness serially divided and developed in time, always escapes our prehension, is never "attainable," as to its reality. It is only when our unconscious consciousness or what might be called super-consciousness comes to itself, is awakened to itself, that our eyes open to the timelessness of the present in which and from which divisible time unfolds itself and reveals its true nature. Tokusan, still uninitiated in the mystery of satori at the time of his interview with the old lady of the teahouse, naturally could not understand what her question purported. His conception of time was gained from his pet commentary by Seiryo, which meant that his understanding could not go beyond logical reasonableness; the distance between this and satori was immeasurable, for the difference was not one of calculability, but of order, of quality, of value. The gap between satori and rationality could never be bridged by concept-making or postulation or abstract reasoning or anything belonging to the order of the intellect (*vijnana*), but by an absolute negation of the reason itself, which means "an existential leap."

6

Another name for satori is *kensho* (見性), "seeing into one's own nature." This may suggest the idea that there is what is known as nature or substance making up one's being, and that this nature is seen by somebody standing against it. That is to say, there is one who sees and there is another which is seen, subject and object, master and guest. This view is the one generally held by most of us, for our world is a rational reconstruction which keeps one thing always opposing another, and by means of this opposition we think, and our thinking in turn is projected into every field of experience; hence this dichotomous world multiplying itself infinitely. *Kensho*, on the contrary, means going against this way of thinking and putting an end to all forms of dualism. This really means reconstructing our experience from its very foundation. What

Zen attempts is no other than the most radical revolution of our world-view.

The rationalistic way of dissolving contradictory concepts is to create a third concept in which they can be harmoniously set up. To find out such a new concept is the work taken up by the philosopher. While it is a great question whether he can finally succeed in discovering an all-embracing and all-uniting and all-harmonizing concept, we cannot stop short of arriving at such a result, as far as our intellect is concerned. Endless and fruitless may be our efforts, but we shall have to go on this way.

The Zen way has taken an altogether different course, diametrically opposed to the logical or philosophical method. It is not that Zen is defiantly antagonistic to the latter, for Zen is also ready to recognize the practical usefulness of the intellect and willing to give it a proper place it deserves. But Zen has advocated another method of reaching the finality of things where the spirit lies at rest with itself as well as with the world at large. It tells us to retreat to our inner self in which no bifurcation has yet taken place. Ordinarily, we go out of ourselves to seek a place of ultimate rest. We walk on and on until we reach God who is at the head of a long tedious series of bifurcations and unifications. Zen takes the opposite course and steps backwards, as it were, to reach the undifferentiated continuum itself. It looks backwards even before the world with all its dichotomies has not yet made its debut. This means that Zen wants us to face the world into which time and space have not yet put their cleaving wedges. What kind of experience is this? Our experience has always been conditioned by logic, by time, and by space. Experience will be utterly impossible if it is not so conditioned. To refer to experience free from such conditions is nonsensical, one may say. Perhaps it is, as long as we uphold time and space as real and not conceptually projected. But even when these basic conditions of experience are denied, Zen talks a certain kind of experience. If this be really the case, the Zen experience must be said to take place in the timelessness of the Absolute Present. Do not ask how this is possible, for its possibility has been all the time demonstrated by Zen. We must remember that the realm of Zen is where no rationality holds good; in fact it supplies the field of operation for it; we can say that with the Zen experience all the rationalistic superstructure finds its solid basis.

Incidentally we may remark that the Christian view of the world starts with "the tree of knowledge," whereas the Buddhist world is the outcome of Ignorance (*avidya*). Buddhists, therefore, negate the world, as the thing most needed for reaching the final abode of rest. Ignorance is conquered only when the state of things prior to Ignorance is realized, which is satori, seeing into one's own nature as it is by itself, not obscured by Ignorance. Ignorance is the beginning of knowledge, and the truth of things is not to be attained by piling knowledge upon knowledge, which means no more, no less, than intensifying Ignorance. From this Buddhist point of view Christians are all the time rushing into Ignorance when they think they are increasing the amount of knowledge by logical acumen and analytical subtlety. Buddhists want us to see our own "original face" even before we were born, to hear the cry of the crow even before it was uttered, to be with God even before he commanded light to be. Christians take God and his light as things irrevocable, imperatively imposed upon them, and start their work of salvation under these limitations. Their "knowledge" always clings to them, they cannot shake this shackle off, they become victims of logic and rationality. Logic and rationality are all well, Buddhists would say, but the real spiritual abode according to Buddhists is found only where logic and rationality have not yet made their start, where there is yet no subject to assert itself, no object to be taken hold of, where there is neither seer nor the seen—which is "seeing into one's own nature."

7

Satori or the "seeing into one's own nature" is frequently confused with nothingness or emptiness, which is a pure state of negativity. Superficially, this seems to be justifiable. For, logically speaking, the mind awakened to the timelessness of time has no content, does not convey any sense of actual experience. As to "seeing into one's own nature," if this means a state of consciousness where there is neither the seeing subject nor the object seen, it cannot be anything else but a state of pure emptiness which has no significance whatever for our everyday life which is full of frustrations and expectations and vexations. This is true as far as our dualistic thinking is concerned. But we must remember that Zen deals with our most fundamental and most concrete experience

lying at the basis of our daily living. Being an individual experience and
not the conclusion of logical reasoning, it is not at all abstract and empty.
On the contrary, it is the most concrete one filled with possibilities. If
satori were a mere empty abstraction or generalization, it could not be
the basis of the ten thousand things. Rationalization goes upwards getting rid of multiplicities step by step and finally reaches a point which
has no width, no breadth, merely indicating a position. But satori digs
downwards underneath the ground of all existence in order to reach the
rock bed which is an undifferentiated whole. It is not something floating
in the air, but a solid substantial entity, though not in the sense of an
individual sense-object. In conformity with the common sense way of
thinking, Zen uses terms frequently liable to be understood that way.
Thus the term "nature" affords good opportunity for misinterpretation.
We are apt to take it for something underlying a phenomenal sense-
object though existing in a much more subtle way, but satori does not
consist in seeing such subtle object; for in the satori-seeing there is
neither subject nor object, it is at once seeing and not seeing; that which
is seen is that which sees, and *vice versa*. As subject and object are thus
one in the satori seeing, it is evident that it is not seeing in the ordinary
dualistic sense. And this has led many superficially-minded people to
imagine that Zen's seeing is seeing into the Void, being absorbed in
contemplation, and not producing anything useful for our practical life.

The great discovery we owe Buddhism, and especially Zen, is that it
has opened for us the way to see into the suchness of things; this is to
have an insight into "the originally pure in essence and form which is
the ocean of transcendental *prajna*-knowledge",—the phrase used by
Gensha (玄沙) in one of his sermons. "The originally pure" is "a stillness
which abides in the present." Buddhists use the word "pure" in the sense
of absolute, and not in that of freedom from dirt and external matters.
"The originally pure" means that which is unconditioned, undifferentiated, and devoid of all determinations, it is a kind of super-consciousness in which there is no opposition of subject and object, and yet there
is a full awareness of things that are to follow as well as things already
fulfilled. In a sense "the originally pure" is emptiness but an emptiness
charged with vitality. Suchness is, therefore, the two contradictory
concepts, emptiness and not-emptiness, in a state of self-identity. Suchness is not their synthesis, but their self-identity as concretely realized in
our everyday experience. What we have to remember here is that the

concept of suchness is not the result of rationalistic thinking about experience but just a plain direct description of it. When we see a white flower we describe it white; when it is a red one, we say it is red. This is simply a factual statement of the sense, we have not reasoned about redness or whiteness, we just see things red or white, and declare them so. In a similar way, Zen sees with its satori-eye things as they are in themselves, i.e., they are seen as such—such as they are, no more, no less, and Zen says so.

We as human beings, Zen proclaims, cannot go any further than this. Science and philosophy will say that our senses are not reliable, nor is the intellect, they are not to be depended upon as the absolutely trustworthy instrument of knowledge and, therefore, that the Zen view of suchness cannot also be regarded as the last source of authority. This analogy, however, does not hold good in the case of Zen, because the satori-seeing cannot be classed under the same category as the sense-information. In satori there is something more, though this something is something absolutely unique and can be appreciated by those only who have had its experience. This is, it is true, the case with all feelings, the feeling that you are an absolutely unique individuality, the feeling that the life you are enjoying now absolutely belongs to you, or the feeling that God is giving this special favor to you alone and to nobody else. But all these feelings ultimately refer to one definite subject known as "I" which is differentiated from the rest of the world. Satori is not a feeling, nor is it an intellectual act generally designated as intuition. Satori is seeing into one's own nature; and this "nature" is not an entity belonging to oneself so distinguished from others; and in the "seeing" there is no seer, there is nothing seen; "Nature" is the seer as well as the object seen. Satori is "mindlessness," "one absolute thought," "the absolute present," "originally pure," "emptiness," "suchness," and many other things. According to the Zen master, our sense-experience alone is not enough, nor is intellection, if we wish to sound the bottomless abyss of reality; satori must be added to it, not mechanically or quantitatively, but chemically as it were, or qualitatively. When we hear a bell or see a bird flying, we must do so by means of a mind christened by satori, that is to say, we then hear the bell even prior to its ringing, and see the bird even prior to its birth. Once the bell rings or the bird flies, they are then already in the world of senses, which means that they are differentiated, subject to intellectual analysis and synthesis, which means in turn that "the originally pure" has been adulterated leading to further and further adulterations, that there is no longer "the full moon of suchness" as seen by Buddhist poets but the one now thickly veiled with dense threatening clouds. Suchness is synonymous with pureness.

8

Gensha (玄沙, 834–908) who flourished towards the close of the Tang dynasty once gave a sermon to the following effect:

"O you monks, have you ever had an insight into the Originally Pure in essence and form, which is the ocean of transcendental *Prajna*-knowledge, or not? If you had no insight yet, let me ask you this: You are now gathered here, and do you see the green hills facing us all? If you say you see them, how do you see them? If you say you do not, how do you say that when the hills are confronting you right here? Do you understand? O monks, it is your Originally Pure in essence and form, which is the ocean of transcendental *Prajna*-knowledge that sees and hears to the fullest extent of its capacity. If you understand, things are such as they are; if you do not understand, things are just as they are. . . ."

Gensha, on another occasion, had this: He came into the Dharma Hall and hearing the swallows twittering said: "They are indeed deeply discoursing on the reality of things, they are indeed talking well on the essence of the Dharma." So saying, he descended the platform. A monk later accosted him: "Today you were good enough to give us a sermon on the twittering swallows, but we are unable to see into its meaning." The abbot said, "Did you understand?" "No, we do not," answered the monk. "Who would ever believe you?" This was the abbot's verdict.

What does this mondo purport? Gensha and his disciples could not but hear the swallows twitter, but the one heard them as discoursing on the deep things of life while the others did not. Gensha's expression, however, is conceptual and we might take him as not being in the midst of his satori but descending upon the level of the intellectual. This is a sort of condescension on the part of Gensha whereby he is practicing the "kind old woman's Zen" as Zen people say.

The following one is better:

Gensha once pointed at the lantern and said, "I call this a lantern, what would you call it?" The disciple replied, "I too call it a lantern, master." Thereupon Gensha declared, "Throughout this great empire of the Tang there is not a person who understands Buddhism."

On another occasion, Gensha was not so critical or so downright. When he called on Santo (三斗), Santo said, "Living long as I do in the mountain retreat so far away from people, I have no cushion to offer you." Said Gensha, "Everyone of us is supplied with one, and how is it that you are not provided with one yourself?" Santo now saluted Gensha, saying, "Please take your seat." Gensha said, "Nothing has been lacking from the start."

The following incident recorded of Gensha's activities as Zen master has something dramatic about it. When his teacher Seppo (雪峰, 822–908) passed away, Gensha being his foremost disciple became the chief mourner. The whole congregation assembled, and the tea-offering ceremony was to take place. Gensha in front of his departed teacher's spiritual tablet lifted the tea cup and asked the congregation: "While our master was still among us, you were free to say whatever you liked. Now that he is no longer here, what would you say? If you can utter a word[4] (suitable for this occasion, on the death of our master), we will consider him faultless; but if you cannot, the fault must be with him. Is there any one who can utter a word?"

He repeated this three times, but no one came forward. Thereupon, Gensha threw the tea cup down on the floor, breaking it to pieces, and returned to his quarters.

Back in his room, Gensha now asked Chyuto (中塔), "How do you understand?" Chyuto said, "What fault did our departed master ever commit?" Gensha did not say anything, he simply turned about and sat against the wall (in the meditation posture). Chyuto began to walk away, when Gensha called him back and said to him, "How do you understand?" It was now Chyuto who turned about and sat against the wall, Gensha, satisfied, did not say anything further.

Death is no trivial incident in human affairs, and the ritual in connection with it is naturally colored with sorrow and deep reflection. Gensha did not forget it and wished to make good use of the occasion for the edification of his congregation. He wanted the latter to air whatever understanding they had concerning the subject of death. He wanted to see how well they had been applying themselves to the mastering of

Zen under the guidance of his master Seppo. Evidently Chyuto was the only person who could "say a word" in regard to the passing of their great master Seppo. The way they, Chyuto and Gensha, demonstrated Zen between themselves was certainly a most unique one, and this proved to be altogether satisfactory to each other, however strange and unapproachable it might appear to outsiders. Let me remind you here of the fact that they have not been committing themselves to all this logically unaccountable behavior just for the sake of appearing so. We must believe that there is such a thing as satori, and that when it is attained, we understand all these words and deeds recorded of the Zen masters in the history of Zen now lasting for over twelve centuries. Zen is still exercising its spiritually beneficial influence among the peoples of the East.

Satori being beyond the limits of reasonable demonstration has no fixed, predetermined, authorized methods of proving itself to the uninitiated. The questioners are induced by every possible means to confront it one day in an abrupt manner. As satori thus has no tangible body to lay hands on, aspirants for it have to evolve it somehow from within themselves. As long as they endeavor to catch a glimpse of it merely from words or acts of the master, it can never be attained. The masters of Zen remain silent in the pulpit and come down without uttering a word. But sometimes they give the shortest possible sermons. Inasmuch as we are endowed with the body, with the tongue, with the hands, all of which are meant to be organs of intelligence and communication, we must be able to make use of them; under proper management they are indeed eloquent and understandable.

Gensha mounted the platform and after a moment of silence gave this out: "Do you know it? Do you now recognize it?" So saying, he went back to his room. Another time, after a silence he simply said, "This is your true man, just this." Still another time his silence was followed by this, "Daruma[5] is present right here, right now. Do you see him, O monks?"

One day Gensha remained too long in silence, and the monks thinking he was not going to say anything began to disperse, when the master called them back and denounced them in the following way: "As I see, you are all cut out of the same pattern, there is none among you who is endowed with any amount of wisdom. When I part my lips you all gather about me wanting to catch my words and speculate on them.

But when I really try to do you good, you do not at all know me. If you go on like this, be sure that great trouble is indeed ahead of you."

On another occasion he was a little better, for he gave this after a period of silence: "I am doing what I can for your edification, but do you understand?"

A monk said, "What should it mean when the master absorbed in silence utters not a word?"

The master said, "What is the use talking in sleep?"

The monk continued, "I wish you would enlighten me on matters of fundamental essence."

"What can I do with a sleepy one like you?"

"If I am sleepy, what about you, master?"

"How could you ever be so senseless as not to know where your pain is?" said Gensha.

Sometimes he would say, "Such a big fellow like yourself, how could you go about wandering one thousand or even ten thousand miles and reaching here still keep on your drowsing and drowsy talk? It would be much better to be just lying down."

Another monk said, "O master, please be good enough to let me have one word of yours pointing at the essence of the matter."

"When you know it, you have it."

"Please be more direct, O master."

"No use being deaf!" replied the master.

When the disciples are earnestly seeking for truth and reality, to call them deaf and sleepy-minded seems to be rather hard and harsh on them. Are the Zen masters such an unkind set of people? Superficially, they are hardhearted indeed. But to those who know what is what about Zen they are most kindly disposed and well-wishing souls. For their remarks come straightforwardly from their satori which is in all sincerity seeking its response in the hearts of the disciples.

9

Seppo (雪峰), teacher of Gensha, was one of the great masters toward the end of the Tang dynasty; his *Sayings* are still accessible. One of his favorite answers was "What is it?" If one should ask him, "What are we facing this very moment?" he would say, "What is it?" This counter-question on the part of Seppo shows how intimately he feels the presence of "it" or "this," he is so desirous to make his questioner apprehend it as intimately as himself, and he does not know how to communicate it without appealing to conceptualism; so he blurts out, "What is this? Cannot you see it? It is right here this very moment. If I resort to words, it is three thousand miles away." "What is this?" is his impatient exclamation. So he says, "Whenever I see my brother-monks come, I say, 'What is this?' and they at once try to be long-tongued. As long as they go on like this, they will not be able to nod their heads until the year of the ass."[6] All Zen masters hate *talking about* "it," for talking means appealing to intellectualization, which will never bring us to the abode of rest.

The master An (晏), the national teacher of Fuchou Province, saw Seppo first in his Zen career. When Seppo noticed An coming by the gate, he firmly took hold of the newcomer, and said, "What is this?" An was all of a sudden awakened to the signification of it, raising his hands high he danced around. Seppo said, "Do you find anything reasonable about it?" An responded at once, "What reasonableness, master?" Seppo patted him and confirmed his understanding.

What Zen masters wish to have us see into, is that unconscious consciousness accompanying our ordinary dualistically-determined consciousness. The "unconscious" so-called here is not the psychological unconscious which is regarded as making up the lowest stratum of our mind, probably accumulated ever since we began to become conscious of our own existence. "The unconscious" of the Zen master is more logical or epistemological than psychological, it is a sort of undifferentiated knowledge, or knowledge of non-distinction, or transcendental *prajna*-knowledge. In Buddhism generally two forms of knowledge are distinguished, the one is *prajna* and the other is *vijnana*. *Prajna* is all-knowledge (*sarvajna*), or transcendental knowledge, i.e., knowledge undifferentiated. *Vijnana* is our relative knowledge in which subject and object are distinguishable, including both knowledge of concrete particular things and that of the abstract and universal. *Prajna* underlies all *vijnana*, but *vijnana* is not conscious of *prajna* and always thinks it is sufficient in itself and with itself, having no need for *prajna*. But it is not from *vijnana*, relative knowledge, that we get spiritual satisfaction. However much of *vijnana* we may accumulate, we can never find our abode of rest in it, for we somehow feel something missing in the inmost part of our being, which science and philosophy can never appease. Science and philosophy do not apparently exhaust Reality; Reality contains more things than that which is taken up by our relative knowledge or its investigation. What is then still left in Reality, according to Buddhism, turns towards *prajna* for its recognition? *Prajna* corresponds to "unconscious consciousness" already referred to. Our spiritual yearnings are never completely satisfied unless this *prajna*, or undifferentiated knowledge is awakened, whereby the whole field of consciousness is exposed, inside and outside, to our full view. Reality has now nothing to hide from us. The Zen master's life-efforts are concentrated in awakening this *prajna*, unconscious consciousness, knowledge of non-distinction, which, like a will-o'-the-wisp, unobtrusively, tantalizingly, and constantly shoots through the mind. You try to catch it, to examine it on your palm, to name it definitely, so that you can refer to it as a definitely determined individual object. But this is impossible because it is not an object of dualistically-disposed intellectual treatment. Hence Seppo's "What is this?" and Gensha's more conceptual "Originally Pure."

"This" is not, however, that dark consciousness of the brute or child which is waiting for development and clarification. It is, on the contrary, that form of consciousness which we can attain only after years of hard seeking and hard thinking. The thinking, again, is not to be confused with mere intellection; for it must be, to use the terminology of Kierkegaard, existential thinking and not dialectical reasoning. The Zen consciousness thus realized is the highest form of consciousness. Seppo's following sermon must be appreciated from this point of view: Seppo appeared in the Hall of Dharma, and, seeing the monks waiting long for his discourse, said: "O monks, the bell is struck, and the drum is beaten, and you are gathered here; but what is it that you are seeking for? What ailments have you been suffering from? Do you know what shame means? What faults have you ever committed? As I notice, there are only a few of you who have arrived at the goal. Seeing this fact, I could not help coming out here and say to you, 'What is this?' O monks, as soon as you enter the gate, I have already finished my interview with you (on this subject). Do you understand? If you do, much labor is saved. Do not, therefore, come to me and try to get something out of my mouth. Do you see?"

The master paused for a while and resumed:

"Even all the Buddhas of the past, present, and future cannot an-
nounce it; the books of twelve divisions cannot convey it. How then
could those who want to lick the old master's sputa have an understanding on the subject? I ordinarily say to you, 'What is this?' and you come
forward trying to gather up whatever drops from my lips. If so, you
can never have an inkling of it till the year of the ass. I say all this just
because I cannot help it. But when I say this, I have already committed
myself to a downright deception . . ."

A monk asked, "How does a simple-minded man pass his days?"

"Drinking tea, eating rice."

"Is this not passing time idly?"

"Yes, passing time idly."

"How not idly can one pass time?" The monk went on.

The master said, "What's that?"

This "What's that?" is all the time kept busy, has no time to lie idly,
but at the same time he passes time leisurely as if no divisible time concerned it, because he abides ever enjoying "the still point of the turning
world." A monk asked, "All things are reducible to the One, but where
does the One go?" The master said, "The cowhide-bound skull!" and
he continued, "If there really be this person (who knows the One), he
is worth—indeed far more than—all the gold we could offer him piling
from earth up to sky. Who says that he is dressed half-naked and just
sustains himself?" So saying, he abruptly exclaimed, "What is this?"

Seppo's "What is this?" is the Absolute Present in which time and
space are merged as one, as a body of self-identity. Another of his
sermons runs thus:

"This understanding does not issue from the lips, from the yellow
scrolls, from the Zen master's quarters. You should apply yourselves
deliberately and find out when you can come across this. If you fail to
catch it in this present moment, you will never get it however many
times you are reborn in hundreds of thousands of kalpas. If you want to
know what eternity means, it is no further than this very moment.
What is this moment? Do not keep on running wild. Your life may
soon come to an end. . . ."

It may not be amiss in this connection to cite some more of Seppo's
mondo in order to see how his satori worked in dealing with various
questions brought up to him by his monks. The questions may not

appear quite appropriate from our modern logically-trained point of view; but we must remember that with Zen people nothing was trivial, everything, including even the smallest incidents of our daily experience, was a matter of grave concern; for even the lifting of a finger, or the opening of the mouth, the eyebrows raised, or the shepherd singing, was pregnant with Zen significance.

Question: "What is our daily life?"

The master raised his *hossu.*[7]

The monk went on, "Is this what it is?"

The master said, "What is this?"

No answer came from the monk.

"What is the present moment?"

"I never had a person who asked such a question."

"I am asking you now, master."

The master called aloud, "O you, mind-losing fellow!"

"What is the personality of the old master?"

"I have never met him."

"How is it that you never have?"

"Where do you expect to see him?"

The monk did not answer.

"What is there beyond words?"

"What do you seek there?"

"I am asking you now."

"I thought you were quite a clever fellow, but I find you have all the time been a dull-head."

"What is the most fundamental of fundamentals?"

"Where did you get the idea?"

"If there were any idea of it, it could not be the most fundamental of fundamentals?"

"What is it then?"

The monk made no answer. Thereupon the master said, "You ask and I will answer."

The monk asked. The master made him take off his monk-robe, and after beating him several times chased him out of the monastery.

"When one tries to get at it, it flies one thousand miles away. What can one do with it?"

"One thousand miles!"

"What shall I do when the ancient frontier-gate does not turn?"
"Has it turned, or not yet?"
"No turning yet."
"Better have it turned."

"I understand this is your saying: 'There is a thing that will save peo-ple in a quiet way, but unfortunately they do not know it.' Now may I ask what this is that quietly saves people?"
"How could you know it?" (You couldn't know it.)

"I heard you say this: 'A room ten feet square contains it.' Now what is that?"
"When you come out of the room, we may consider it."
"Where is it this very moment?"
"Have you come out of the room, or not yet?"

"What (shall I do) when I plan to go back to my native place?"
"Where are you this very moment?"
The monk gave no answer.

"According to the ancient master, when you return to the root, you understand. Now what is the root?"
"The radish root, the cucumber root."

"What does it mean when they say, 'Follow forms and you lose the essence'?"
"Lost!"

"It is said that wherever we look around, we hit upon enlightenment, what does it mean?"
"This is a fine post."

At the end of the summer session, the master (Seppo) sat in front of the monks' quarters. Seeing the monks gathering about him, he raised his staff and said, "This staff of mine is meant for people of the second and third grades." A monk asked, "What would you do if the first grade one should turn up?" The master lost no time in striking him.

When Gako (鵝湖), one of Seppo's disciples, became keeper of a small temple, a certain government official came to see him. Noticing a *hossu*, the official took it up and said, "I call this a *hossu*, but what would you call it?" Gako said, "It is not to be called a *hossu*." The officer said, "There are so many Zen masters nowadays noted for their wisdom, and why don't you start on your pilgrimage?" Gako now realizing his incompetence left his temple and came to Seppo. The latter took him in and said, "How is it that you are here again?" Gako told him about his interview with the government officer whom he failed to satisfy. Seppo said, "Ask me then." Gako repeated the story, whereupon the master uttered the verdict, "A *hossu*!"

"The Sai-in is dead, where is he bound for?"

"It is not you alone but the entire world who knows not where he's bound for."

When Seppo saw Gensha, one of his best disciples, he said this: "When Jinso the teacher died, a monk came to me and asked, 'Where will he be gone?' I said, 'It is like ice melting into water'." Gensha replied, "I would not say so." Seppo said, "What should you say?" Gensha said, "It is like water returning to water."

When Kakwan (可觀) had his first Zen interview with Seppo, Seppo said, "Come on nearer." So he advanced and made a bow. The master without saying a word raised his leg and stepped on the prostrating monk. This made the monk all of a sudden come to a realization. Later when he made his abode at the Horinho in the Nangaku mountains, he gave this: "When I was with Seppo I was given a kick by the master, and ever since my eyes are not opened. I wonder what kind of satori it is." Let me ask, why this remark by Kakwan who evidently had satori under Seppo's foot? Is to *satoru* not to *satoru*? Is to know not to know? Is to be free and master of oneself not to be free and master of oneself? Are affirmations and negations self-identical? Does satori consist in sitting quiet and doing nothing? If you do something, that is, if you act at all, you commit yourself to one thing or another, to a negation or to an affirmation. Does this mean going out of satori and losing it? Is this just sitting quiet really doing nothing? Is not this doing nothing also doing something? Death itself is doing something. There is no such thing as pure negation, for a negation is going to lead to another negation or to an affirmation—they are mutually conditioning. Satori is indeed beyond all logical analysis.

A monk newly arrived at Seppo and the master asked, "Where do you come from?"

"I come from Isan."

"What has Isan to say?"

The monk said, "When I was there, I asked him about the meaning of the First Patriarch's coming from the West (over to China). But he kept on sitting in silence."

"Did you approve of it, or not?"

"No, I did not."

Seppo said, "Isan is an 'old Buddha' (meaning great master), you go straight back to him and confess your fault."

Reikwan Osho (靈觀和尙) always kept his gate closed and sat by himself in meditation. One day Seppo thought of calling on him. He knocked at the gate. Kwan came out and opened it. Seppo lost no time in taking hold of him and demanded, "Is this a simpleton or a sage?" Kwan spitting, said, "This impish fellow!" and releasing himself from the grip pushed him out and shut the gate again. Seppo said, "It is not in vain to find out what kind of man he is."

10

Now I think we can fairly well characterize what Zen satori is:

It is to be with God before he cried out, "Let there be light."

It is to be with God when his spirit moved to give this order.

It is to be with God and as well with the light so created.

It is even to be God himself, and also to be his firmament, his earth, his day and night.

Satori is God's coming to self-consciousness in man—the consciousness all the time underlying human consciousness, which may be called super-consciousness.

Satori is not knowledge in its commonly understood sense.

Satori goes beyond knowledge. It is absolute knowledge in the sense that in satori there is neither the knowledge of subject nor the object of knowledge.

Satori is not a higher unity in which two contradictory terms are synthesized. When a staff is not a staff and yet it is a staff, satori obtains.

When the bridge flows and the water does not, there is satori.

Satori is not an act of intuition as long as there are traces in it of a dualistic conception.

Satori is intuition dynamically conceived. When you move with a moving object, when you are identified with it, and yet when you are not at all moving, a certain state of consciousness—super-consciousness—prevails, which is satori.

When an individual monad is perceived reflecting the absolute or as the absolute itself, there is satori.

Every moment we live is, therefore, eternity itself. Eternity is no other than this instant. They are mutually merged and identical. This state of perfect interpenetration is the content of satori.

Satori does not perceive eternity as stretching itself over an infinite number of unit-instants but in the instant itself, for every instant is eternity.

Satori may be defined as dynamic intuition.

Psychologically speaking, satori is super-consciousness, or consciousness of the Unconscious. The Unconscious is not, however, to be identified with the one psychologically postulated. The Unconscious of satori is with God even prior to his creation. It is what lies at the basis of reality, it is the cosmic Unconscious.

This Unconscious is a metaphysical concept, and it is through satori that we become conscious of the Unconscious.

Satori is Ummon's light possessed by each one of us. And, as he says, when we want to lay hands on it, there is utter darkness. Satori refuses to be brought up onto the surface of our relative consciousness. This, however, does not mean that satori is a thing altogether isolated. To *satoru* means to become conscious of the Unconscious, and this Unconscious is all the time along with consciousness.

Satori makes the Unconscious articulate. And the articulated Unconscious expresses itsef "logically" incoherently, but most eloquently from the Zen point of view. This "incoherency" indeed is Zen.

The cosmic Unconscious in terms of space is "Emptiness" (*shunyata*). To reach this Emptiness is satori. Therefore, when things are surveyed from the satori point of view, Mount Sumeru conceals itself in one of the innumerable pores on the skin. I lift a finger and it covers the whole universe.

PART TWO

4

Torataro Shimomura

D.T. Suzuki's Place
in the History of Human Thought

I THINK THAT ONE of D.T. Suzuki's great achievements, historically speaking, was the opening up of a path to the essential spirit of Mahayana Buddhist and especially Zen thought for the intellectual world of the West.[1] In Oriental thought, especially in Buddhism, there is something which would have remained completely closed off to those Western scholars who know of no other approach to understand it except through linguistic or philological study. This is because in Oriental thought there is something beyond verbal expression, denying conceptual understanding; moreover, this is precisely the case with its most crucial essence. Therefore, I must say that the way to an understanding of Oriental thought had remained fundamentally closed off to the West. And it must be said that it was D.T. Suzuki, through his own deep Zen Awakening[2] and training, together with his understanding of Western languages and thought, who was first able to open up a path by which Westerners could enter into the thinking of the Orient. Even if someone else had such qualifications it is not likely that they could have gone as far as he did.

D.T. Suzuki's work was not simply a matter of introducing Zen thought to the West. It seems that not enough attention is paid to this. If one does not deeply consider the problem involved in conveying Zen thought in Western terms and the importance of that problem, then one cannot comprehend the greatness of D.T. Suzuki's achievements. It must be understood that this is not merely a matter of the history of Japanese thought, but of world thought. The so-called introduction of Zen thought to the West by D.T. Suzuki actually involved the task of building a bridge to span the gulf between Eastern and Western thought, which are not only different in their traditions but are even mutually conflicting and contradictory.

For there is, in fact, a fundamental difference between East and West concerning the most serious problems of being human, our ultimate problem. For instance, regarding such things as life, death, and God, the viewpoints of East and West fundamentally oppose each other. In the West, death is simply the end of life, so life is always the only problem—how to *live well* is the only problem. But in the East *life-and-death* is always the problem; even in our everyday language, "attaining rebirth" (*ojo*) means death. In the West, God is thought of as absolute Existence, but in the East, God is thought of rather as absolute Nothingness (*mu*). In the West, religious faith transcends the intellect, but in Buddhism that transcendence takes place through "Satori" or "Awakening"; to that extent, religious transcendence is a matter of a special kind of intellect. There is the question of what the nature of this special kind of intellect is, of course, but it is at any rate still a problem of the intellect [and not faith].

We must consider how it is possible to find a path between such fundamentally opposing thought. There is no common standard between East and West. Usually the generally accepted procedure is to make an interpretation of the Oriental thought based on some specific philosophical system of the West, or to attempt an extremely superficial identification by means of finding some external similarities between the two. By doing this, however, the originality of Zen thought is utterly lost.

D.T. Suzuki did away with such approaches once and for all and instead, emphasized the fundamental difference and distinction. He did away with the Western tendency to give as rational an interpretation as possible, of trying to approximate the Western way of thinking and offer a consistent method. Instead, he put emphasis on the fact that Zen thought is, in opposition to the Western rational way of thinking, an irrational, non-rational way of thinking. This is an important first step in gaining a basic understanding of the true Zen thought of the Orient. To explain Oriental thought on the basis of Western thought or by borrowing Western ideas—that is a Western interpretation. This is possible so long as there is some common ground, but insofar as there is a fundamental difference such an approach will entail distortion and misunderstanding.

First of all it is necessary to break away from the Occidental standpoint in order to understand the *originality* of Oriental thought. At the same time it is not possible to convey Oriental thought to the West, which is different in nature, simply from the Oriental standpoint. It is necessary to liberate Zen thought from the distinctly Oriental standpoint and to open up for Zen a universal, worldwide basis. Put simply, we must take a philosophical standpoint. Actually, such a problem and process is often encountered in the history of philosophy.

For example, a similar problem can be found in the relation between Greek and Christian thought. When they encountered each other, the Greeks attempted to understand the Christian religion as "the philosophy of Christ." Philosophy became the avenue of approach. However, Christianity negates and denies philosophy, particularly Greek philosophy which is based on "reason." Because of this there was a long history of confrontation and discord; not until the thirteenth century was Thomas Aquinas able to establish a system which brought them into harmony. Here Christian philosophy reached a kind of completion. But then, such a meeting and reconciliation can be said to have been easy in comparison with our present case in the Orient. This is because Christianity had been established in the realm of Hellenistic culture. St. Paul, the first Christian systematic thinker, grew up surrounded by Hellenistic culture and was educated in it. Remembering this alone it should be sufficient to understand why I speak of it as being easier than in our case.

East and West, however, are completely separated by their respective geographical, ethnic, and historical traditions. There is a real gap between the two. Western thought, which began in Greece, recognizes the highest manifestation of reason in verbal expression, while we in the Orient recognize the highest wisdom through the negating and transcending of all statements. Just considering this one point, I think the difference between the two and the extreme difficulty of bringing them together in any form becomes sufficiently clear.

Let us consider a bit more concretely how the thought of an incongruous tradition has been understood, with an example from the history of Western thought. In this instance the necessity of a fundamental *conversion* in the way of thinking can be seen. In Greek thought existence is finite. The Greeks thought of all existence as possessing form, as "Idea." Everything that had form was finite. For the Greeks everything without exception was finite. Time as well as space, humans of course, and even the gods were finite. Therefore, for the Greeks the infinite did not exist. As that which was not limited and thus without determination, the infinite was less than existence, prior to existence. Such an "infinite" could not be thought of as positive in any way but only as something negative.

In Christianity, however, God as the Creator is infinite Being, absolute Being. The Greek gods were not creators but simply "form-givers." The Creator creates being out of nothingness, but the Greek gods which form beings merely give order to chaos; for them matter is already there and cannot be created. The redemption of the sinner, which is the core of the Christian faith, being the salvation of one who from the first is not worthy of salvation, is accomplished solely through God's love. Salvation has nothing whatsoever to do with human collaboration, effort, or works. God as Savior is *almighty* and must be an infinite Being. Such an "infinite Being" which is the basis of Christian thought could not be understood at all according to Greek thought; it is irrational. How can this infinite Being be *comprehended?*—Western thinkers have struggled for a long time with this.

The first and most basic problem is to realize the fundamental distinction between the finite and the infinite. As long as we try to understand the infinite by means of an analogy with the finite we cannot help turning it into something finite. No matter how we may extend or enlarge that which is finite, it remains finite. The very great is not the infinitely great. That which is without end, the endless (*endlos*) also is not the infinite. No matter how endless it is, no matter how far you take it, the thing itself is still finite—it does not go beyond being finite even though it is without end.

The truly infinite is not the extension of the finite, it is the negation of the finite (*unendlich*). When this is realized the first step toward a positive understanding of the infinite can be taken. This realization is that the infinite cannot be understood. Without such a realization the infinite will never be understood, i.e., realizing that the infinite cannot be understood actually becomes the first step toward a positive under-

standing of the infinite and can serve as a basis. This is extremely paradoxical. However, if this paradox is not broken through it is impossible
to understand the infinite.

Westerners must pass through the same kind of paradox to understand
Oriental and especially Zen thought. Before anything else we all must
realize the existence of a basic difference, or rather opposition, in our
respective ways of thinking. It is necessary to clarify how irrational
Oriental thought is and how difficult it is to understand by means of
Western thought. And then one must grasp that Mind (*shin sho*) which
considers the irrational as rational. D.T. Suzuki's approach, and what
most of his efforts were directed toward, was an extolment of this character of the Oriental mind. For this reason, even when he described Zen
Mind[3] he did not in the least interpret or explain Zen psychologically;
rather he emphasized that such an approach was meaningless. This emphasis on the meaninglessness of the psychological approach opened
up a path to a positive understanding of Zen. The presentation of scholars
prior to D.T. Suzuki, and even his contemporaries—not just Westerners
but Japanese scholars as well—were mistaken or at least not thoroughgoing in this respect.

To show that Zen thought cannot be understood according to
Western rational thought clarifies at the same time the restrictions
and limitations of Western thought. With the above-mentioned problem of the infinite, I suggested that realizing the infinite cannot be
understood becomes the first step to an undersanding of it. That the
infinite cannot be understood means that it cannot be understood
according to the logic of the finite. What is contradictory in the realm
of the finite is not contradictory in the realm of the infinite. That what
is contradictory in the realm of the finite is not contradictory in the
realm of the infinite, in fact, constitutes nothing other than the essence
of the infinite. For example, with finitude it is a contradiction for whole
and part to be equal, but it is of the essence of the infinite that whole
and part are equal. It is a contradiction for a finite circle to have numerous centers, but that precisely is the essence of an infinite circle.
The logic of the finite is not the only logic; there exists a logic of the
infinite—this simply cannot be understood without a breaking out of,
or a conversion from, the finite way of thinking, by realizing the re-
stricting boundaries of finite logic.

A similar problem can also be said to exist concerning the relation between Western and Eastern thought. And it should be said that with the realization of this basic conflict and distinction, for the first time a path can be blazed between them. For this reason it is not possible to introduce Zen thought to the West simply because one is versed in Western culture and has Zen Awakening. A basic confrontation must be made, and through devoting ourselves to the basic distinctions, for the first time a bridge can be built. This is nothing but a worldwide standpoint transcending both East and West, a philosophical standpoint in its true sense. For this reason D.T. Suzuki's work can be called philosophical and he himself a philosopher.

Philosophy originally arose in Greece and developed in the West, but if it is simply limited to this, it is not true "philosophy." When we have a universality transcending all particularity, something worldwide transcending East and West, then for the first time we have "philosophy." So-called Western and Eastern philosophy express nothing more than a difference in the character of philosophical thought; two kinds of philosophy do not exist.

Philosophy was first given form by the Greeks. To that extent it is Greek philosophy. However, because it had a worldwide nature, it was philosophy. Because no other philosophy existed at that time except for Greek philosophy, it was *the* philosophy (*Die* Philosophie). However, as soon as a philosophy based on Christian thought emerged, Greek philosophy was no longer "*the* philosophy" (*Die* Philosophie). Greek (Augustinian and Thomastic) philosophy had to admit its own limitations. Then Christian philosophy, which transcended and included Greek philosophy, became philosophy. This was, indeed, a development of philosophy. Through its encounter with Christian thought, philosophy turned increasingly inward and deepened. Historically this first took the form of an interpretation of Christian thought according to Greek philosophy. But Christian thought includes something in its essence which cannot be rationalized, something irrational according to Greek thought. If a rationale is forced upon it, the originality of Christian thought will be lost. To establish a true Christian philosophy after the basic distinction between Greek philosophy and Christian thought was realized, a philosophy had to be established which tried to rationalize what had been considered irrational according to Greek philosophy. But for this to be "philosophy" it had to become a universal, worldwide philosophy in which not only Christian but Greek philosophy are included. In later ages this came to be called Christian philosophy, but at that time it was simply "philosophy." What is limited to so-called Christian philosophy must not be designated *the* philosophy (*Die* Philosophie), even if, as a historical fact, Christian philosophy must have represented "philosophy" at that time.

Our problem now is analogous. For us—we who come out of the tradition of Oriental thought—Western philosophy including both Greek and Christian philosophy is not *the* philosophy (*Die* Philosophie). If it does not include our Oriental thought as well, it is not our "philosophy." Following ancient Greek and then medieval and modern Christian-toned European philosophy, the formation of the next stage of philosophy can be said to be our new philosophical task. This is nothing other than "philosophy" being formed as Greek philosophy, then developing into Christian philosophy, and now trying to evolve again anew. But then again, if this is merely *our Oriental* philosophy, it is not yet "philosophy." As Christian philosophy was formed through the mediation of Greek philosophy, this next stage of ours must be formed through the mediation of the previous two. This will be our philosophy and yet not simply a philosophy peculiar to the Orient. A particularistic philosophy is not philosophy; it must be a universal philosophy of the whole world (*the* philosophy, *Die* Philosophie). As mentioned above, Greek philosophy was not simply the philosophy of Greece; at the time it *was* philosophy. That it came to be called Greek philosophy meant that it had already ceased being philosophy as such. If our philosophy is to be a philosophy with the Zen thought of the Orient as its core, then it will first become philosophy when it is understood by the world. And it must become world philosophy (*Die* Philosophie), not just Oriental philosophy.

This is our task, our mission. To do this we must establish a more comprehensive philosophy in which the irrational according to Greek and Christian philosophy becomes rational, just as Christian philosophy had been considered irrational according to Greek philosophy, but then established a comprehensive philosophy which tried to make the irrational elements of Christianity rational. D.T. Suzuki's work must be said to be the basis for such efforts. Needless to say, his work was not limited simply to introducing Zen thought to the West.

From this vantage point, D.T. Suzuki's work was not just a matter concerning the history of Oriental thought but the history of world thought. His task became a matter of giving Zen thought a philosophical form. Of course, he himself never claimed to be a philosopher and he probably never thought of himself as philosophizing Zen thought; but whether he had that intention or not, objectively and historically speaking his work had such a significance. Several years ago I attended a philosophers' conference in England. When the philosophy professors there spoke about Japanese philosophy, D.T. Suzuki's name came up, and I saw firsthand how he was regarded as a leading Japanese philosopher. And he was in close contact with the philosophical efforts of representative philosophers of modern Japan, such as Kitaro Nishida (1870–1945) and Hajime Tanabe (1885–1962). Yet this problem is not a task solely for Japanese philosophers; it really is a task for philosophers all over the world today. The recent so-called "Zen boom" in the West is not merely a passing fad or superficial phenomenon; it is indicative of a deep demand in the modern world. The fact that it has become such a popular phenomenon suggests this. Philosophers such as Heidegger, who genuinely think about the source of traditional philosophy, are aiming at the task mentioned above from the domain of the problem of philosophy itself. While such philosophers cannot of course be said to be intentionally directing themselves toward Zen thought, they are nevertheless heading in that direction.

What I have said above deals with the historical significance of D.T. Suzuki's labor, but what about the significance for the history of our Oriental thought?

A century has already passed since Japan opened its doors to the West after a long period of isolation. The questions what and how much of Japanese thought were accepted by the West during that time are important for measuring the present status of Japanese thought in the world today. Of course, the true value of Japanese thought cannot be determined through what is known or accepted by the West or how it is evaluated. What has true value in itself cannot be dependent upon the West's evaluation. That which has true value, however, must not limit itself to some geographical specificity, but must be capable of being evaluated on a worldwide basis and also able to stand up to such an evaluation. To accomplish this we must take our stand in the common world arena. A path to worldwide understanding must be opened.

Here music and the arts are a most advantageous expedient. Through this avenue of immediate sense experience, music and the arts can have a worldwide immediacy. Actually, for we Japanese as well, the arts were what could be most quickly and widely understood. Perhaps ukiyo-e[4] has served as a forerunner here. As is already well-known, among the French impressionists such pictures were not only understood but ac-actually exerted a great influence on them. The West's evaluation of ukiyo-e even motivated the Japanese themselves to re-evaluate it.

However, ukiyo-e is not really a legitimate and serious form of paint-ing within our art history; rather it is a "light" or "shallow" art, so it would not be acceptable if the true value of our art were to be judged by ukiyo-e. I do not think our legitimate and orthodox paintings can be understood as simply as our ukiyo-e can. Especially Chinese and Japa-nese traditional, legitimate painting cannot be truly appreciated by the West merely through immediate sense experience because Western paintings are generally realistic whereas Oriental paintings have a meta-physical and symbolic character and a "thought" behind them.

Ukiyo-e does not have such a character; it possesses a much more common or popular entertaining quality, and the colors, lines and composition introduce a wealth of refinement, delicacy and lyricism. While possessing a specifically Japanese quality, it can at the same time be immediately and universally understood. Not only that, ukiyo-e, being evaluated highly as art in this way was largely dependent on historical circumstances, in which it evoked a strong and sympathetic response during the period of "impressionism." This should be called a historical "encounter," the good fortune of historical coincidence, be-cause it is questionable whether ukiyo-e would have received the same response had it been introduced to the West earlier or later than it was. Certainly the excellence and originality of ukiyo-e, which is a result of our painting tradition, would not have been possible without this back-ground. In this sense ukiyo-e is a satisfactory embodiment of the charac-ter of our art, but no one would agree to our art being evaluated with ukiyo-e as an exemplar nor, I think, would we want that.

And if even the immediacy and sensitivity of our art other than ukiyo-e is not easy to understand, then certainly an understanding of our thought, which is accessible merely through the medium of a language belonging to a completely foreign system, is difficult for the Westerner. And on top of this, our finest thought is inexpressible through language; verbal expression is itself negated. For these reasons an understanding of

Oriental thought is extremely difficult. Concerning our philosophical thought, it could even be said that right up until recent years its very existence was unknown to the West.

But do we really have some kind of philosophy for which we can ask and expect Westerners' understanding? Here our concept of "philosophy" becomes the problem. In the strict sense of the term, "philosophy" for us meant that academic study which entered our country beginning at the start of the Meiji era (1868–1912). In fact, for we Japanese "philosophy" meant "Western philosophy." And the situation has in essence remained unchanged even today. As soon as the philosophical thought fashionable in the West was introduced into Japan, we accepted it as it was, with almost no thought to asking our own philosophical questions. Our philosophical study consisted mainly of learning Western philosophy. Even today in our universities, what is studied and lectured on under the name of "philosophy" is Western philosophy; when Oriental philosophy is meant, a qualifying term is added, such as Chinese philosophy or Indian philosophy.

Further, the Oriental philosophy that is thus studied amounts merely to a historical and philological study of the texts of the past; actual philosophical problems in the authentic sense are not even considered. In this sense it is not yet Oriental philosophy in its authentic sense. Not only that, because "philosophy" originally did not exist in the Orient, in the strict sense our study of Oriental thought is not even a study of the history of Oriental philosophy; so-called Oriental philosophy is nothing but a mere attempt to re-interpret Oriental thought as "philosophy." Such a situation has been basically limited by the fact that "philosophy" was for us an entirely new and foreign enterprise. Actually "philosophy" arose in Greece and then developed in the Western tradition. What we today call Oriental philosophy is nothing but a re-interpretation of the Oriental thought from this standpoint of Western philosophy.

The problems of "philosophy" are the ultimate problems concerning human beings, the world, and God. In the Orient as well the speculation upon such problems is, of course, not at all lacking; on the contrary, speculation about these problems in the Orient has been even deeper than in the West. Nevertheless, it was not "philosophy." In the Orient these kinds of problems were always dealt with from the standpoint of religion and ethics, not as an independent, pure academic discipline. As mentioned, the study of "philosophy," even the concept of it, really did not even exist. The Japanese term *tetsugaku* was coined in the beginning of the Meiji era as a translation for the Western term "philosophy." In China also, this Japanese term coined in written characters was introduced and is used there.

Japanese scholars spent the entire Meiji era endeavoring to understand the logic and method of this newly introduced "philosophy." A philosophy of the Japanese people, i.e., giving philosophical form to the problem of one's own self based on the actual experience of the Japanese, was not something to be expected at once. Therefore, philosophy for us at that time was merely an academic study, not anything more than a kind of critique of the formal, logical conformity in the thought of Western philosophers. The first Japanese person that could be said to have had his own philosophy was, as is common knowledge, Kitaro Nishida; other than him we have had very few "philosophical" thinkers.

However, such a situation, such a process, is not limited to Japan alone; the same thing has also occurred in the West. When the Romans took up Greek philosophy, when Christianity tried to develop its own philosophy, and again in modern times when various peoples tried to develop their own philosophies—all involved a similar process. But these cases are far simpler than ours in the Orient because there is some continuity. In our case not only the historical tradition, but the race, language, customs, religion and ethics are all entirely foreign and without continuity. In the beginning of the Meiji era, "philosophy" was new to Japanese thinkers and they approached it with fresh curiosity and accepted it as one integral part of "Western civilization and enlightenment."[5] We cannot imagine how difficult it must have been to understand the thought of a completely different linguistic and conceptual system. In comparison with this, natural science, which deals with matter, was relatively easy to comprehend; but the difficulty in the understanding of something of a completely conceptual basis, like philosophy, which has to be grasped solely thorough the medium of language with all its historical and traditional implications, cannot for a moment be compared, for example, with the translation of a *A Primer on Anatomy*.[6] And further, the two-thousand-year-old philosophical tradition in the West is different from science. The entire Meiji era was spent just trying to understand all this, and the formulation of a positive Japanese philosophy was possible only after mastering it.

Philosophy naturally poses the ultimate problem of man and sets it up according to precise concepts and logic, but it is not just objective knowledge; philosophy is subjective, existential thought through which we can live. We must develop our own philosophy or we have no right to call it "philosophy." The understanding of Western philosophy has so far remained an objective understanding, not a subjective understanding which is a philosophy of the subjective self. The traditional thought of man, world, and God as it is experienced in the Orient cannot possibly be systematized with the concepts or logic formulated in Western philosophy. This is similar to when Christianity encountered Greek philosophy, and yet our case is even more foreign.

Our philosophical task was first to understand the "philosophy" which had completely eluded our grasp and then make it our own. We also have made modern Western thought more or less our own through "Western civilization and enlightenment," and yet underneath the surface we possess an ancient cultural tradition rooted in Buddhist and Confucian thought with a profundity and greatness in no way inferior to Greek thought or Christianity. But this originally was not "philosophy." Creating a philosophy out of these various experiences was *our* philosophical task. And our new contribution to philosophy, to world philosophy, will be our next philosophical task. Greek philosophy upon encountering Christianity accomplished *Aufhebung*, a "self-negation-preservation," and thus philosophy was deepened. In modern times this philosophy, through its encounter with the thought of the Orient, should proceed anew to the next stage.

Through the encounter with Oriental thought, the new problem which we are entrusted with in philosophy is the thought of Nothingness. Up until now this concept has been lacking in Western philosophy. In Greek philosophy the infinite was merely a negative concept and something without limitation; as such it is not anything at all. Likewise, whether in Greek or Christian philosophy—in Western philosophy as a whole—Nothingness was merely nonexistent. On rare occasions mystics have considered it, but only as a fragmentary idea within mysticism. Neither Greek nor Christian philosophy had the logic or methodology to understand Nothingness—absolute Nothingness—positively. This is why the original, next stage of philosophy must be established with motives and questions different from those of Greek and Christian philosophy.

But the difficulty in doing this will be even greater than the evolution from Greek to Christian philosophy. This is because in such thought of Nothingness all concepts, language, and logic are ultimately denied. Generally speaking, religious thought takes the ultimate to be beyond verbal expression. But in Christianity it has been clearly stated that "In the beginning was the Word ... the Word of God." However, in Buddhism the ultimate teaching is always conveyed "wordlessly," as in "Shakyamuni's twirling a flower and Kashyapa's smiling."[7] Moreover, in the Orient absolute Nothingness is not merely expounded in religion, but is living in all life and in all thought. The basis of existence is Nothingness. And existence is the manifestation of Nothingness. In Western philosophy God or infinite Being exists; the basis of existence is existence. In the Orient the truly infinite or absolute is absolute Nothingness. Ultimate truth is established where all language and concepts are negated. Thus, if "philosophy" must be conceptual knowledge, and if it must be conceptually and logically expressed, it is only natural that our traditional thought has not developed into philosophy but rather has negated it.

For all that, to try to develop *our philosophy* from this point of view is to attempt the impossible; so is it meaningless? After all, Buddhism with its principle of Nothingness has produced many, many scrolls of *tripitaka*, the "Three Baskets" of the Buddhist canon consisting of sutras, regulations and discourses; as a matter of fact, Zen, with its doctrine of "No dependence on words or letters" has left behind a large amount of Zen literature. As is well-known, the paradox that "all people have the Buddha-nature and yet we all must undergo hard practice," constitutes the fundamental doubt of Buddhists. If the philosophy of Nothingness is our philosophy and if without it we would have none, then should we give up philosophy? If we think it is impossible or meaningless to try and develop the philosophy of Nothingness, that means we recognize only established Western philosophy as legitimate; from that standpoint then, it really would be impossible and meaningless. Is a philosophy which makes the irrational rational and the meaningless meaningful the new philosophy? Nishida initiated this new philosophy and provided a foundation for it. At least he was able to make a start. Whether he intended it or not, his philosophy must be recognized as an epoch in our history of thought.

The fruit of D.T. Suzuki's labors also is of such a range, as is the profound historical significance of his thought. His achievements as a Buddhist scholar also are undoubtedly great, but if we limit his achievements to that he would not necessarily stand out as a singularly unique scholar. D.T. Suzuki's greatest contribution was not just as a Buddhist scholar but as a philosopher who transcended Buddhism. This meant considering Buddhism from a standpoint which transcended Buddhism. It involved thinking about Buddhism in a worldwide, universal manner. On this point his efforts were similar to the philosophical efforts of Kitaro Nishida and Hajime Tanabe. The reason D.T. Suzuki was a world citizen lies not merely in such things as his living abroad for a long time and authoring works in Western languages, or in his being known and respected abroad. It was due to the fact that he opened up Zen thought to the world through those works. Westerners really are indebted mainly to D.T. Suzuki for opening up this path to an understanding of Mahayana Buddhism, and especially Zen which is its essence. What is it that distinguishes his accomplishments as a philosopher—if I may presume to call him that—from those of Nishida and Tanabe? Perhaps it is, put simply, that while the efforts of Nishida and Tanabe were directed toward Zen *logic*, D.T. Suzuki's efforts were directed toward Zen *mind*.[8]

This is not something that a philologist could do; it is not even in his repertoire. Needless to say, the mind is something living, not at all abstract, and it absolutely cannot be grasped outside one's own actual experience. It is the same as being able to express or convey the beauty of music only through written words and literature without listening to it for oneself. Zen, particularly, is based entirely on the actual fact of one's actual Awakening. Zen thought, as well, is not based on any intellectual understanding but on one's actual Awakening. Because of this, trying to explain Zen other than as an expression and unfolding of one's own Awakening is utterly meaningless.

D.T. Suzuki's emphasis on elucidating Zen Mind rather than Zen logic was something that had to wait for him to be done, and it was valuable and necessary. Without an elucidation of Zen Mind, Zen would be merely empty paradox, devoid of meaning. "Philosophy" has still been accepted in Japan as something merely formal and abstract, fit only as subject matter for lectures because we lack a philosophical mind which is its basis, or womb, and depend only on logic from beginning to end. For this reason no positive, concrete philosophical accomplishment has come out of Japan.

However, D.T. Suzuki's explication of Zen Mind is not, as already mentioned above, a *psychological* interpretation of Zen. He was trying to show Zen Mind itself, not give a psychological interpretation of it. And that is a completely different matter. He himself thoroughly abandoned psychological interpretation. Zen is Mind which has eradicated all reason. It is due to the essence of Zen that he elucidated Zen Mind itself and did not merely give a psychological explanation of Zen. Zen Awakening itself has no relation to the psychological approach toward it; the very meaning of process in this context can only be clarified through Zen Awakening. The thorough denial of a psychological interpretation is due to the fact that the Zen Mind itself fundamentally denies any psychological interpretation and any mind which is explained in such a manner. It was because of this that D.T. Suzuki repeatedly emphasized that the Zen koan is only a paradox for rational thought, and is a method of breaking through such rational thought. It is the presentation of consciousness prior to [the breakup into subject and object of reflective] consciousness. This is not merely the unconscious. Unconsciousness is that which has not yet been made conscious. Consciousness prior to consciousness is that consciousness which has negated consciousness. It is consciousness which is *no longer* conscious. Conscious without being conscious, it is an absolutely negating consciousness. It could also be spoken of as *unrestricted* consciousness.

It was precisely Nishida's philosophy that dealt with that which was presented by D.T. Suzuki as Zen Mind in terms of Zen logic. I think it can be said that with Suzuki, Nishida, and Tanabe, Japanese philosophy genuinely became Japanese philosophy.

The Zen logic of Nishida's philosophy, likewise is not a logical interpretation of Zen. It is not at all interpreting Zen according to some established logic, such as Hegelian dialectical logic. It is the formation of a logic of Zen Awakening itself, the formation of a logic springing forth from the Zen Awakening. This is a completely new formation of logic. It is formed not by a logic which developed out of previous philosophy, but aims at a logic transcending all logic, and including it as well.

After a preparatory stage of understanding Western philosophy (which entered Japan during the Meiji era) and mastering its methods, the development of a Japanese philosophy must be said to have been initiated by the Zen Mind of D.T. Suzuki and the Zen logic of Nishida and Tanabe. But this Japanese philosophy is based on the Oriental mind and experience, and must still be established as a worldwide philosophy. And if we, who already know about the existence of philosophy from ancient to modern, by confronting and connecting with this philosophy, do not include as much of it as possible, what we develop will not be appropriate for a contemporary philosophy. Our philosophy is not simply Oriental philosophy; it must be a world philosophy which has transcended Oriental philosophy.

Whenever we read D.T. Suzuki's works we should think deeply about where that refreshing source which we constantly perceive comes from. It is not a mere impression. The events he narrates are concerned with ancient thought, and yet one feels a freshness because that thought is alive and that means new. And we, who have been exposed to Western thought and thus are not merely Oriental people, feel something alive and fresh in his writings. This shows that his writings are of a worldwide nature.

Buddhist concepts have already become a dead language. Being understood only as technical terms of the specialist, completely unconnected with our own present thoughts and feelings—they certainly are a dead language. That we can feel a freshness from and sympathize with D.T. Suzuki's narrative is because there they really are no longer Buddhist terms but become, so to speak, an international language. That we now can sympathize with his words and thoughts is because he expressed them in an international language.

We are now modern, and "modern man" has the character of a world citizen. That an interest in Zen now exists in the West means that it is possible for Zen both to gain worldwide understanding, which transcends the Orient, and to possess universality.

Long ago, Xuanzang [Hsüan-tsang](602–64), a Chinese scholar-monk, traveled to India at the risk of his life to obtain the Dharma. In the twentieth century this Dharma spread to the West through D.T. Suzuki.

5

Christmas Humphreys

Dr. D.T. Suzuki and Zen Buddhism in Europe

THE SCHOOL OF ZEN BUDDHISM is now well-known in Europe. A score of books are available in several languages; articles on the subject increasingly appear in well-known journals, both specialist and popular in appeal, and the word *Zen* is entering the English language.

References are made to it in all connections, from lectures on serious subjects to jokes in weekly periodicals. Advanced thinkers in the field of philosophy, psychology, and religion study its teaching, and books and articles are beginning to appear in which comparison is made between these teachings and aspects of Western thought. Out of this quantity of material, much of it displaying very little appreciation of the specifically Zen contribution to the mind's development, there is at least a proportion which has reached an awareness that Zen has a unique contribution to make to the mental field in the West, and that this element is more than a new way of thought—it is a way beyond thought. This discovery is a shock to all but the highest thinkers, for to them the realm of the intellect is the level of mind in which enlightenment, however they may regard that term, is to be found. That Truth should lie beyond the reach of thought is to the average mind an idea so indigestible that it is at once rejected. That the few should be willing to consider the possibility is the opening of a door through which the Western mind may one day march to its own salvation.

This new discovery, long hinted at by the mystics, but in language and symbol beyond the thinking intellect to grasp, is thanks to the work of one man, and he is Dr. D.T. Suzuki. This is a proposition beyond the field of opinion; it can be proved. The author of this article was working in the field of Buddhism in 1920, and as the historian of Buddhism in England[1] can speak for the half century preceding. In 1924 the Buddhist Society in London was born, and began to build up a library. Let us look at those books in it which cover the subject of Zen Buddhism.

Before the publication of Dr. Suzuki's first series of *Essays in Zen Buddhism* in 1927 the literature available to the public was as follows. *The Religion of the Samurai*, by Kaiten Nukariya (1913); a chapter, "The Zen Cult in Japan," in E.J. Harrison's *The Fighting Spirit of Japan* (1913); seven pages in Coomaraswamy's *Buddha and the Gospel of Buddhism* (1916); a valuable 20–page pamphlet by Arthur Waley on *Zen Buddhism and its Relation to Art* (1922), and passing references to the Zen schools as one of the Buddhist Schools of Japan. In the Journal of the Pali Text Society appeared in 1906 Dr. Suzuki's *The Zen Sect of Buddhism*, and in 1912, as the sole "Zen Scripture," Gemmell's translation of the *Diamond Sutra*. And that is all, or at least all that a young man, eager to learn more of this wondrous Zen, could find to assuage his thirst. Of the attempted practice of Zen technique, or of the first steps to achieve the Zen experience, there was none.

Then, in 1927, came the first of the *Essays in Zen Buddhism*, avidly seized and read by the few who shared the same thirst. Published by Luzac & Co. of London for the Eastern Buddhist Society of Kyoto, this epoch-making volume, with its essays on Satori, on Practical Methods of Zen Instruction, and the now famous Cow-herding Pictures, made an enormous impression on its readers. Here was a door to a new world within the mind; here was the first attempt not only to tell the West in detail about the Chinese and Japanese School of Zen Buddhism, but to show the way, or at least existence of the way, to its essential experience. Other works followed rapidly. *Studies in the Lankavatara Sutra* (1930) was followed by the sutra itself in 1932. In 1933 came the second series of *Essays in Zen Buddhism*, and the third in 1934. In that memorable year came also the *Introduction to Zen Buddhism* and *The Training of the Zen Buddhist Monk*, and in 1935 the *Manual of Zen Buddhism*.

To his collection of books was added in 1938 the first edition of *Zen*

Buddhism and its Influence on Japanese Culture (now republished as *Zen and Japanese Culture*), and then came the war. This was the end of what we may call the first sowing of the seed of Zen in the Western mind. Let us look at the fruits of this sowing.

In 1930 appeared Dwight Goddard's *The Buddha's Golden Path*, described as "A Manual of Practical Buddhism Based on the Teachings and Practices of the Zen Sect," and as the author was a close friend of Dr. Suzuki this may be called the first attempt by a Westerner to interpret his teachings. Meanwhile Mr. Wong Mou-lam was working on an English translation of the *Sutra of Huineng* [Hui-neng], and a free version of this was included in Dwight Goddard's *A Buddhist Bible*, published in the U.S.A. in 1932, the London edition of the sutra by the Buddhist Society not appearing until 1944. In 1936 appeared in London *The Spirit of Zen* by Alan Watts, then just twenty-one, and Mr. Watts has ever acknowledged that although he has since studied Zen with other Japanese scholars in the U.S.A., his grounding came from Dr. Suzuki.

Let us pause to consider the author of this generous contribution to Western thought. His full biography has yet to be written, and the present author is gathering material for the attempt. But from the viewpoint of the West, which looks to a man who has dedicated his life to teaching the West the principles of Zen Buddhism, the outstanding dates and facts are as follows.

Born in 1870 in north Japan of a line of doctors, several of whom had been lay *roshi*, he entered Tokyo University in 1890, but his heart was early set on Zen, and he spent most of his time at the feet of the Zen master, Imagita Kosen, and his successor, Shaku Soen, in Engakuji, Kamakura, where he later lived. While so studying he was invited to Chicago to assist Dr. Paul Carus in the Buddhist publications of the Open Court Publishing Co. He therefore redoubled his efforts in Zen, and within the year achieved his Zen enlightenment under Shaku Soen. In 1897 he crossed to the U.S.A. to work with Dr. Carus, and spent the next eleven years abroad. In 1900 appeared his first major work, his translation of *The Awakening of Faith*, and when he arrived on a visit to London in 1906 his scholarship had preceded him. His command of English, already good, was improving all the time, as is shown by his article on Zen in the Journal of the Pali Text Society for 1906, and articles contributed to *The Monist* of Chicago which formed the basis of his *Brief History of Early Chinese Philosophy*. His *Outlines of Mahayana*

Buddhism was published in London by Luzac & Co. in 1907, and his trip to Europe of 1908 made clear the trend of his mind and the nature of his life's mission.

This was no less than to make known the teachings of Zen Buddhism to the Western world, and in this field he has been, as already shown, the unchallenged pioneer. As a teacher he is unique as a scholar-practitioner, a man who, having gained his Zen experience at the feet of a Master, dedicates his life to attempting to teach what he far more than intellectually knows. There are scholars writing of Zen who have never attained a Zen "experience," in the sense of satori; there are masters of Zen who make no attempt to teach outside their monasteries. Dr. Suzuki alone teaches to the world in several languages what he knows of his own experience. Learned in Chinese, Sanskrit, Pali and his own Japanese, he reads German easily and has a remarkable and up-to-date knowledge of English literature on the subjects akin to his own. *The Eastern Buddhist*, founded in 1921, was largely meant for Western consumption, and when the first volume of *Essays in Zen Buddhism* appeared in London in 1927, the power of its subject was equaled by the acknowledged scholarship of its author.

The subject was too recondite for the many, and the book was only avidly read by the few whose minds were ripe to consider the "nonsense" which lies beyond the limitations of conventional sense. But the seed was sown, and the author's appearance at the Queen's Hall in London in July 1936 for the World Congress of Faiths was of profound importance in showing the West the fusion of a man and his teachings. His visit to the Buddhist Society on July 20 made a link which has never been severed, for the Society, through the present writer, is the London agent for his writings, and it has been his "home" in Europe ever since.

Then came the war. Dr. Suzuki spent it writing in his home in Kamakura. The Society, containing already a number of his unacknowledged pupils in the field of Zen, converted its meditation group, founded in 1930, to the study of Zen. But all things come to an end, even a war, and in 1945 the stage was set for the second sowing of Zen propaganda, if there be such a thing. The present writer arrived in Japan within a few months of the war, and spent seven months there. Having found Dr. Suzuki, he took down at his dictation an English version of the famous two lectures to the emperor, which was later published by the Buddhist Society as *The Essence of Buddhism*. *The Doctrine of No-Mind*, originally devised as a commentary on the *Sutra of Huineng*, was likewise brought to Europe for publication, followed soon after by *Living By Zen*. The firm of Rider & Co. were entrusted with the collected ·works of Dr. Suzuki, and before long some nine volumes were available in a uniform edition. Meanwhile Dr. Suzuki had embarked on a long series of visits to the U.S.A., which amounted to a stay of several years. In 1953 he came to Europe with his constant companion and secretary, Miss Mihoko Okamura, without whose help and devotion in difficult times we might not have had Dr. Suzuki with us for so long. He came again in 1954, and again for a longer stay in 1958, traveling long distances to visit leading European minds. The meetings with Carl Jung of Zurich were especially fruitful, and Dr. Suzuki's interest in Western psychology has borne fruit in his contribution to *Zen Buddhism and Psychoanalysis* (Harper), which appeared early in 1960.

This "second sowing" of Zen in Europe helped to produce a remarkable harvest. R.H. Blyth's *Zen in English Literature* was published in Japan in 1942—with acknowledgment to Dr. Suzuki—and was also made available in London about 1948. My own *Zen Buddhism* appeared in London in 1949. True, Dr. Suzuki on reading it murmured sadly, "I suppose you in the West *have* to be so intellectual," but that may well be a fact to be faced. In 1953 appeared three books which did *not* come from the inspiration of Dr. Suzuki, and they were the first of such to be written on Zen since Arthur Waley's pamphlet, already mentioned, in 1922. Eugen Herrigel had lectured on Zen and the art of archery before the war, but it was only in 1953 that his expanded book on the subject appeared in American and English editions. The First Zen Institute of New York published *The Development of Chinese Zen* by Heinrich Dumoulin S.J., translated and edited by Ruth Sasaki, which is a major work in bringing Zen to the West, and in the same year notes on the teachings of Nyogen Senzaki, a contemporary of Dr. Suzuki who had spent nearly all his life in California, were published under the title *Buddhism and Zen* by the Philosophical Library of New York. The fact that these three works, and the second volume of a *History of Chinese Philosophy* (Fung Yu-lan), are the only books circulating in England on Zen which make no acknowledged debt to Dr. Suzuki, is in itself a further proof of the present writer's claim that the coming of Zen to Europe is virtually the work of one man, and he the subject of this Festschrift.

In 1951 there was published in French Dr. Hubert Benoit's *La Doctrine Suprème*, which appeared in English in 1955 as *The Supreme Doctrine*. So frankly is this an attempt to consider Zen in the light of Western ideas, based on Dr. Suzuki's then-known teaching, that the author asks his readers to study at least the former's *Zen Doctrine of No Mind* before considering his own work. This book, perhaps the first to be written on this subject, has had a wide sale in both languages, and a considerable influence on all concerned with Zen for the West.

Meanwhile, the Buddhist Society in London was making available to the public the scriptures which are the most studied in Zen monasteries, the *Diamond Sutra*, the *Platform Sutra of Huineng*, the works of Huang Po and Huihai, and Dr. Conze's *Selected Sayings from the Perfection of Wisdom*. But the group in London, which is, so far known, the pioneer class in Europe to study and meditate on the principles of *zazen*, has had the privilege of visits from a series of Zen *roshis* from Japan, who in turn had the opportunity to examine and criticize the work of the class. The first was Mr. Masato Hori, of Myoshinji, in 1953, followed the next year by the Ven. Sogen Asahina of Engakuji, Dr. Suzuki's own monastery. At Easter, 1958, Dr. Shin'ichi Hisamatsu seemed as surprised as he was delighted with the quantity of material available in English for the study of Zen, and with the strenuous efforts of the class to prepare themselves, in the absence of a master, for that day when one should arrive. In August, 1959, the Ven. Daiki Tachibana of Daitokuji himself took the Zen class, and formed his own impression of its worth as a group of self-appointed disciples of Dr. Suzuki, attempting to apply the Zen procedure to their own Western lives.

But books were appearing by authors having no direct contact with a Zen master, and making no acknowledgment in terms to the work of any one author on Zen. Such have been Dr. Lily Abegg's *The Mind of East Asia*, a too-little recognized attempt to build another bridge between East and West; Aldous Huxley's *Perennial Philosophy* is full of Zen, with quotations from Dr. Suzuki's *Studies in the Lankavatara Sutra*; while the works of L.C. Beckett, a revered member of our Zen class, are a pioneer attempt to collate Zen thought with Western thinking. Her *Neti Neti* roused considerable interest; her *Worlds Unbounded*, which includes a collation of the latest views in astronomy with extracts from the *Lankavatara Sutra*, is very remarkable, and in a later chapter she adds herself to the list of those attempting to introduce the viewpoint of Zen to the growing science of psychology. Dr. Suzuki's friendship with Dr. Carl Jung of Zurich is well known, and the latter wrote a Foreword to the former's *Introduction to Zen Buddhism*. Here is one of the potentially most fruitful meetings in modern history, the leading mind in Western psychology and that of the school of Zen. From this link at high level the field widens downwards. Dr. Suzuki's own lectures in Mexico in 1957, which appear with others in *Zen and Psychoanalysis* (Harper, 1960), is an attempt to build a more difficult bridge, between the work of Freud and Zen. Others are working in London on the synthesis of Zen and psychology, including Dr. Graham Howe and Dr. Jeanne Palmer. And now one of the leading psychiatrists in London, Dr. Henry V. Dicks, in the course of a lecture in Vienna in 1959 under the auspices of the World Federation for Mental Health, chose for his subject the daring and provocative title "Mental Health in the Light of Ancient Wisdom," giving credit to the works of Dr. Suzuki and his followers for the source of his knowledge of the latter.

This one lecture may be the proverbial straw in the wind which shows the way the wind is blowing. Western psychology is at present bound in a tight circle of concepts, and when one of its advanced practitioners attempts to break the circle, his efforts may lead to a closer rapprochement between the two great fields of mental and spiritual development.

In science, the breakthrough is most noticeable of all, though how much may be attributed to Zen influence is impossible to say. Curiously enough, this progress is most noticeable in the very large and the very small; in astronomy, whose province is the visible universe, and in physics where the analysis of the atom is reaching the point of No-matter, and hence of the Mahayana concept of the Void. In philosophy, using the term vaguely, there is a noticeable loosening of the bonds of the intellect, and an increased willingness to view the possibility of a breakthrough to No-thought. The intellect, all-powerful until recent times, is losing its grip, and the faculty of the intuition, long held to be but a mode of thought, is beginning to be realized as the power of direct awareness of a Truth beyond words and conceptual thought. Again, to what extent this recent development has been influenced by the new Zen thinking is a matter for argument. For the influence functions, as it were, on three levels; a knowledge of Zen Buddhism, the practice of Zen technique, and the attainment of some measure of that enlightenment of mind which in full measure is known as satori. And the persons influenced may be either thinkers and writers, or those who seek the path which leads to enlightenment, and in each of these the effect may be on the conscious or the unconscious mind. An example of the first may be works of "Weiwuwei," as a distinguished Irish writer likes to be known. Digesting the works of Dr. Suzuki, he has reproduced in *Fingers Pointing to the Moon* and other works his intuitive reaction to that teaching. An example of the second "level" is the Zen class of the Buddhist Society, while the unconscious in innumerable and unexpected places throws up fragments of a Zen awareness which are easily distinguishable from the mystical tradition in European thought.

But in Europe the teaching in the printed work was followed by the man. Dr. Suzuki is much more than the exponent of a well-known system of spiritual teaching. He embodies the fact that the teaching leads to the end it seeks. For none doubts that he is a great teacher in his own right, and even were he to be divorced from any particular school of thought he would still be widely read, and eagerly listened to by those with the privilege of meeting him.

It is true that he has been criticized in Japan and elsewhere, not only at scholastic level, by those apparently unable to appreciate that Zen experience is quite beyond the analysis of the intellect, but for attempting to teach the barbarian-many the secrets of the enlightened-few. This line of attack, that he has dared to make Zen understandable to the West, and attempted to explain the unexplainable, is reminiscent of the attacks by the Brahmins of the day on the Buddha, for making known to all men what the Brahmins jealously guarded for the advantage of the few. But the West is grateful to the man who has given sixty years of his life to explaining, patiently, unceasingly, in book after book, the elements of a new thought-alignment with a view to achieving that which lies beyond even the noblest thinking. He is a bridge-builder, whose bridge may in the end be used by all.

Meanwhile, the books of those who have learned such Zen as they know from his writings and presence continue to appear, and will continue to appear, including the present writer's *Zen Comes West*, which is an attempt to face the problem which now faces the future of Zen in Europe. Zen masters and *roshis* will continue to visit Europe, to select pupils able to study in Japan, to lecture, and to assist existing classes to work fruitfully on the right lines. More Western writers will digest their own Zen reading and meditation and give it forth again in Western form, even though the Japanese Zen masters still complain that the approach is too intellectual. In time Zen *roshis* will come to Europe and stay. In time there will be European *roshis*. These are the distant fruits of the patient sowing of one man, who has offered the light at so high a level that all in the West must climb to reach it. For Zen cannot be stained, or degraded or harmed. It is Truth in its own dwelling place. And the way to it is now established as part of the fast-evolving thought of the West. It may be that in twenty years Zen will be recognized as the most powerful single factor in that evolution of the first half of the twentieth century. If so, it will be thanks to the ceaseless and untiring efforts of one man, Daisetz Teitaro Suzuki.

6

Luis O. Gomez

D.T. Suzuki's Contribution
to Modern Buddhist Scholarship

S INCE ITS INCEPTION in the middle of the nineteenth century, Buddhist scholarship in the Western style has found itself torn between the highly specialized disciplines that form the backbone of its rigor and genius—Sinology, Indology, Japanology, and Anthropology. Modern approaches to Buddhism have also wavered between a certain, sometimes grudging, recognition of the universal values inherent in Buddhist spirituality, and a skeptical, if not hostile attitude toward those aspects of the tradition that seem less rational or more intuitive. These are not accidental or whimsical idiosyncrasies of the scholarly tradition, but safeguards that have proven their value in the course of time with the contribution of French, Japanese, English, and German scholarship to our understanding of traditional Buddhism. However, this cautious, critical eye of modern erudition may fail to appreciate fully the contribution of more synthetic minds. Its pinpoint accuracy may obscure the significance of a latter-day Renaissance mind such as that of Daisetz Teitaro Suzuki.

His work opened the doors of Zen Buddhism (theory and practice) and of Buddhism generally to many of us in the present generation—whether we came to have this interest by way of some mysterious affinity born in the isolation of the provincial fringes of Western culture, or pulled by the rushing torrents of the counterculture, or by a purely erudite interest in an exotic subject. Many of us have gone through a

"Suzuki stage" in our lives, when we devoured everything we could find that bore the revered name.

Some, like myself, may have outgrown this naive stage by entering an adolescence of disappointment and rejection. We have learned to see through the shortcomings of his attempts to Westernize Zen. This has come about at times through the words of other towering giants, such as S. Yanagida, who showed us the difference between the modern eclecticism of Suzuki, Hisamatsu, and Nishida, and the message of classical Chan [Ch'an] and Zen literature. Some of us have also tested our prized gold on the furnace of traditional Zen practice, or on the touchstone of the Indian textual tradition. Then, finding that our idol was not the demigod we thought he was, we have abandoned him for more specialized and cautious works of scholarly research.

But I would hope that all of those who have gone from sheer, uncritical adoration to unconditional, arrogant rejection, will recover their senses. In the sphere of intellectual growth—as in coming of age and reaching adulthood—one must discover with the passing of time the personal sense of gratitude, and the full appreciation for strength in the midst of human limitations that bring back into a new light the ennobling sentiment of filial piety. My own debt of gratitude to D.T. Suzuki is not limited to an enthusiastic but brief first exposure to Buddhism. My initial encounter with his work was through a Spanish translation of his *Introduction*. This came at a stage in my college career when, having read a few excerpts of Pali Nikaya texts, I was ready to move away from Deussen and the *Upanishads* to Buddhism (to meet shortly thereafter with the works of another giant—Edward Conze). This was followed by a brief look into the *Essays*, which whetted my appetite for the Indian Mahayana Sutras. Then came the great discovery: *The Training of the Zen Buddhist Monk* and the *Manual of Zen Buddhism*. In spite of all that has been said about suzuki's cerebral approach to Zen (much of which I believe is true), it was through his work that I first understood the centrality of meditation, and the practical and religious dimensions of Zen Buddhism.

I distinctly remember how I, hardly nineteen at that time, clung to *The Training* as the answer I had "so long" sought. Each new reading brought an added thrill and a youthful (quite proud) feeling of certainty and devotion. I carefully colored the figures of the pantheon in the *Manual*, and I had the Evergreen paperback bound in elegant dark blue

(only to be thoroughly disgusted to find that the binder had desecrated
the holy book by stamping my name on the spine). That was also the
time when I heard about Suzuki's visit to Mexico and his exchanges with
Erich Fromm—I also then read the Fromm-DeMartino volume. I was
exhilarated by the thought that two of my interests (and idols) would
have met, and that they had found common ground on the soil of a
Spanish-speaking country. Years later I would realize the naiveté of my
enthusiasm. I would see how simplistic were the metaphors of approach
and interaction, how superficial were many of the statements in those
books. I shared with some of my contemporaries the embarassment of
discovering that much of our interest in Buddhism had begun with an
image that was somewhat inaccurate and romanticized. Still, in retro-
spect I cannot ignore the process that Suzuki's works set in motion.

Our generation owes Suzuki more, however, than just the initial
spark of youthful enthusiasm. In many ways he is a model of scholarship
and a pioneer in the field, in spite of all that may be said with hindsight.
Only because we stand on the shoulders of D.T. Suzuki can we now see
beyond. It is easy to forget, in the maze of generalizations and attempts
at comparative philosophy, how much in the *Essays* is based on sound
and extensive scholarship into the documentary history of Zen. Some
may appreciate his excerpts from the writings attributed to the first
Patriarchs or his comments on Dahui's [Ta-hui's] interpretation of the
koan, but it is only when one examines his Japanese-language contributions that one fully realizes the amount of research that went into the
writing of the *Essays*. Much of his work on the Dunhuang [Tun-huang]
fragments, for instance, is available only in Japanese (now in the first
volumes of his collected works). His writings in English, with their
conscious effort to digest for the Western reader, contain only a faint
reflection of the magnitude and depth of his scholarship in this area.

In the field of Indology, Suzuki's erudite mind is more evident to
the Western reader. His edition of the *Gandavyuha Sutra*, imperfect as
it is (unavoidably, given the poor manuscript tradition available to us),
clearly forms the basis for his analysis of the symbolism of Maitreya's
"Tower." Perhaps more significant were his works on the *Lankavatara
Sutra*, the fruit of the painstaking labors of many years. He produced a
Sanskrit-Tibetan-Chinese Index, an English translation, and the most
extensive commentary ever published in English for any Buddhist text.

Again, given the limitations of the Nepalese scribal tradition and the shortcomings of the Nanjio edition, Suzuki's work has certain limitations, but it is works such as his that lay the foundation for subsequent studies. Without his pioneering work we would still have an unacceptable gap in our knowledge of Mahayana and the early Lanka School of Chan. As it is, more than a quarter of a century after he began his publication of this sutra we still have at our disposal only Nanjio's edition, and Suzuki's translation, study, and index. One last area in which it is easy to forget the value of his work—again, in part out of adolescent arrogance, as Suzuki as yet has not been fully superseded—is that of the interpretation of Pure Land Buddhism. It is perhaps reasonable to take issue with some of his speculative flights on the connection between the koan and the *nembutsu*, but I do not think we have yet appreciated the full import of his investigation of surrender as selflessness, and true self as no self (in *Shin Buddhism*, for instance). The value of these interpretations for the future of dialogue and reconciliation among Buddhists, and of interfaith dialogue with Christians, has yet to be appraised justly and expressed forcefully by modern-day Buddhists.

One may remember Suzuki as the leading figure among those who brought Zen to the West, or as the prophet-missionary of *Zen and Japanese Culture*. But he was also a man open to a variety of cultural and religious forms, truly a man of the post-war twentieth century. How could I forget, for instance, that it was him, through his translations from the *Myokoninden* (in *Buddhist and Christian Mysticism*), who first brought me to a more just appreciation of Pure Land, and to awakening from the complacent slumber of many years of estrangement from Christianity. We also tend to forget his contribution, as editor and project director, to other tools we take for granted: The *Tibetan Tripitaka*, *The Eastern Buddhist*, and the translation of Shinran's *Kyogyoshinsho*.

All of this points to a scholar of many faces: a prolific writer, a genius of synthesis, and a missionary of sorts, coexisting in the same body with a critical philologist. Perhaps some of his weaknesses stem from this complex combination of talents and interests. Yet one cannot deny that his strength is to be found precisely in the rare phenomenon of so much energy combined with a truly cosmopolitan mind capable of delving into the most diverse cultural and linguistic traditions. Furthermore, if Suzuki sinned out of naive enthusiasm, this was the unavoidable price he paid for a sense of commitment for the universal value and meaning of his subject of study—a quality that has become so rare among scholars of our age.

After the infantile stage of uncritical admiration for the man of genius, after the subsequent stages of growth—further study, development of a sense of objectivity and criticism, then rebellion and reflection—one must come back to Suzuki the man with a new sense of respect. The fallen idol becomes a real human being, and his true stature becomes all the more clear when it is seen among the shortcomings of his methods, his Zeitgeist, and his humanity. Then, to want to go beyond D.T. Suzuki is to admire him all the more. Without ever meeting the man, in his work we can speak to him, and be reminded that greatness is not the domain of demigods, but of that spiritual animal bound by body and history, which we call the human person.

7

Larry A. Fader

D.T. Suzuki's Contribution to the West

> How many varieties of garlands can skilled hands
> fashion with the same flowers?
>
> —*The Dhammpada*

BUDDHISM AND ZEN were introduced to the West during the episode of interreligious, intercultural encounter that started at the end of the nineteenth century. This time of sharing is unusual in the history of such contact insofar as it was accomplished more through genuine dialogue than by economic hegemony, political expansion, or displays of military might. Consequently, the West was able to consider Eastern teachings openly, exploring how Buddhism and Zen either contradict or concur with more familiar approaches to life.

D.T. Suzuki was a towering figure during this period of discovery. Indeed, even to describe him now as "the man who introduced Zen to the West" is to rehearse a truism. Despite our general familiarity with Suzuki's role as promulgator of Zen, there is yet a need to survey the many aspects of Western culture which were profoundly influenced by this extraordinary man and his teachings. In the following discussion, Suzuki's contribution to the West is presented together with some of the significant responses it engendered.

Suzuki was many things to many people. To some, he was a curiosity: soft-spoken, slight, an Asian living in a hemisphere still unaccustomed to Easterners. To others, he was a teacher with a particular talent for expressing difficult concepts in clear language and appropriate metaphor. He was seen as scholar and translator, religious thinker, philosophical psychologist, spiritual mentor, aesthetician and popularizer.

95

Suzuki brandished no sword. Indeed, he followed his teacher, Abbot Shaku Soen, in this respect. In 1893, with the world arming for military conflict, Shaku Soen—the first Zen master to venture to the West— warned delegates to the Chicago World's Parliament of Religions that the times dictated mutual respect instead of belligerence.[1] Similarly, Suzuki presented his ideas in the forums of intellectual discourse where internal coherence and applicability determine persuasiveness. Although the Japanese scholar never avoided the differences between, for example, Buddhism and Christianity, neither was conquest his objective.

On the other hand, Suzuki faced a difficult task. He attempted to teach of "emptiness," "non-rationality," and "ego-death," to a culture which, on the whole, places priority on the struggle between good and evil. Suzuki's interpretation of Zen was couched in language that defied the paradigms to which the West had long since grown used to; he professed "intuition" (although specifically defined) within a world-view nurtured by technology and the "ratiocination" of Aristotelian logic.

Intellectual challenges, no matter how graciously they are presented, seldom remain on the level of intellect alone. Since the categories through which we know and order the world are also the bases of our feelings of security, to call these into question—even just by offering intellectual alternatives—is to produce an "existential" effect, to "shake the foundations." Thus, Suzuki's interpretation of Zen was an implicit invitation for the West to conjure up its own presuppositions and reassess its very identity.

This fundamental questioning may be seen in terms of the West's definition of "religion." Historically, the dominance of the monotheistic traditions—Christianity, Judaism, Islam—in Euro-American civilization has been almost complete. Although Westerners had glimpses into the existence of "non-Western" traditions prior to the twentieth century, it was not really until the Chicago Parliament that Eastern religions were accepted into the arenas of religious discourse. But prying open the categories meant in turn questioning the basic assumption that religions are by definition "theistic," (i.e., they maintain the existence of a "Father" God who is Creator of the world). Minus this concept, a tradition was previously considered pagan or heathen, and was not treated as a religion at all. Western theological debate was therefore usually confined to questions of which sect or theology best explains God and His relation to the human realm.

But Buddhism, Zen, Daoism [Taoism], (and, some would argue, even the "theism" of Hinduism) do not precisely fit into Western theological categories. Buddhism has no "Father" God, and wherever it does select a "theological" form of expression, it is referring to something conceptually different than the Western God. Since Suzuki was such a major figure in the introduction of Buddhism and Zen, we may infer that he contributed to a basic paradigm change in the West.

There were of course many who attempted to dismiss Buddhism and Zen from the outset. One need only look at the controversies which ensued from the Chicago Parliament to realize how threatening Eastern religious philosophies were to traditional clergy and theologians. On the other side of the ledger, however, the number of important religionists who accepted the challenge of Suzuki's "new" ideas is remarkable.

Earliest among these was Paul Carus. Noted author, publisher, and editor of *The Monist* and *The Open Court*—two of the most influential journals around the turn of the century—Carus arranged and financed Suzuki's initial stay in the United States. Paul Carus was devoted to the task of making Eastern religious texts available to the West. Thus, immediately upon Suzuki's arrival in 1897, the young Japanese scholar's expertise was applied to translating and interpreting Buddhist and Daoist manuscripts. Much of the material published under Carus' name from 1897 until the Chicago publisher's death bears the unmistakable mark of Suzuki's influence.

W.T. Stace attempted to argue that mysticism transcends the bounds of particular cultural and historical contingencies. But in his early volume, *Time and Eternity* (1952), there is virtually no mention of non-Western cultures. Clearly, the narrow scope of Stace's data severely weakens the book's main thesis. *Mysticism and Philosophy* (1960) is far more complete, however. In it, Stace attempts to organize various different mystical positions, including Buddhism and Zen, into a coherent whole in order to analyze "mystical experience."

This change can be attributed to Stace's exposure to Suzuki's books and articles. In *Mysticism and Philosophy*, all references to Zen are from Suzuki, whom he labels a "Zen mystic." Stace further points to Suzuki as the model for any mystic who wants to use religious language consistently. In the West, Stace argues, mystics feebly attempt to defend their claims rationally, explaining away apparent inconsistencies. They therefore often miss the paradoxical nature of reality which mysticism unlocks. Suzuki's use of logic, on the other hand, is not apologetic. The Japanese scholar does not hesitate to employ paradoxical statements while attempting at the same time to make sense of them by pointing to "intuitive experience." Suzuki "speaks with only one voice, whereas the Western mystic is double-voiced."[2]

Fr. Thomas Merton's influence on modern Christianity is well known. What is less acknowledged, however, is the extent to which Father Merton underwent a profound change toward the end of his life as a result of his study of Eastern thought. D.T. Suzuki was a primary catalyst in that process.

Merton's approach to Eastern religions was open-minded. He seriously entertained the possibility of uniting his belief in Christianity with Truths gleaned from Buddhist, Daoist, and Zen philosophy and literature. Merton's rendition of *The Way of Chuang Tzu* as well as his *Asian Journals, Mystics and Zen Masters,* and *Zen and the Birds of Appetite* represent a whole-hearted attempt to understand the essence of Eastern thought and to make it his own.

Perhaps the most extraordinary of these writings is the dialogue with Suzuki which Merton includes in *Zen and the Birds of Appetite.* In this series of letters, one perceives both Father Merton's intense yearning for spiritual enlightenment and his personal difficulties sustaining belief in Christian theological myths. Suzuki suggests that Merton may find an answer by focusing on the latter's own concept of Godhead—a notion that points beyond the symbols and ideas which have ensnared the Christian author's spirit. One also perceives Merton tenaciously clinging to the personal aspect of Grace, which, according to Suzuki, prevents him from plunging into the abyss out of which emerges freedom.[3]

Although Suzuki was a lay monk as a youth in Japan, he deviated from the traditional Zen path, studying both Eastern and Western philosophy and becoming comfortable with the methodological rigors of objective scholarship. Included among his academic contributions to the West are a prodigious output of interpretive books and articles; translations from Chinese, Japanese, Sanskrit and Pali, and three journals, *Zendo, The Eastern Buddhist,* and *The Cultural East* (edited in conjunction with R.H. Blyth).

Given Suzuki's academic approach, it is understandable that his influence would be felt strongly in Western Buddhist scholarship. Not only did he translate Buddhist and Zen materials into English, but he also had a significant effect on such other translators as Paul Carus (already mentioned), Dwight Goddard, Edward Conze and R.H. Blyth. His interpretation of Zen aroused a great deal of controversy among such scholars as Heinrich Dumoulin and Hu Shi over the importance of viewing Eastern philosophy in its historical and cultural contexts. Finally, Suzuki inspired many other scholars to present Zen in a systematic, discursive manner.

The late Professor Charles A. Moore of the University of Hawaii indicates the significance of Suzuki's "academic" interpretation of Zen: "Suzuki in his later years was not just a reporter of Zen, not just an expositor, but a significant contributor to the development of Zen and to its enrichment.... A great man, a great scholar," he continues, "does not merely repeat the past; he develops and enriches the past by bringing to it the new insights of his own genius."[4]

Dr. Suzuki's earliest English-language translations were done in collaboration with Carus. They worked together on Laozi's [Lao Tzu's] *Tao Te Ching, Amida Butsu, T'ai-Shang Kan-Ying P'ien,* and *Yin Chin Wen.* Despite the difficulty of these projects, Suzuki had time to pursue his own studies as well. In 1900, just three years after coming to America and at thirty years of age, he published a translation from the Chinese of *Açvaghosha's Discourse on the Awakening of Faith in the Mahayana.* This project required expert linquistic and dialectical skills; and the many variations among available manuscripts demanded impeccable scholarly method. Once published, this translation established the youthful Suzuki's scholarly reputation.

During the same period, Suzuki made a careful study of the Dunhuang [Tun-huang] manuscripts, especially *The Gandavyuha* (another philosophical text), and translated lectures given by Shaku Soen during the latter's tour of the United States. Shaku Soen's talks were also edited and published as *The Sermons of a Buddhist Abbot.*

Although English renditions of the sayings of Zen masters frequently appear in all of Suzuki's writings, his next important translations were not published until the 1930s. The most significant of these include *The Lankavatara Sutra* (1932) and a commentary on this text entitled *Studies in the Lankavatara Sutra* (1930). His translation of *The Gandavyuha Sutra* was published in 1934, and in 1935 the first edition of his influential *Manual of Zen Buddhism* was completed.

Thus, by the mid-1930s Suzuki had made a sizeable amount of

Zen material available to Westerners who could not deal with Buddhist texts in their original languages. That this was significant to the Western understanding of Zen is clear from the response of Mrs. Rhys Davids, then a leading scholar in the field of Buddhism. In *A Manual of Buddhism* (1932), she attests to the importance of Suzuki's *Lankavatara Sutra*: "D.T. Suzuki has recently published an English translation of the Lankavatara Sutra . . . . It is chiefly on this Sutra that what is known as Zen Buddhism is based."[5] Similarly, Edward Conze, another respected scholar of the Mahayana school of Buddhism, attests to the importance of Suzuki's contributions: "In the thirties D.T. Suzuki put Ch'an, or rather Zen, on the map, and for long he was the only source of what we in the West believe we know about Zen."[6]

With the publication of *Manual of Zen Buddhism*, Suzuki believed that he had brought to the West a set of materials necessary for a well-rounded understanding of Zen. *The Manual* was intended to complement his earlier *Introduction to Zen Buddhism* in which the essential teachings of Zen are discussed philosophically and *The Training of a Zen Monk* in which monastic rituals and practices are described.

Suzuki's scholarly respectability gained him access to audiences which might otherwise have turned a deaf ear. On the other hand, some Westerners for whom Zen meant sitting cross-legged or koan study (Philip Kapleau, or the followers of Shaku Sokatsu, Sokei-an Sasaki and Nyogen Senzaki, for example) rejected Suzuki's intellectual approach offhand.

Suzuki used logic to bring his readers or listeners to the point where reason does not avail. To some—most notably journalist, novelist, and philosopher Arthur Koestler—this was untenable, a contradiction in terms. In 1960, Koestler published *The Lotus and the Robot* and a series of articles in which he derides Suzuki's philosophy as "ambiguous," "vague," "at best an existential hoax, at worst a web of solemn absurdities."[7]

D.T. Suzuki's contribution to the West penetrated far beyond the areas of religious dialogue and Buddhist scholarship. The fields of psychology and psychotherapy also benefitted from his teachings. In particular, Suzuki had a profound influence on psychoanalysts Carl Jung, Erich Fromm, and Karen Horney.

Carl Gustav Jung is perhaps the most influential figure in the realm of psychology to have drawn from D.T. Suzuki's interpretation of Zen.

Jung authored the Foreword to Heinrich Zimmer's 1939 German translation of Suzuki's *An Introduction to Zen Buddhism*[8] (originally published in English in 1934), met Suzuki during the 1953 "Eranos meetings" in Zurich, invited the Zen scholar to lecture at the psychoanalytic institute in Switzerland, and entered into a heated argument with Suzuki's critic, Arthur Koestler, in *Encounter* magazine.

Jung disagreed with some aspects of Zen Buddhism. He nevertheless found it an important source for clarifying some obscure psychoanalytic concepts and for guiding his patients in their understanding of analysis. Jung therefore wrote to Suzuki, "Zen is a true goldmine for the needs of the Western psychologist."[9] Once, confronted by a patient who was having difficulty responding to psychoanalysis, Jung advised the man to read "something about Zen Buddhism" in order to understand Jungian psychological thought and "what you're up against."[10] Quite a prescription coming from a psychologist of Jung's stature!

The central Zen concept of "making whole" or, to use Jung's phrase, "psychic healing" exercised the psychotherapist. Jung stressed that Zen is more important to Westerners than Hinduism because it is free from the highly technical terminology and physical techniques of Indian religious practice which divert one from the true goal of attaining egolessness. Rather, "The attainment of wholeness requires one to stake one's whole being. Nothing less will do; there can be no easier conditions, no substitutes, no compromises."[11]

Jung emphasized the difficulty (if not the impossibility) of Westerners' attempts to understand the Oriental religious approach. He cautions that we are dependent on the structure of logic and science, and warns that our primary task is to build up "our own Western culture, which sickens with a thousand ills."[12] On the other hand, he also admits that the "satori experience" has its parallels in "those few Christian mystics whose paradoxical statements skirt the edge of heterodoxy or actually overstep it."[13] With the exception of these Christian mystics, Jung asserts, there is nothing in the West which approaches the profundity of satori in Zen: "If we discount the sayings of our Western mystics, a superficial glance discloses nothing that could be likened to it even in the faintest degree."[14]

In contrast to Jung's approach is the humanistic psychology of Erich Fromm. Fromm was also influenced by Suzuki, but in different ways. Whereas Jung dealt with Zen Buddhism as an aspect of his psychological thought, Suzuki's influence touches closer to the core of Fromm's thought. Fromm organized an influential workshop on Zen Buddhism and psychoanalysis in Cuernavaca, Mexico, and incorporated many concepts which resemble Suzuki's interpretation of Zen into his psychoanalytic writings.

The Cuernavaca workshop of 1957, held at Fromm's Mexico home, brought together eminent psychologists expressly for the purpose of exploring Zen Buddhism and psychoanalysis. As such, it marks an important point of contact between thinkers in the field of psychology and D.T. Suzuki's interpretation of Zen. Suzuki addressed the gathering, and his speeches were later published as "Lectures in Zen Buddhism" together with Fromm's address entitled "Psychoanalysis and Zen Buddhism" and that of Richard DeMartino entitled "The Human Situation and Zen Buddhism," in a volume which Fromm edited and called *Zen Buddhism and Psychoanalysis.*[15]

Fromm organized the Mexico meeting and issued the invitations to its participants as a result of his feeling that psychotherapists—and in particular, psychoanalysts—were at that time "not just interested, but deeply concerned" with Zen.[16] This "concern," Fromm believed, was a new and potentially important development in the attitude of psychologists. His own address to the workshop, reformulated, as he says, because of "the stimulation of the conference," includes language and ideas that may be traced to Dr. Suzuki's Cuernavaca lectures.

Erich Fromm first learned of Zen Buddhism through Suzuki's writings, and later, by attending Suzuki's lectures at Columbia University during the 1950's. Fromm considered himself Suzuki's student in the traditional sense that he read the latter's writings and attended classes. Fromm also saw himself as Suzuki's student in the more subtle sense that he learned about Zen merely by being in the Japanese scholar's presence. Of the effect that Suzuki had on his and his wife's Zen studies, Fromm writes: "Sometimes we thought we had understood—only to find later that we had not. Yet eventually we believed that the worst misunderstandings had been overcome and that we had understood as much as one can with the limited experience which is our lot. But undoubtedly whatever understanding of Zen we acquired was helped not only by what Dr. Suzuki said or wrote, but by his being."[17]

Psychoanalyst Karen Horney is an important yet elusive case in the Western response to Suzuki's interpretation of Zen. For, although her interest in Suzuki's thought was great, her sudden death in December of

1952 leaves us with little documentation of her reactions after studying his works and traveling with him to Japan.

Dr. Horney's interest in Zen grew out of her early disillusionment with Western religious forms, according to Dr. Jack Rubins. Horney was also close friends with Paul Tillich who was becoming interested in Zen at that time. She often attended Tillich's sermons at St. John the Divine, in New York City. By the end of the 1940s, Horney had read Aldous Huxley's *The Perennial Philosophy* and Eugene Herrigel's *Zen in the Art of Archery*, and was heavily influenced by Eastern thought.[18] It is therefore not surprising to find that her formulation of psychoanalysis contains many interesting parallels to Asian religion in general, and, specifically, to Zen.

In addition, it is possible to extrapolate from Horney's last writings and the accounts of those who knew her that she was changing the fundamental direction of her thought as a result of her studies of Zen, and her association with D.T. Suzuki. The beginnings of this change may be seen in a paper Horney delivered in February of 1952 (shortly before her trip with Suzuki and others to Japan), entitled "The Paucity of Inner Experiences."[19] Here, Horney stresses the need for each individual to be in touch with an inner, non-objectified "whole self." The loss of one's inner orientation forces a person to defend himself by substituting external rules, intellectualization, and other external dependencies. These in turn further obscure the inner experiences, leading one to a state of unfulfillment, anxiety, and feelings of the futility of life.

In the same article, Horney also experiments with terminology found in Suzuki's writing, especially the notion of "emptiness" or "nothingness." For her, "the unawareness of inner experiences gives a person a feeling of emptiness or nothingness which in itself may or may not be conscious. But whether this feeling is conscious or not, it is in any case frightening."[20]

It was in Japan that Zen took on an aspect of crucial personal importance for her, according to her travelling companion, Richard DeMartino. Horney stayed overnight at a Zen monastery, conversed with psychiatrists interested in Morita therapy, visited temples and gardens, purchased Japanese art, and met Zen master Shin'ichi Hisamatsu. Suzuki arranged most of her itinerary. Her attitude toward Zen at the beginning of the trip was casual, according to DeMartino; but by the time she left Japan in August she had been convinced of its great importance and set out to create a new psychotherapeutic form which would take its teachings into account.[21]

Zen is associated with many traditional cultural forms in Japan. Yet another of Suzuki's contributions was to make some of these—haiku, Zen painting, calligraphy, photographs and descriptions of flower arranging, translations of noh and kabuki drama, swordsmanship and an understanding of the Way of Tea—more accessible to the West. Although his books and articles were laced with stories and examples from the arts, Suzuki's major work on the topic is *Zen Buddhism and Its Influence on Japanese Culture*.[22]

Just as the philosophical formulation of Zen inspired a re-examination of Western thought-patterns, so these artistic forms—new to the Occident—changed the way many Westerners conceive of aesthetics. Novelists, painters, musicians, and poets drew both from Zen cultural forms and from the philosophy which are their underpinning.

Perhaps the most radical artistic transformations of all were spearheaded by composer John Cage (a founder of the Avant-garde movement) and potter Bernard Leach (who altered the direction of modern ceramics). In both cases, Suzuki's contribution is significant.

Cage is among the most controversial and influential figures in the Western music world. During 1945–46 he "first became seriously aware of Oriental philosophy" through the writings of Ananda Coomaraswamy, Aldous Huxley, and Sri Ramakrishna. This concern expressed itself in *Sonatas and Interludes* in which the "permanent emotions" of Indian thought were probed.[23] Although subsequent works display this generalized interest in the Orient, Cage eventually became more interested in Zen.

Cage first studied Zen with D.T. Suzuki during the late 1940s, visiting the scholar in Japan three times. Although he also attended lectures by Nancy Wilson Ross and Alan Watts, it is primarily from Suzuki and Suzuki's writings that he learned about Zen. Cage's numerous publications are punctuated with stories of the Zen masters taken from Suzuki, and often include reminiscences of personal encounters with the Japanese scholar.

Many of the concepts central to Cage's aesthetic are rooted in the composer's understanding of Suzuki's writings. Cage himself attests "without my engagement with Zen (attendance at lectures by Alan

Watts and D.T. Suzuki, reading of the literature) I doubt whether I would have done what I have done."[24]

Bernard Leach, generally considered the father of modern ceramics in the West, made an intensive study of the pottery of China, Korea, and Japan as well as Eastern thought. Although Leach came under the direct influence of Soetsu Yanagi and Hamada Shoji, D.T. Suzuki's teachings were instrumental in reshaping the aesthetics on which his pottery is based.

Leach writes of Suzuki: "I knew him profoundly. He, as much as any man, introduced me not only to Zen, but also to Jodo Shinshu Buddhism." The artist further states his gratitude to Suzuki for contributing to his ability to use pottery as a form "of adoration of the essence of life," and for helping him express through ceramics "a quietude of form or quiet seeking of Truth."[25]

Suzuki's contribution permeated Western culture on the popular level as well. Especially during the 1950s, Zen was being read and discussed by a broad spectrum of the population in the United States and Europe. Although distinctions arose between "beat" and "square" Zen, even the leaders among the popularizers paid allegiance to Suzuki.

Buddhist meditation and study groups sprang up throughout the West. In particular, the Buddhist Society—a British organization loosely associated with the earlier Buddhist Society of Great Britain and Ireland and the Buddhist Lodge—attracted several individuals who became significant contributors to Zen's popularity.

Among American groups, Suzuki was most closely associated with the Cambridge Buddhist Association. Although he was revered by members of this organization, his own choice was to remain a teacher and scholar rather than assume the posture of a "Zen Master."

Suzuki's influence on the Buddhist society increased as the group expanded. His writings were published in the society's original *Buddhist Review* as well as the later *Buddhism in England* and the still current *Middle Way*. In 1936, Suzuki was a featured participant in the World Congress of Faiths, held in London and organized by the Buddhist Society's leadership. According to Christmas Humphreys, founder of the Buddhist Lodge, and a prolific author of books and articles on Buddhism, Suzuki was "judged by many to be the most popular figure at the Congress."[26] Eventually the Society changed the focus of its meditation group from "Buddhist meditation to Zen meditation."[27] The basis for this change was, in Humphreys' words, "Dr. D.T. Suzuki, whose name is all but coterminus with Zen as known and practised in the West."[28]

Such personalities as Humphreys, Alan Watts, A.C. March, H.P. Blavatsky, and Edward Conze came under Suzuki's influence through the British group. The Buddhist Society, in turn, became an important publishing outlet for Suzuki's articles and books, with Humphreys as their editor.

Among the popularizers of Zen in the West, Alan Watts deserves special mention because of the many people who came under his influence. Watts studied D.T. Suzuki's interpretation of Zen extensively, and viewed himself as continuing within the framework of Suzuki's teachings. During the 1950s, when Zen was at the height of its popularity, Watts' name was virtually synonymous with the "beat" culture associated with Zen.

Watts claims never to have had "a formal teacher (*guru* or *roshi*) in the spiritual life—only an exemplar whose example I have not really followed because no sensitive person likes to be mimicked. That exemplar was Suzuki Daisetz—at once the subtlest and simplest person I have known."[29]

While a teenager in England, Watts became active in the Buddhist Lodge of the Cambridge branch of the Theosophical Society, and in 1930, Humphreys introduced the young Watts to Suzuki's writings. Watts consequently wrote, *The Spirit of Zen* to "clarify and popularize" Suzuki's "enigmatic thoughts."[30] In the Preface to the first edition, Suzuki's contribution is affirmed: "It is to him that we of the West owe almost all of our knowledge of Zen."[31] *The Spirit of Zen* draws heavily from Suzuki's translations and other material contained in the three series of *Essays in Zen Buddhism*.

Watts first met Suzuki in 1936 while the latter was in London for the World Congress of Faiths. Watts describes Suzuki as "unofficial lay master of Zen Buddhism, humorous off beat scholar, and about the most gentle and enlightened person I have ever known; for he combined the most complex learning with utter simplicity. He was versed in Japanese, English, Chinese, Sanskrit, Tibetan, French, Pali, and German, but while attending a meeting of the Buddhist Lodge he would play with a kitten, looking right into its Buddha-nature."[32] Again, Watts refers to Suzuki as a "naive intellectual—wisely foolish, gently disciplined, and simply profound."[33]

Watts published over twenty full-length books, ranging in scope from Zen to Christian theology and practice, to comparative psychotherapy. He produced and performed radio broadcasts on the West Coast devoted to religious and philosophical questions and was involved in the founding of the Esalen Institute—a retreat devoted to alternate means of achieving personal wholeness and well-being.[34]

Watts also helped inspire an entire generation of "beat" poets and writers, including, for example, Allen Ginsberg, Jack Kerouac, William Burroughs, Gary Snyder and Neal Cassady. These writers perceived themselves as following the path of Zen masters Han Shan and Shi Teh [Shih Teh] in search of freedom. The book which epitomized the "beat" movement, Kerouac's *Dharma Bums*, chronicles events in their lives and their experiments with Buddhist ideas.

Ginsberg, who was also directly influenced by Suzuki, writes about a visit to Suzuki's home on the very day that *The Dharma Bums* was published: "On the way to the publisher's party, Kerouac, myself and Orlovsky visited D.T. Suzuki at his house in New York on a spur-of-the-moment phone call, sat in his study, composed haikus on a Sesshu print on his wall, and drank green tea with him that he prepared—he saw us downstairs to bid adieux from his door opened on the front stoop, waving goodbye, saying to us 'Don't forget the green tea.' "[35]

Suzuki believed that the Beat Generation, also called the "San Francisco Renaissance Group" had misunderstood his interpretation of Zen. "Spontaneity," wrote Suzuki, "is not everything, it must be 'rooted'."[36] Indeed, the Japanese scholar was aware that while Zen was entering into the vernacular of Western culture, it was also being watered down and misrepresented. In the same article he states, "Zen is at present evoking unexpected echoes in various field of Western culture: music, painting, literature, semantics, religious philosophy, and psychoanalysis. But as it is in many cases grossly misrepresented or misinterpreted, I undertake here to explain most briefly, as far as language permits, what Zen aims at and what significance it has in the modern world, hoping that Zen will be saved from being too absurdly caricatured."[37]

Suzuki did not attempt to win larger audiences by diluting concepts or compromising his intellectual integrity. But neither did he write or speak in technical terms meant only for the seasoned scholar. As a result, lay readers and some of the West's most rigorous thinkers found his presentation of Zen palatable.

One can hardly begin to catalog the names of the significant Western personalities who reaped the fruits of Suzuki's contribution. Add to those discussed above, for example, thinkers of the stature of Martin Heidegger, James Bisset Pratt and Arnold Toynbee; writers and artists like Jackson Pollack, Herbert Read, Rudolf Ray, J.D. Salinger, Merce Cunningham, Jackson MacLow or Dizzy Gillespie; philosophers of religion such as John Cobb, Richard DeMartino or Huston Smith. Then include the many people who were influenced ephemerally, indirectly, or as part of the larger movement of Western culture in general. In one way or other, Suzuki touched them all.

Daisetz Teitaro Suzuki was first and foremost a master teacher—one who could accurately assess his readers or listeners and then respond to them with complete appropriatness. Perhaps herein lies the reason why this diminutive scholar from Japan could make a profound contribution in so many areas of Western culture. "Emptiness" was his message as well as his medium. To the question, "How many varieties of garlands can skilled hands fashion with the same flowers?" we may well respond, "What is the meaning of Suzuki's coming from East to West?"

8

Masao Abe

The Influence of D.T. Suzuki
in the West

I N THE WEST, as well as in Japan, Suzuki Sensei has often been regarded exclusively as an exponent of Zen in the twentieth century.
He was, however, a many-sided individual and a thinker of con-
summate synthesis rarely found in our times. One of his earliest books
in English is entitled *Outlines of Mahayana Buddhism*, and the significance
of Mahayana Buddhism was his major concern from the outset. He carefully studied the *Lankavatara Sutra*, and published a translation, index,
and exegesis of the Sutra. The *Gandavyuha Sutra* and Huayen [Hua-yen]
Buddhism also were subjects of persistent interest and research throughout his life.[1] In addition, he was deeply involved in Pure Land Buddhism
and produced invaluable studies and translations of its literature.[2] Still
another concern and achievement was his introduction and new interpretation of Japanese culture to the West.[3] All of these fields, including
Zen, were grasped by Suzuki Sensei from the perspective of "religious
experience" which can be universally realized by human beings. Thus
he often compared Zen and Pure Land Buddhism with Christianity,
particularly Christian mysticism.[4] When I comment on Suzuki Sensei's
influence in the West I should refer to all of his major works, but it
is far beyond the scope of the present essay to do so. I will remark.
therefore, primarily on the subject of his influence in the West focusing
on his contribution to Zen, while touching on other aspects of his work
only tangentially.

It is worthy of note that the twelve years between 1897 and 1909, that is, the period between Suzuki Sensei's twenty-seventh and thirty-ninth years, were of fundamental importance in making possible his eminent later activities, which had such a profound effect on the Western intellectual world. Though he spent the last fourteen months of this period in England and on the Continent, most of this time he lived in the United States, where he resided with Paul Carus in La Salle, Illinois.[5] There, while translating Açvaghosha's *Discourse on the Awakening of Faith in the Mahayana*, Suzuki Sensei was deeply involved in a study of Western psychology and religious thought, particularly that of William James. In England, he was engaged in translating Swedenborg's *Heaven and Hell* into Japanese. During the thirty years or so after this period, that is, during the period ending just a few years before the beginning of the Pacific War, the three volumes of *Essays in Zen Buddhism*, the English translation of the *Lankavatara Sutra*, and the companion volume expounding the Sutra, and his other important works in English, were successively published.

Dr. Margaret H. Dornish, a scholar in religious studies who is currently lecturing on Eastern religions at Pomona College in Claremont, California, wrote her doctoral dissertation nearly twenty years ago about the early period of D.T. Suzuki. Her research can be regarded as the first step in Western study of Suzuki Sensei's thought. In recent years, Dr. Larry A. Fader, Professor of Religion at Trinity College in Hartford, Connecticut, and Dr. William LaFleur, Professor of Japanese Literature and Buddhism at the University of California at Los Angeles have also been studying D.T. Suzuki and his early contacts with Western thinkers. Since Suzuki Sensei's early period abroad and his works of this period are relatively little known in Japan, it will also be necessary there to undertake research into this period of his life, in order to comprehensively understand Suzuki Sensei's thought and, in particular, in order to clarify the nature of his effect on Western thinkers. These early English writings became the driving force of his ultimately widespread intellectual influence on the West.

It was not until some years after World War II, however, that Zen thought—as expounded by Suzuki Sensei—came to exercise such a remarkable influence on broad segments of American and European society. Before the war, his various books had been highly regarded in the West by only a small number of people of spiritual vision and by some philosophical thinkers, but the books had not truly been disseminated to the broad intellectual community. So it was, in the midst of the waves of sudden change in world history, with the order of Western society so shaken to its roots by the war, that the luminous body of Zen—which Suzuki Sensei had deeply immersed Western society in before the war—began to emit its own original light. In those days, when many people in Europe and America were seized with anxiety, doubt, and despair over the failure of their traditional system of values, Zen emerged to suddenly impress a large segment of the intellectual community, and began to provide new hope for people's broken spirit. Many individuals sensed in Zen the light of an entirely new life, and set out determinedly to grope toward this vision. Suzuki Sensei's unflagging round of lectures and speeches after the war, at universities in America and in various parts of Europe, played an important role in spurring on this movement, as did his activities as an author in English, which continued to be prolific well after the war.

A strong interest in Zen thus developed in the West, not only among scholars and thinkers, but among a widely diverse group of people. The movement was most notable in the United States, where a broad variety of Zen-influenced experiments were happening in painting, music, dance, and the literary arts, especially in poetry and in the novel. A so-called Zen Boom unfolded across the spectrum of the intellectual world especially in the 1950s. In addition to Suzuki Sensei's writings, his free and buoyant Zen personality almost invariably caught up those who came in contact with him, functioning as a force transcending words, opening people's eyes to the true nature of Zen Buddhism. It reached a point in the United States where publications from the *New York Times* to popular magazines were running pictures and interviews featuring D.T. Suzuki.

The effect of Zen was all-pervasive. Investigation and analysis of these Zen influences is not only important to our understanding the relationship between Zen and the spiritual life of Western man—or the problems of prior modes of contact, exchange, metamorphosis, and synthesis of Eastern and Western thought—it is also necessary from the standpoint of the future exchange of ideas between East and West. To take up these matters here, however, is not possible, since it is beyond the scope of this essay. But even if we restrict our view of Suzuki Sensei's influence to the sphere of scholars and thinkers, an event at the Second East-West

Philosophers' Conference in 1949 illustrates how highly regarded Suzuki was in intellectual circles. At the conference, Dr. Gregg A. Sinclair, former president of the University of Hawaii, divided the attending scholars into two groups according to whether or not they were familiar with the works of D.T. Suzuki. That this could happen at all during an international academic conference notwithstanding, this episode suggests just how significant Suzuki's thought was, and is, from the perspective of exchange of ideas between East and West, and it foreshadowed the immeasurable influence his thought is likely to exercise in the future.

The "Zen boom" however, is over. Instead, a more quiet and serious interest in Zen has been gradually penetrating Western, and especially American, soil. On the one hand, careful historical studies of Zen and its doctrinal background, and translations of original Zen literature are being conducted. On the other hand, increasing numbers of serious *zazen* practitioners have been gathering at Zen centers which are emerging at many locations in the West.

In the West as well as in Japan, however, Suzuki Sensei's works have not escaped criticism. For example: Suzuki presented only Rinzai Zen, neglecting the important stream of Soto Zen, including its remarkable Japanese promulgator, Dogen. Suzuki characterized Japanese culture as if it has been nourished only by Zen, overlooking other religious influences such as Shingon, Tendai Pure Land, and Shinto; Suzuki's approach was generally subjective, not based on careful historical and textual studies. To some extent, these criticisms are undeniably correct. I think, however, that, before hastening to make a definitive evaluation of Suzuki Sensei's significance upon intellectual history we must consider at least two points.

First, a comprehensive and integral evaluation of his writings should include the entire corpus of nearly ninety titles originally published in Japanese[6] and nearly thirty volumes originally published in English. Just as many Japanese students are unfamiliar with D.T. Suzuki's English writings as most Westerners, including scholars, are not acquainted with D.T. Suzuki's works in Japanese—his careful studies of the Dunhuang [Tun-huang] manuscripts of Chan [Ch'an][7] and publication of critical editions of important Zen texts, for example.[8]

Second, a penetrating examination of the inner motivation underlying Suzuki Sensei's activities over a long lifetime is needed. Was he motivated primarily by an academic spirit of inquiry, or by a missionary attachment to Zen Buddhism, or by a broader desire to generally introduce Oriental thought to the West?

To help resolve these issues and to try to understand the real significance of Suzuki Sensei in intellectual history, I want, rather, to consider for a moment D.T. Suzuki's "image" as he was perceived by Westerners.

It is natural that Suzuki Sensei's activities in the West, spanning a period of more than half a century, should have evoked many different reactions. As I mentioned before, he was lauded as well as criticized in diverse ways, and the most conspicuous reactions might be summarized in the following three ways.

First, there are people, and not just a few, who understand Suzuki Sensei to have been a Buddhist missionary, or Zen evangelist, working to spread Buddhism in the Western world. When they say "evangelist," they are not using the term in an occupational sense, and, in most cases, their viewpoint includes an attitude of respect. Nevertheless, those who are unshakeably fixed in their Christian beliefs may, in judging Suzuki Sensei to have been an evangelist for Buddhism and Zen, view his activities and his wide influence with caution, or sometimes react against him. There are even those who label his activities a Zen "missionary attack" on the Western intellectual class, or a Buddhist "invasion" of the Christian world.

Second, among scholars of East Asian studies, Buddhism, and religion, certain individuals, while acknowledging the great role of Suzuki Sensei in introducing Eastern ideas to the West, criticize his interpretation of Buddhism and Zen as having been subjective and unscholarly. They say that D.T. Suzuki was a popularizer but not a scholar. Those who subscribe to this view, are, of course, speaking from their own perspective concerning the meaning of "scholarship" and "scholar." In most cases, it is historical research and textual scholarship, or, put broadly, an "impartiality," as prescribed by the positivistic method, which constitute the standard of judgment.

Third, other people say that D.T. Suzuki, in his writings and speeches, presented the marvelous quality of satori—Zen enlightenment, or "awakening"—but did not lend particular weight to the importance of *zazen* practice (seated meditation). Suzuki, they claim, was a Zen thinker, but not a *roshi* (Zen master). This is a point of view found among those who have gone to Japan and to some extent dedicated themselves to Zen practice, or those who have practiced *zazen* at Zen centers, or similar facilities, in other countries.

Naturally the three preceding issues are not an exhaustive description of the ways in which Westerners have responded to D.T. Suzuki. Yet it is unquestionably the case that his activities have been perceived, and his work evaluated and criticized, from the three perspectives I have mentioned. What then was the true meaning of D.T. Suzuki for the West? And what was it that truly provided him with the internal motivation to undertake his life's work?

Between 1955 and 1957, while studying at Columbia University, I was able to sit in on the lectures presented by Suzuki Sensei every week. He was there at that time as a visiting professor. I was also blessed with the good fortune to have the opportunity to visit him frequently at his residence at the Okamuras' house on Ninety-fourth Street. There he would give me personal instruction and I could listen to him talk in a more informal atmosphere. On these occasions Suzuki Sensei would tell me from time to time something about his personal motivations.

He would say that many people of the Christian religion go to foreign lands, where they strive to propagate their faith despite enduring numerous hardships. In Buddhism, however, though there have been those who have risked their lives to travel to India or China seeking the Buddhist Dharma, very few have risked their lives to transmit the Dharma. In the future, he would say, this must change. When I heard Suzuki Sensei himself make these statements—there in New York, in a far corner of America—it was as if a thousand-pound weight had been brought to bear on my chest.

There was, without question, a strong sense of mission behind Suzuki Sensei's efforts to transmit Buddhism, and Zen, to the West. I also believe that he never lost the feeling, as an Asian, that it was indeed the religious legacy of Buddhism and Zen in Asian civilization which Asians could most significantly contribute to the rest of the world. His encounters with Westerners were all grounded in this state of mind.

It was nevertheless not merely a sense of mission, or pride as an Asian, or even scholarly drive, which provided Suzuki Sensei with his real internal motivation. I believe that behind his activities there resided a religious Awakening. As a youth, under the guidance of Zen Master Shaku Soen, he had become deeply realized through penetrating into the root-source of the universe of life-and-death. His "motivation" derived from no other than this realization. It was what he later referred to in his writings variously as "No-Mind," "*prajna*-intuition," "cosmic unconsciousness," "spiritual perception," *nin* (true Man) or *myo* (wonder). This awakening functioned within Suzuki Sensei as an overwhelming Buddhist spirit of "vow," aimed at bringing everyone to awaken to this same Reality. In this quest, there was no distinction between East and West. His scholarly study of Buddhism was undertaken in order to further this work; it was not the other way around. His efforts to introduce Zen to the West also derived from this commitment; he was not simply trying to increase the exposure of Zen teachings. His awareness of himself as an Asian was due to his having found, within the Asian tradition, this "Root-Awakening," which is not ultimately something confined to East or West.

In this sense, Suzuki Sensei was more than anything else a citizen of the world. He was a citizen of the world who intensively lived the first of the Four Buddhist Vows: "However innumerable living beings, I vow to save them all." His repeated criticisms of the dualistic way of thinking and the tendency toward seeking power and control, especially evident in the West, were also due to this commitment to bringing others to Awakening. In the light of such compassionate devotion, to characterize him with a narrow missionary consciousness or scholarly impartiality misses the mark. His frequent talks about satori are certainly explicable in the same terms. He did in fact talk at times about Zen monastic life, but he did not stress the necessity of *zazen* in particular. Furthermore, he did not himself act as a teacher of *zazen* or koan practice for those Westerners who gathered about him as seekers of Zen. I think it was probably his feeling that duties of this kind should be entrusted to those who were properly qualified to fulfill them. It seems that Suzuki Sensei wanted to behave thoroughly in keeping with his own proper sphere, and not to exceed its boundaries. However, in situations such as the question-and-answer periods after his lectures or in his bearing in daily conversations, there was vividly apparent an unimpeded freedom of response that concealed a combative sharpness. This was a characteristic of such depth that it often caused those who came in contact with him to realize suddenly that they were, fundamentally, caught up in their own attachments.

At the Fourth East-West Philosophers' Conference in 1964, sponsored by the Philosophy Department of the University of Hawaii in Honolulu (this was to be the last East-West Philosophers' Conference that he would attend), Suzuki Sensei introduced, in the course of a public lecture, the Zen story of Kwasan beating the drum.[9] Then he said that if he were asked "Well, why is it that you brought yourself all the way across the Pacific to come here?" he would answer, "I'll show you why in *my* own way [emphasis added]." He next pounded on the rostrum with his fist. In this way he was attempting to engage each one of the hundreds of people in the overflowing audience at the Kennedy Theater in an authentic Zen dialogue.

For Suzuki Sensei, it was not necessary to undertake Zen dialogue in a private room, in the prescribed manner that a *roshi* would employ in a Zen monastery. And he did not hold that *zazen* was absolutely necessary for the attainment of enlightenment. Clearly, to Suzuki Sensei, Zen is not a system of *dhyana* (meditation). He thus emphasized the awakening to *prajna*-intuition which is originally functioning in us, even apart from *zazen*.

The number of people pursuing *zazen* practice in North America and Europe has grown progressively larger in recent years. There is a movement away from Zen as an intellectual pursuit to Zen as a practice. This is an important transformation if Zen is to take root in the West. Nevertheless, *zazen* practice will have little to do with what Suzuki Sensei spoke of as *prajna*-intuition if *zazen* is something pursued as a quietude that stands in opposition to the uproar of modern culture, or if it ends at mere "meditation." To simply view Suzuki Sensei as a Zen thinker who did not expound on religious practice is to fail to appreciate that force which most deeply motivated his life—in the same sense that one would fail to understand that force by simply viewing Suzuki Sensei as a Zen missionary to the Christian world. Behind the dedicated activity that characterized Suzuki Sensei's long life, something was indeed at work which cannot be neatly categorized under a heading such as the one used here: "The Influence of D.T. Suzuki in the West."

Upon reflection, I think that we must not stop at merely cherishing the memory of Suzuki and praising the great strides that he took. Nor should we simply criticize or reject him just by pointing out the bias innate in his approach. Those who have been involved with him personally or with his writings—positively or negatively—must come to appreciate that what motivated D.T. Suzuki was the spirit of the vow to attain, together with one's self and all others, "Awakening"—and thereby open up a new spiritual vista in which Easterner and Westerner can work hand in hand to fulfill humanity. It is important for us, too, to share that spirit of "vow" and try to materialize it in our own way.

PART THREE

9

Thomas Merton

D.T. Suzuki: The Man and His Work

> On peut se sentir fier d'être contemporain d'un
> certain nombre d'hommes de ce temps...
>
> *Albert Camus.*

W E ARE LIVING in a very unusual age. It is therefore no great
wonder that there have been unusual men in it. Though
perhaps less universally known than such figures as Einstein
and Gandhi (who became symbols of our time) Daisetz Suzuki was no
less remarkable a man than these. And though his work may not have had
such resounding and public effect, he contributed no little to the spiritual
and intellectual revolution of our time. The impact of Zen on the West,
striking with its fullest force right after World War II, in the midst of
the existentialist upheaval, at the beginning of the atomic and cybernetic
age, with Western religion and philosophy in a state of crisis and with
the consciousness of man threatened by the deepest alienation, the work
and personal influence of Dr. Suzuki proved to be both timely and fruitful: much more fruitful than we have perhaps begun to realize. I do not
speak now of the rather superficial Western enthusiasm for the externals
and the froth of Zen (which Dr. Suzuki himself could tolerantly but
objectively evaluate) but of the active leaven of Zen insight which he
brought into the already bubbling ferment of Western thinking in his
contacts with psychoanalysis, philosophy, and religious thought like
that of Paul Tillich.

There is no question that Dr. Suzuki brought to this age of dialogue
a very special gift of his own: a capacity to apprehend and to occupy
the precise standpoints where communication could hope to be effective.

121

He was able to do this all the more effectively because one felt he was entirely free from the dictates of partisan thought-patterns and academic ritualism. He was not compelled to play the complex games by which one jockeys for advantage in the intellectual world. Therefore, of course, he found himself quite naturally and without difficulty in a position of prominence. He spoke with authority, the authority of a simple, clear-sighted man who was aware of human limits and not inclined to improve on them with huge artificial structures that had no real significance. He did not need to put another head on top of his own, as the Zen saying goes. This of course is an advantage in any dialogue, for when men try to communicate with each other, it is good for them to speak with distinct and personal voices, not to blur their identities by speaking through several official masks at the same time.

It was my good fortune to meet Dr. Suzuki and to have a couple of all too short conversations with him. The experience was not only rewarding, but I would say it was unforgettable. It was, in my own life, a quite extraordinary event since, because of the circumstances in which I live, I do not get to meet all those I would meet professionally if I were, say, teaching in a university. I had known his work for a long time, had corresponded with him, and we had had a short dialogue published, in which we discussed the "Wisdom of Emptiness" as found comparatively, in Zen and in the Egyptian Desert Fathers. ("Wisdom in Emptiness"— A dialogue between Daisetz Suzuki and Thomas Merton, in *New Directions 17*, New York, 1961.) On his last trip to the United States I had the great privilege and pleasure of meeting him. One had to meet this man in order to fully appreciate him. He seemed to me to embody all the indefinable qualities of the "Superior Man" of the ancient Asian, Daoist, Confucian, and Buddhist traditions. Or rather in meeting him one seemed to meet that "True Man of No Title," that Zuhang Zi [Chuang Tzu] the Zen Masters speak of. And of course this is the man one really wants to meet. Who else is there? In meeting Dr. Suzuki and drinking a cup of tea with him I felt I had met this one man. It was like finally arriving at one's own home. A very happy experience, to say the least. There is not a great deal one has to say about it, because to speak at length would divert attention to details that are after all irrelevant. When one is actually there with a person, the multiple details fall naturally into the unity that is seen without being expressed. When one speaks of it secondhand there are only the multiple details. The True

Man has meanwhile long since gone about his business somewhere else.

Thus far I have spoken simply as a human being. I should also speak as a Catholic priest and monk, brought up in a certain Western religious tradition but with, I hope, a legitimate curiosity about and openness to other traditions. Such a one can only with diffidence hazard statements about Buddhism, since he cannot be sure that he has a trustworthy insight into the spiritual values of a tradition with which he is not really familiar. Speaking for myself, I can venture to say that in Dr. Suzuki, Buddhism finally became for me completely comprehensible, whereas before it had been a very mysterious and confusing jumble of words, images, doctrines, legends, rituals, buildings, and so forth. It seemed to me that the great and baffling cultural luxuriance which has clothed the various forms of Buddhism in different parts of Asia is the beautiful garment thrown over something quite simple. The greatest religions are all, in fact, very simple. They all retain very important essential differences, no doubt, but in their inner reality Christianity, Buddhism, Islam and Judaism are extremely simple (though capable as I say of baffling luxuriance) and they all end up with the simplest and most baffling thing of all: direct confrontation with Absolute Being, Absolute Love, Absolute Mercy or Absolute Void, by an immediate and fully awakened engagement in the living of everyday life. In Christianity the confrontation is theological and affective, through word and love. In Zen it is metaphysical and intellectual through insight and emptiness. Yet Christianity too has its tradition of apophantic contemplation or knowledge in "unknowing" while the last words I remember Dr. Suzuki saying (before the usual good-byes) were "The most important thing is Love!" I must say that as a Christian I was profoundly moved. Truly *prajna* and *karuna* are one (as the Buddhist says) or *caritas* (love) is indeed the highest knowledge.

I saw Dr. Suzuki only in two brief visits and I did not feel I ought to waste time exploring abstract, doctrinal explanations of his tradition. But I did feel that I was speaking to someone who, in a tradition completely different from my own, had matured, had become complete, and had found his way. One cannot understand Buddhism until one meets it in this existential manner, in a person in whom it is alive. Then there is no longer a problem of understanding doctrines which cannot help being a bit exotic for a Westerner, but only a question of appreciating a value which is self-evident. I am sure that no alert and intelligent

Westerner ever met Dr. Suzuki without feeling something of the same.

This same existential quality is evident in another way in Dr. Suzuki's vast published work. An energetic, original and productive worker, granted the gift of a long life and tireless enthusiasm for his subject, he has left us a whole library of Zen in English. I am unfortunately not familiar with his work in Japanese or able to say what it amounts to. But what we have in English is certainly without question the most complete and most authentic presentation of an Asian tradition and experience by any one man in terms accessible to the West. The uniqueness of Dr. Suzuki's work lies in the directness with which an Asian thinker has been able to communicate his own experience of a profound and ancient tradition in a Western language. This is quite a different proposition from the more or less trustworthy translations of Eastern texts by Western scholars with no experience of Asian spiritual values, or even the experience of Asian traditions acquired by Westerners.

One reason for the peculiar effectiveness of Dr. Suzuki's communication of Zen to the West is that he had a rather remarkable capacity to transpose Zen into the authentic totalities of Western mystical traditions that were most akin to it. I do not know how deep an acquaintance Dr. Suzuki had with the Western mystics, but he had read Meister Eckhart pretty thoroughly. (I may mention in parentheses that I agree with Dr. Suzuki in his final position about Zen and Mysticism, in which he elected to say that Zen was "not mysticism" in order to avoid certain disastrous ambiguities. But this question still calls for further study.)

Although Dr. Suzuki accepted the current rather superficial Western idea of Eckhart as a unique and completely heretical phenomenon, we must admit, with more recent scholarship, that Eckhart does represent a profound, wide, and largely orthodox current in Western religious thought: that which goes back to Plotinus and Pseudo-Dionysius the Areopagite, and comes down in the West through Scotus Erigena and the medieval school of St. Victor, but also profoundly affected Eckhart's Master, St. Thomas Aquinas. Having come in touch with this relatively little-known tradition, Suzuki found it congenial and was able to make good use of it. I found, for example, that in my dialogue with him mentioned above, he was able to use the mythical language in which the Fall of Man is described, in the Bible and the Church Fathers, to distinct advantage psychologically and spiritually. He spoke quite naturally and easily of the implications of the "Fall" in terms of man's alienation from himself, and he did so in just the same simple natural way as the Fathers of the Church like St. Augustine or St. Gregory of Nyssa did. If the truth be told, there is a great deal in common in the psychological and spiritual insight of the Church Fathers and in the psychoanalytically-oriented Christian existential thinking of men like Tillich, himself more influenced than many realized by the Augustinian tradition. Dr. Suzuki was perfectly at home in this atmosphere and perfectly able to handle these traditional symbols. In fact he was far more at home with them than many Western theologians. He understood and appreciated the symbolic language of the Bible and the Fathers much more directly than many of our contemporaries, Catholics included, for whom all this is little more than an embarrassment. The whole reality of the "Fall" is inscribed in our nature in what Jung called symbolic archetypes, and the Fathers of the Church (as well as the Biblical writers too no doubt) were much more concerned with this archetypal significance than with the Fall as an "historical event." Others besides Dr. Suzuki have, without being Christians, intuitively grasped the importance of this symbol. Two names spring to mind: Erich Fromm, the psychoanalyst, and that remarkable and too little-known poet, Edwin Muir, the translator into English of Franz Kafka. I do not think Dr. Suzuki was the kind of person to be bothered with any concern about whether or not he was sufficiently "modern." The "True Man of No Title" is not concerned about such labels, since he knows no time but the present, and knows he cannot apprehend either the past or the future except in the present.

It may be said that all Dr. Suzuki's books are pretty much about the same thing. Occasionally he will draw back and view Zen from the standpoint of culture, or psychoanalysis, or from the viewpoint of Christian Mysticism (in Eckhart) but even then he does not really move out of Zen into some other field, or even take a radically new look at his subject. He says very much the same things, tells the same wonderful Zen stories perhaps in slightly different words, and ends with the same conclusion: Zero equals infinity. Yet there is no monotony in his works and one does not feel he is repeating himself, because in fact each book is brand-new. Each book is a whole new experience. Those of us who have written a great deal can well admire this quality in Dr. Suzuki's work: its remarkable consistency, its unity. Pseudo-Dionysius says that the wisdom of the contemplative moves in a *motus orbicularis*—a circling and hovering motion like that of the eagle above some invisible quarry, or the turning of a planet around an invisible sun. The work of Dr. Suzuki bears witness of the silent orbiting of *prajna* which is (in the language of the same Western tradition of the Areopagite and Erigena), a "circle whose circumference is nowhere and whose center is everywhere." The rest of us travel in linear flight. We go far, take up distant positions, abandon them, fight battles and then wonder what we got so excited about, construct systems and then junk them, and wander all over continents looking for something new. Dr. Suzuki stayed right where he was, in his own Zen, and found it inexhaustibly new with each new book. Surely this is an indication of a special gift, a special quality of spiritual genius.

In any event, his work remains with us as a great gift, as one of the unique spiritual and intellectual achievements of our time. It is above all precious to us in the way it has moved East and West closer together, bringing Japan and America into agreement on a deep level, when everything seems to conspire to breed conflict, division, incomprehension, confusion, and war. Our time has not always excelled in the works of peace. We can be proud of a contemporary who has devoted his life to those works, and done so with such success.

10

Erich Fromm

Memories of Dr. D.T. Suzuki

I N ATTEMPTING TO WRITE a few words of memories of Dr. Suzuki I am struck by the paradox that it is so difficult to write memories about him precisely because I see him so alive before me. How can one write "memories" about a man who has just left the room for a moment, and whose presence is felt with all vividness?

I write these lines in the garden of our house in Cuernavaca (Mexico) where Dr. Suzuki stayed with us for several months, exactly ten years ago. Here he sat, walked, read, conversed, and although it is ten years ago, the strength and radiance of his personality makes him ever-present.

Should I write about his never-failing kindness, about his firmness and truthfulness, his concentration, the absence of vanity and Ego in him? Those who knew him, know all this; and for those who did not know him, words like these cannot mean much. Perhaps I should mention his ever-present interest in everything around him. He was delighted to see a Mexican rug, or piece of pottery, or silverware. It was not only a matter of seeing it, but of touching it, feeling its texture and its form. He gave life to everything by his interest, by his active relatedness; a person, a cat, a tree, a flower—they all came to life through his own aliveness. The following story may illustrate this: when he had been in Mexico two years before, he visited the house of a friend and colleague of mine, Dr. Francisco Garza, and admired the beautiful garden with its many old trees. Two years later, when he returned and visited Dr. Garza's home again, he looked at one of the trees and asked: "What happened to the branch of the tree that was here last time?" Indeed, a branch had been cut off, but Dr. Suzuki remembered that branch and missed it.

Should I give an example of his thoughtfulness? He always wanted to make us a gift of a Japanese stone lantern. But there were many difficulties entailed in packing it, shipping it from Japan to Mexico, and finally in getting it through the Mexican customs without our having to pay the import duties, a point upon which Dr. Suzuki insisted. While all these circumstances delayed the matter, he never forgot it. Just at the beginning of this year I received a letter from Dr. Suzuki stating that the lantern had been shipped, that he had found a way to pay the import duties, and mentioning the kind of place that would be best to place it in our garden. Indeed, the lantern arrived as he had wished; I am looking at it as I write this; but Dr. Suzuki had died before I could confirm the arrival of his gift.

Should I write about the effect his very presence had on me, on my wife, and on so many other friends and colleagues? His love for life, his freedom from selfish desires, his inner joy, his strength, all had a deep effect. They tended to make one stronger, more alive, more concentrated. Yet without ever evoking that kind of awe which the great personality so often does. He was always himself, humble, never an "authority"; he never insisted that his views must be followed; he was a man who never aroused fear in anybody; there was nothing of the irrational and mystifying aura of the "great man" about him; there was never a sense of obligation to accept what he said because he said it. He was an authority purely by his being, and never because he promised approval or threatened disapproval.

My wife and I first became acquainted with Zen through his books, and later by attending his seminars at Columbia University in New York; after that, by many conversations here in Mexico. Sometimes we thought we had understood—only to find later that we had not. Yet eventually we believed that the worst misunderstandings had been overcome and that we had understood as much as one can with only the limited experience which is our lot. But undoubtedly whatever understanding of Zen we acquired was greatly helped not only by what Dr. Suzuki said or wrote, but by his being. If one cannot put in words what being "enlightened" is, and if one cannot speak from one's own experience, Dr. Suzuki's person represented it. He himself, his whole being, was "the finger that points to the moon." I told him many Chassidic stories which he enjoyed and appreciated in their close connection with Zen thinking. One of them illustrates what I am trying to say with regard to him: A Chassid is asked why he comes to visit his master; does he want to hear his words of wisdom? "No," he answered, "I just want to see how he ties his shoelaces."

While Dr. Suzuki stayed here in Cuernavaca, he participated in a one-week workshop on Zen Buddhism and Psychoanalysis organized by the Mexican Psychoanalytic Society. About fifty psychoanalysts from the United States and Mexico participated, mainly because this was a unique opportunity to hear several lectures given by Dr. Suzuki, to hear his remarks in the discussions, and perhaps more than anything else, to be in his presence for a whole week. And indeed, his presence was responsible for a remarkable phenomenon. As one might have expected, the meeting began with the usual distraction due to over-emphasis on thoughts and words. But after two days a change of mood began to be apparent. Everyone became more concentrated and more quiet. At the end of the meeting a visible change had occurred in many of the participants. They had gone through a unique experience; they felt that an important event had happened in their lives, that they had woken up a little and that they would not lose what they had gained. Dr. Suzuki participated in all the sessions with punctuality and interest. He never made a concession of thought in order to be "better understood," but neither did he insist or argue. He was just himself, his thinking firmly rooted in his being. The hours of the sessions were many, the chairs were hard. All he needed was to be alone from time to time. One day Miss Okamura and my wife were looking for him; they could not find him anywhere, and just as they began to become a little worried they saw him, sitting under a tree, meditating. He was so relaxed that he had become one with the tree, and it was difficult to see "him."

I have often wondered about the unique quality in Dr. Suzuki. Was it his lack of narcissism and selfishness, his kindness, and his love of life? It was all of these, but often I have thought of still another aspect: the child-like quality in him. This needs some comment. The process of living hardens the heart of most people. As children we still have an open and malleable heart; we still have faith in the genuineness of mother's smile, in the reliability of promises, in the unconditional love which is our birthright. But this "original faith" is shattered sooner or later in our childhood. Most of us lose the softness and flexibility of our hearts; to become an adult is often synonymous with becoming hardened. Some escape this fate; they keep their heart open and do not let it harden. But in order to be able to do so, they do not see reality fully as it is. They become as Don Quixote, seeing the noble and the beautiful where they are not; they are dreamers who never awaken fully to see reality including all its ugliness and meanness. There is a third solution, but an exceedingly rare one. The persons who take this road retain the softness of a child's heart, and yet they see reality in all clarity and without illusions. They are children first, then they become adults, and yet they return to being children without ever losing the realism of adulthood. This is a difficult way, and that is why it is so rare. I believe it was this which characterized Dr. Suzuki's personality. He was hard as rock and soft as wax; he was the realistic, mature man, who was able to look at the world with the innocence and faith of the child.

Dr. Suzuki was a "radical," by which I mean that he went to the root. And the root, for him, was man. His humanity shone through the particularity of his national and cultural background. You forgot his nationality, his age, his "persona" when being with him. You spoke to a man, and nothing but a man. It is because of this that he will be present always; a friend and a guide whose physical presence was secondary to the light which radiates from him.

11

Ernst Benz

In Memoriam

D AISETZU SUZUKI is the person whom I can least imagine to be no longer in the land of the living.

I first had the opportunity to meet him in 1946–47 and had the pleasure to meet him again on various occasions in Ascona, Marburg and Japan. He gave me the impression of an immutable "present" radiated by his personality and unaccompanied by any sign of outer change. I also met him on his travels, in Ascona, Marburg, or Kyoto, but, unlike all other travelers, he never gave the impression of being a transit passenger, a person who had to hasten on to another place because he had something more important to do there. On the contrary, he was always completely present, as if he were always there, and radiated an aura of presence to those around him. Whereas constant moving from place to place has a devastating effect on most travelers' relationship to the universe, Suzuki was so in tune—in his heart and innermost being—with the order of the cosmos, that even his frequent journeys within this universe could not upset his physical and spiritual equilibrium.

I remember how once at the end of an Eranos conference in Ascona all the participants hurried off in all directions to every continent while Daisetz Suzuki (who was staying up in the Casa Eranos) delayed his departure by one day because the following night was the August full moon, and he wanted to enjoy calmly contemplating it over the Ticinese mountains, and its reflection in Lake Maggiore from the terrace of Casa

Eranos. Would a European have wanted to delay his departure because of the full moon? But he just sat on the roof contemplating the full moon as the world turned on its axis.

This relates to the point for which I'm most grateful to Suzuki, namely, his ability to convey to his listeners the experience of the eternity of the moment. Perhaps this is precisely the essential theme of Zen philosophy, which has already betrayed itself when it becomes philosophy, and whose essential meaning consists in allowing the contemplative to experience the eternity of the moment and to cause him to exclaim, "That's it! That's right!" This is an experience which we are increasingly deprived of by our entire Western lifestyle. It is not only the element of haste, the need to scatter ourselves, that prevents us from perceiving the essence of life (the irretrievable instant of its pure realization) but also the fundamental orientation toward the future inherent in Western thinking—the specifically Judeo-Christian haste—which prevents us from grasping and experiencing the moment in its eternal grandeur and imperishability. Faust's words, "Could I but say to the moment, 'Stay awhile, you are so beautiful',", best expresses this specifically Christian eschatological aspect of Western culture—which always strives for a future, transcendental goal, senses this goal as near at hand, tries at times to tear it down from heaven above in a revolutionary upsurge and to anticipate its realization—but never fully reaches this goal.

I have never known anyone further removed from Faust's words than Daisetz Suzuki. He was a master of the sovereign art of addressing each moment with the words, "Stay awhile, you are so beautiful." Of course, this was the result of his mastery of an art to which he had dedicated his entire life by means of rigorous, concentrated meditation. However, he had the lucidity to perceive this result of his lifelong struggle not as the successful outcome of his own efforts but as a gift of grace.

These leaps into timelessness always occurred in an instant on the most improbable occasions in his presence. I remember how once my wife and I were standing with him and his charming Japanese secretary on the elevated terrace next to the Marburg University church gazing at the Lahn valley below and the wooded mountains beyond, when a cat ran over the parapet wall. We had been talking about transmigration of the soul and Suzuki used the appearance of the cat to illustrate the fundamental difference between the attitude toward animals of a Christian—for whom a cat is merely a cat—and a Buddhist, who, upon contemplating this cat, cannot help thinking that this animal might be the reincarnation of his grandmother. In this way the cat on the wall suddenly became an object and symbol of a comparative religious study in which Suzuki depicted the pre-eminence of the Buddhist attitude to animals so convincingly—and showed us so impressively that there were no insuperable barriers, within the fraternity of creatures, between humans and non-humans—that we finally almost believed this cat to be capable of anything. The whole explanation was, however, not an exercise in apologetics but merely a friendly discussion about a cat.

The second thing for which I'd like to thank Suzuki is the corresponding experience of a new vision of the transience of this world. The sovereign freedom with which Suzuki could capture the moment with quasi-mystical power, and switch at will into the joyful enthusiasm of "That's it! That's right!" revealed itself against a background of a curious, and yet typically Buddhist, melancholy, which knows something about the irresistible evanescence of all existence but assumes such evanescence right from the start. Even in the greatest and most beautiful forms it takes note of it and frequently adapts to it. It is the experience of the irresistible flowing and gliding past of phenomena, the Heraclitic experience of "You never step in the same river twice."

This Buddhist melancholy, which I'd like to call "the melancholy of karma"—and in which the knowledge of the implacable succession of cause and effect, even in the ethical domain, is rooted—is also the basis of that peculiar Buddhist humor which Suzuki possessed in such an entrancing way. It has often been asserted in connection with Kierkegaard that only Christ could have a sense of humor because true humor presupposes the conquest of the world and that the cross forms the basis of that sovereign distance from the world which humor implies.

This exclusive reasoning does not stand up to scrutiny. There is also a specifically Buddhist humor which sees the world from the standpoint of its conquest achieved in *samadhi*, the world in the light of nirvana, as it were. Instead of the sovereign conquest of the world with the cross as its symbol, Buddhism has the sovereignty which confronts all being with the transcendental void, which is the origin and goal of existence. The wise succeed, as it were, in "cocking a snook" at karma and escaping from the stream of evanescence to recognize the eternal ideal of the transcendent in the glistening reflection of the waterfall of earthly phenomena.

I am also grateful to Suzuki for drawing my attention to the occurrence of such experiences in the realm of Christian mysticism. With his subtle intuition Suzuki ascertained genuine transcendental experiences in the realm of Christian mysticism; experiences related to his own. Thus he discovered—especially in Meister Eckhart—some similarities to the mystical experiences of Zen Buddhism, although in my opinion he went too far in asserting, from his essentially non-historical Buddhist standpoint, that the specifically Christian aspects of Meister Eckhart's thinking were superfluous, and thus dispensable, additions to his Christian Zen mysticism. This is in fact not possible since his sense of history was founded on his basic understanding of the incarnation and cannot be separated from his image of Christ. Nevertheless, it seems to me that Suzuki's achievement of discovering in Christian mysticism genuine points of departure for a comparison with Buddhist mysticism is so great that his somewhat missionary zeal to turn Meister Eckhart into a Zen Christian can be accommodated. This is precisely the great spiritual-historical significance of Suzuki, the constant discovery of points of reference for mutual understanding between Eastern and Western piety and spirit.

I also realized through Suzuki what role Buddhism as a whole could play in the spiritual condition of today's world. There is no doubt that because of Christian thinking and its eschatological orientation toward a historical goal, worldly activity has gathered momentum and left humanity in a condition of acute inner restlessness. Even the idea and practice of revolution derives from the Christian understanding of history: is not a revolution merely an attempt to establish the promised, future kingdom of God with human power, according to human plans and by means of force?

I could imagine that, in view of the frantic acceleration of the development of historical circumstances in all areas of life, manifested through the Christian understanding of mankind, history, and the universe, and apparently rushing to its end at an alarming, ever-increasing tempo, Buddhism might have the salutary effect of a brake, insomuch as it directs our thoughts, which are obsessed with the future, and science, which is likewise obsessed with forecasting and controlling the future, back to the eternity of the moment and enables man—provides him with the means—to step back from the raging current of events and phenomena and consider them from a transcendental perspective. Buddhism, with its art of the "eternal instant" and its "Stay awhile, you're so beautiful" seems to me, moreover, to fulfill an important function for modern Japan too, not only in the cultural sphere but the economic sphere as well. Since the Meiji period Japan has adopted the secularized, Western eschatological thinking of economic and technical progress and has been strengthened by American cultural and economic influences. Today it needs its own Buddhist tradition in order not to lose itself in the Judeo-Christian haste which was half freely chosen and half imposed by circumstances.

Precisely because I first got to know Suzuki in his old age as a *puer aeternus* and had the honor of contributing to a journal celebrating his 90th birthday, I was fully expecting to do the same on his 100th birthday and never imagined that he himself would no longer be alive.

May these grateful memories serve in place of congratulations on his 100th birthday.

12

Wilhelm Gundert

A Sower of Seeds

I
N ORDER TO FIND SOME EXPLANATION for the astonishing phenomenon of Dr. Suzuki's lifework it may be helpful to look again
upon the time in which he was born and upon the outstanding
factors which molded his character in early years. In 1870, his year of
birth, his country, under the leadership of the Emperor Meiji, had just set
out on its new course of radical modernization. His father, a hereditary
physician ranked in the feudal samurai class, had been divested of his
annual grant of rice. The family was left in utter poverty. There were no
means to give the boy an education in medicine for which he seemed to
have a talent. But, at eighteen, he managed to become a teacher in the
little school of a fishing village, teaching arithmetic, reading, writing,
and a sort of Japanized English, which he had picked up from textbooks of the lowest standard.

There appear in this development three characteristic traits: his samurai inheritance which counts for courage, faithfulness, and devotion;
his talent for the medical art or, in a broader sense, for clear and keen-
eyed observation, attested to by his bodily appearance—the forward
stretched position of the head, the lively piercing eyes, the listening ears,
the scenting nose; and, a symptom of the early Meiji era, his interest in
things abroad—in English, which, as he fancied, should be taught even
in the remotest fishing village. At the back of all these qualities we
perceive a deep-rooted optimism coupled with a happy tinge of sheer

naiveté, trusting that in any case the difficulties on the way are there just to be mastered. It is this quality which later led his master to bestow on him that most significant surname, "big simplicity," *Daisetz.*

His mother's death left him alone and free to follow now his inmost inclinations. He went to Tokyo to attend informally the new Imperial University. But what attracted him much more, was a new revival of Buddhistic energies centering in the famous Zen monastery, Engakuji, of nearby Kamakura. The leading spirit there was Shaku Soen, only eleven years older than himself, of a most noble, sensitive, indomitable mind, highly trained throughout his youth by the hardest work as well as by a most severe Zen master, and moved by a clear vision of the needs of Buddhism in this time of crisis. He saw the inundation of his country by things foreign, the decline of Buddhist faith and life to mere formality.

Shaku Soen resolved to counteract this very real danger with his utmost effort. After having got his master Kosen's attestation, he refused to settle down immediately, as usual, in a temple position. In spite of his great poverty he went to Tokyo for three years to study English, "a thing of no use anywhere for Zen," as his master wrote him, and then put in another three years' preparation by a stay among the fellow Buddhists in far-off Ceylon to learn to read the Pali scriptures and to understand the differences between their conception of Buddhism and his own. It was for him a time of countless hardships and privations. On his return in 1892 he was at once elected as superintendent of the Engakuji and all its affiliated monasteries. And it seems that Shaku Soen from the start became aware of his new disciple's particular abilities and began to put some hopes in him. The next year, in 1893, there was a gathering of singular importance to take place, the World's Parliament of Religions in Chicago, a welcome opportunity to give the world a first idea of what Far Eastern Buddhism was worth. Shaku Soen was resolved to cross a second ocean. He had Suzuki translate his manuscript, which was prepared as an address to be delivered at the Parliament. A year later by the intermediation of Shaku Soen, he rendered *The Gospel of Buddha* by Paul Carus into Japanese.

Such was the beginning of Suzuki's career as the foremost interpreter of Zen for Western nations. And things developed in a way which made it possible for him to get for this, his destiny, the very best equipment he could wish for. During the congress, Shaku Soen had become acquainted with Mr. Hegeler, the millionaire owner of a zinc company in Illinois, who together with his son-in-law, Dr. Paul Carus, managed a publishing house devoted to religious and scientific books and periodicals. As Dr. Carus was in need of a translator, Shaku Soen knew no better man to recommend to him than his young companion. This implied the double confidence that, on the one hand, four years of genuine Engakuji Zen training in the case of this young man would suffice to make him "waterproof" against whatever influences came from outside, and, on the other hand, that there was no better way to counteract a danger than to meet it at its starting point. There has existed since times of old in the community of Buddhist teachers a sort of prophecy called *vyakarana* (in Japanese, *juki*), work allotment. A master has an insight into his disciple's possiblities and accordingly allots to him a special mission. Shaku Soen's answer to Mr. Hegeler was nothing less than *juki* put into practice.

Suzuki spent the next eleven years at the Open Court Publishing Company working with Dr. Paul Carus proofreading, editing, translating from Chinese and Japanese, mastering Sankrit as well. He also accompanied his master Shaku Soen on lecture tours in the United States as secretary and translator. During this tour he met an American lady, Beatrice Erskine Lane, whom he later married in Japan. He published his first important book, *Outlines of Mahayana Buddhism* in 1908.

Then, at last in 1908, he left America, copied Sanskrit documents for some time in Paris, translated Swedenborg from English into Japanese in London, and then returned to Kamakura for further studies under the guidance of Shaku Soen. He was now 38 years old and had already gained a reputation as a unique interpreter of Zen and Buddhism in general to the West. He kept it up for fifty-eight years more incessantly teaching, writing, and lecturing wherever he was welcome, always in that unobtrusive, quiet attitude which did so much to win his hearers.

His literary work, prolific as it is, knows of no other topic but Zen, and Zen again. Even his style of editing is typically Zen-like. It is without a system, it shows no reasoned plan; it is a causal series of "essays" and "studies." Some of his books perhaps may disappoint professional scholars. If so, it will not be the author's fault, but that of Zen itself, of which the author is just the congenial organ. And if you turn from his more popular essays to those on difficult subjects, e.g., to his *Studies in the Lankavatara Sutra*, you will admire the author's skill in grappling with the intricacies of those dialectic problems and the lucidity of his solutions. His translations of Chinese and Japanese are not in every case verbally correct, but they always hit the mark, and this is, after all, what matters. In cases of complicated passages we never find him at a loss to work out a shortcut which leads directly to the goal.

The range of the audiences he visited for lectures and discussions was as broad as was his knowledge. He went and spoke of Zen wherever he was welcomed, be it to philosophers, to theologians, or to psychologists. Some anxious people had misgivings; what has Zen to do with psychoanalysis, they asked. But he was not deterred, he knew what he was doing. It is just like Suzuki Daisetz to have discovered all those points of contact between psychotherapy and Zen. Nobody but he, however, saw more clearly the undeniable difference between those two in origin and outlook.

But criticism of Suzuki's apparent unconcern went further. In Germany, a very learned professor of the science of religion has recently reproached him for having more than any other writer contributed to the modern tendency of Westernizing the Far Eastern Zen and of depriving it of its essentially religious character. And as a proof of his assertion he points to the deplorable phenomenon of Zen snobbism which recently became a fashion both in America and Europe.

Now, to begin with "Zen snobbism," it suffices to remember the familiar parable in Chapter 13 of the "Gospel According to Matthew":

> Behold, a sower went forth to sow; and when he sowed, some seeds. . . fell upon stony places, where they had not much earth; and forthwith they sprang up, because they had no deepness of earth, and when the sun was up, they were scorched, and because they had no root, they withered away.

Apparently the truth of this example already has begun to realize itself. A friend of mine who recently returned from the United States told me of the owner of a bookshop whom he had met and asked about the present situation of his trade. The bookseller's laconic answer was: "Zen is out, sex is in."

Suzuki Daisetz was a sower of extraordinary energies and perseverance. He continued what his master Shaku Soen at the Parliament of

Chicago in 1893 had begun more than seventy years before: namely, to draw the attention of humanity to the phenomenon of Zen, and nothing more. This is a perfectly legitimate undertaking from the Western point of view.

But critics may go further, asking: What about Suzuki's legitimacy within his own confine, in Zen? Was the seed he sowed true Zen or false? Here lies a trap for specialists in the science of religions. Every religion establishes for its adherents a standard of its own. You cannot encounter a Christian with a Buddhist measure. And a follower of Zen can only be judged by a Zen measure. Do we really know what the Zen measure is? Did not perhaps Suzuki Daisetz know a little more about it? At any rate he readily confessed himself to be a sinner, because through all his life he spoke and wrote of things transcending speech and script. It was in this sense also, I suppose, that he signed his works with his most enigmatic surname. "Daisetz" can at the same time mean "of great simplicity" and "a great simpleton." He confessed his sins, but went on "sinning." He represented in himself a genuine Zen koan, enigmatical indeed for Western forms of thought. It has a striking similarity with the eighth Example of the *Hekiganshu*, where Suigan, after having spoken all the summer long, asks his hearers whether he had not lost his eyebrows. Three of his old comrades make their remarks about him, one rather negative, the other positive, the third one, Ummon, cuts them short. "Barrier (*kwan*)," he says and bars discussion about things which lie beyond it.

Incidentally, it might be useful to remember that, generally speaking, the attitude of Buddhism toward "outsiders" is much more lenient than that of other religions, including Christianity. But gaining the assent of others, a certain adaptation, the use of "skillful means" (Sk., *upaya*, Jap., *hoben*), is not only recommended—for instance in the *Saddharma-pundarika*—but has been practiced in degrees compared to which those innocent connivances on Suzuki Daisetz's side just count for nothing.

As regards myself, I must confess that I for many years have underestimated the high significance of Suzuki Daisetz's personality and work. The change came only after I had formed the resolution to study the *Hekiganshu*, of which, in spite of its supreme importance, no complete translation was at hand. I had begun with incomplete editions, current in Japan, which disappointed me, and had ordered Kato Totsudo's big commentary from Japan. Just about that time, in September 1954, Dr. Suzuki appeared in Germany for lectures at Marburg University and at Stuttgart. I had the honor of interpreting for him. One of his points in speaking was that Zen prefers spontaneous action to worded explanation. "We need not tell a good friend that we like him. A friendly tap will do." Saying this, he tapped my shoulder and the audience was delighted.

He agreed with my discontent over incomplete editions of the *Hekiganshu*, saying that in fact such books did not deserve that title (which is quite true, because they leave out just the most important part of Engo's contribution to Setcho's collection). On the way to Stuttgart in the railway car, he read a Chinese book in a Chinese binding: it was a Japanese edition of the *Hekiganshu* in two volumes. At Stuttgart, when we parted, he took them out, wrote on each his dedication and presented them to me quite unceremoniously. In whatever he did there was not a shadow of ado. But for me it was, first of all, the decisive encouragement which I needed to take up the work. And in the course of years, it changed into a sort of mandate binding me to carry on in spite of all the difficulties implied. I need not add that from this time his books became to me quite indispensable, especially his studies on the sutras from which Zen derives its views; my admiration for his scholarship reached its height through the study of his books on the *Lankavatara-Sutra*.

But to conclude, I must report a personal experience of the summer 1954. While he was sitting with me in the lobby of a hotel, a woman, apparently distressed, approached and asked entreatingly to be received. As she knew no English, I served as interpreter. The details of the conversation are omissible. But what I never can forget is the quiet, sober, sympathetic attitude in which the eighty-four-year-old modest gentleman listened to her penetrating questions, the smooth and simple kindliness of his appeasing, comforting, encouraging replies and the serene vivacity of his look. He had his hands folded on the table, and at the end he drew his right hand out and held it almost hesitatingly toward her. At last she grasped it, and we parted. In July 1966, when I informed her that the venerable man had died, she answered, "He, at that time, saved my life."

We are living in an age when East is no more East and even West is no more simply West. The streams of life, of faith, of human brother-hood are flowing all around, and gradually they float historical barriers away. It is a situation which calls, on every side, for a broad mind in particular, and all the more, for deep and firm reliance on and in the ground in which our lives originate and in which alone we are at home.

13

Shin'ichi Hisamatsu

*Mondo: At the Death of
a "Great-Death-Man"*

I T WAS MY MOST REVERED TEACHER, Dr. Kitaro Nishida, who in
1920 first introduced me to Dr. Daisetz Suzuki. Ever since that time,
for a period of some forty-five years, I have received Dr. Suzuki's
many kindnesses in the Dharma. I thus have not only respected Dr.
Suzuki as my "Uncle-Teacher in Dharma" but have also felt personally
very close to him. Then, early on the morning of July 12, 1966, he
suddenly passed into nirvana after suffering severe abdominal pain from
a strangulation of the intestines.

Looking back upon his life, I cannot help but feel the deepest reverence
for him. Because of my own illness, I regretfully could not attend his
funeral. I sent instead the following telegraph of condolence: "Billions
of kalpas apart; [yet] not a moment separated." Seven weeks later, after
the customary mourning period, we of the F.A.S. Zen Institute held on
September 4, 1966, midday of the fall intensive *sesshin* period, a solemn
memorial service for Dr. Suzuki, at Reiun'in, Myoshinji.

On this occasion, I suddenly gave out a cry and held a last mondo
with Dr. Suzuki.[1] This mondo and the memorial discourse which was
presented after it now follow:

Ohhhhhhhhh . . . !
This ONE who hurts!
Are you suffering?

143

It's all right,
Thank you!

Dr. Suzuki, throughout his lifetime of nearly one century, consistently concentrated on the study of Zen in a unique way. For him, study and practice were one and the same. He also sought, through his proficient command of English, to promote the spread of Zen abroad. Thus did he enable Zen, which had been unique to the Orient, to be known all over the world and, more than that, to nurture man's spiritual life and thereby to contribute to mankind profoundly and widely. This is truly an immense joy for the Dharma.

About ten years ago, when I went abroad, visiting various areas, including the United States, Europe, Egypt, the Near East, the Middle East, and India, I was surprised to find that wherever I went the celebrated name of Dr. Suzuki was known as that of a sage of the East and that Zen was known in an inseparable connection with his name.

It is unavoidable that in the mode and degree of people's knowledge about him there are differences between the deep and the shallow, the right and the wrong, the approving and the critical. Nevertheless, the reputation of a person like Dr. Suzuki, who is universally known for his unique religious and cultural contribution, not only is unprecedented in Japan but is rare in the whole world. It may not be overstating the matter to say that he was one of the greatest treasures of the world as well as a national asset to Japan. No wonder the unexpected report of his death saddened people at home and abroad, causing them to mourn for him.

Confronted with his passing, how can we properly comprehend the so-called death of this man-of-the-universe? Even when we contemplate death in its ordinary sense—the death of ourselves or of others—we find, if we reflect deeply, that it is far from easy to know how to respond to it. Much more difficult is it, therefore, to know how to grasp the kind of death which an ordinary understanding of death does not exhaust, as in the case of Dr. Suzuki's death. Upon his dying, a great many people are reported to have made calls of condolence and to have been present at the funeral. But I wonder how they took the death of this man beyond life-and-death—the death of Dr. Suzuki as a "Great-Death-Man." I believe this is a matter of deep concern to us all.

Until now, Zen, as is well known, has taken up the problem of "life-

and-death" not as a mere object of speculation but as the most crucial, total concern of the living-dying subject himself. Not only in Zen but also in Buddhism in general, the problem of life-and-death has been considered to be the primary problem. Death does not exist apart from life; life is not separate from death. Life is attended by death; death accompanies life. Thus death alone is not the absolute crisis; life also is a crisis. Hence we have in Buddhism such expressions as *Shoji jidai,* "The Great-Matter of life-and-death," or *Shoji no ichi daiji,* "The single most important matter—life-and-death." As to the term "life-death" (or life-and-death), it is quite a problem what implication it carries. It carries in it more than its literal meaning. It can possibly include the whole of humankind, or indeed, the whole world. Otherwise we could not say, "The Great-Matter of life-and-death."

The problem of life-and-death cannot be said to be of a crucial or absolute nature if it implies anything partial, such as something physiological or psychological, or if it implies anything particular which is distinguished in terms of right and wrong, good and evil, likes and dislikes, and so on. Here we see the reason why a thorough existential inquiry into the implication of the term "life-and-death" is necessary. Such an existential inquiry into the meaning of the term is exactly the same as an existential inquiry into the matter of life-and-death itself. The problem here, therefore, is not a particular or individual problem; nor is it a problem which, even when it does include everything, can be treated in a merely objective manner. It is really the crucial problem of existential subjectivity. Its solution will, therefore, mean at the same time the ultimate solution of the whole problem of man. As regards Dr. Suzuki's death, any ordinary way of encountering it is quite unsatisfactory when we think of him as one who has expounded the life-death problem to the world.

I think some of us may have heard that Shakyamuni, when he was entering into nirvana, said to his disciples assembled round him: "If anyone among you should say that I am now entering into nirvana, he will not be my disciple. Nor will he be my disciple who should say that I am not entering nirvana." According to Shakyamuni, either affirming or negating his entrance into nirvana makes one fail to be his disciple. Zen early took this up as a koan.[2] How should we, as well as Shakyamuni's disciples, meet this situation right at this moment? If ordinary people had heard Shakyamuni say the above on his entering into nirvana at his death, many of them might have been puzzled and might have grumbled the common place grievance: "We don't understand those ambiguous words of yours; they are beyond our apprehension." But how should a disciple of Shakyamuni cope with the Buddha's death so that he may be a true disciple? This is a very important matter.

In ninth-century China there lived a famous Zen master, Xiangyan Zhixian,[3] who said: "If on the way you meet an accomplished man, greet him with neither speech nor silence." Xiangyan meant that in meeting a person who has attained Awakening or nirvana, neither speech nor silence will do. How, then, should we greet an Awakened person? This question must also be considered to imply a total, ultimate problem in it, and not anything merely particular, such as having recourse to words or keeping silent.

If we are unable to answer the challenge of Shakyamuni on his death-bed, we cannot help but treat Dr. Suzuki merely as a man who was born and who died in an ordinary manner. Although his great achievements are too many to enumerate, a mere praising of them will not truly extol the man himself. I would rather say that unless we can extol him truly in terms of his Awakening, his achievements cannot be given their finishing touch and gain their true significance.

People with one accord admire Dr. Suzuki, saying that he was not only an unprecedented national asset to Japan but a priceless treasure of the world. But this is not the end. For those of us who concern ourselves with an existential self-inquiry, with a thorough inquiry into the world and history, the problem of how to face Dr. Suzuki's nirvana is a problem. Basically speaking, however, the same can be said about any True-Man's death.

Here is another case in which the same problem was taken up by a Zen Master, Daowu Zongzhi[4] by name, in the same ninth-century China. Once Daowu, accompanied by his attendant Jianyuan Zhong-xing[5] went to mourn the death of a person he had known. Jianyuan, the attendant, rubbing the coffin in which the dead person had been placed, asked his master, "Is this one alive or dead?" In the ordinary sense, there was no doubt that the person was dead, but Jianyuan was in quest of the solution of the life-death problem, and had to ask this seemingly nonsensical question. To this, Master Daowu immediately responded: "I won't say 'alive'; I won't say 'dead'." This response indicated the same point as the above declaration of Shakyamuni. (Similar instances have often occurred in Zen since its earliest days.) Master Daowu, although asked the same question again and again, just kept on saying, "I won't say! I won't say!" Jianyuan, when he heard his master's answer, is said to have realized what his master really meant. Now, what do you suppose he realized?

As to the way of encountering death, there is not only the apparently negative answer, "neither alive nor dead," but also seemingly affirmative ones. In tenth-century China there lived a Zen master named Dasui Fazhen.[6] When asked, "How are you at the time when life-death arrives?" he answered promptly, "When served tea, I take tea; when served a meal, I eat the meal." I am afraid some people might take this to be beside the point. But, on the contrary, this hits the bull's eye.

In Zen there are many instances such as this; but we do not necessarily have to take them only from the past. We are directly confronting here and now the "arrival of the life-death" of Dr. Suzuki. Is then Dr. Suzuki alive or dead? How is the death of a person who has attained the Great Death, which is beyond life-and-death, to be taken? How is his life to be understood? How are we to respond to this?

I have made my last mondo face to face with Daisetz-*koji* (Zen layman). How have you taken it? For myself, I have thereby expressed my utmost reverence for and gratitude to the late Dr. Suzuki. This is none other than "Billions of *kalpas* apart; [yet] not a moment separated."

> Who is this hurting ONE!?
>
> If you want to see "ME" at my last,
> First die a Great Death!
> For "I" make no response to your calling;
> "I" present no sight to your eye,
> No sense to your touch,
> No image to your conception.

14

Keiji Nishitani

Remembering Dr. Daisetz T. Suzuki

OVER THE YEARS I VISITED Dr. Suzuki on many occasions, but not once did he appear nervous or tense. There were times during our talks when he would get fired up over the subject, but I never felt he became overly enthusiastic or forced the issue. There was always a gentle presence about him, like trailing clouds. The impression I got of his buoyant appearance was just as many others have mentioned. It was just the opposite of the severe, penetrating-to-the-bone presence which one felt from, say Kitaro Nishida.[1] How I miss the frank and open atmosphere between these two school buddies in which I was able to share the several times I was present when they met and talked together.

When I recall the ever-calm and open personality of Dr. Suzuki, and then consider the enormous accomplishments throughout his life, they just do not fit together; I am sure I am not the only one who feels puzzled by this. With Dr. Nishida I could easily sense his great achievements from his personality. While both men accomplished something outstanding, Dr. Suzuki always seemed perfectly ordinary.

But in the depths of such ordinariness there was, without doubt, a fervent passion. In common parlance, he had a task to fulfill; it was, however, an unlimited task. In his final years he often said that he would like to do this and that while still alive, that he could not die until these things were completed. He even mentioned on occasion that he was sure he would live until that work was done. In these words I felt a kind of unlimited vow, or perhaps I should say a tireless and unbounded determination. One could even say his limitless life went beyond the bounds of his physical body. Such boundlessness possessed a religious quality. Thus what I designated above as his "unlimited task" was a religious one.

Perhaps the seed of this task lay in his awakening of a religious mind and determination to do Zen practice in his student days. I do not know what made him decide to do Zen practice, but it must certainly have been the problem of his own salvation. During his Zen pursuit, however, the conviction arose in him that he must transmit the way of Zen to the West and, in its turn, to all mankind. This was his realization of the first of "The Four Great Vows,"[2] namely, "All beings without limit I vow to save." Since then, the activities throughout his life were the actualization, in its truest sense, of the Bodhisattva Way, which is one of:

Going in search of Awakening.
Returning to save all sentient beings.

In other words, his activities were within historical actuality in its true sense, and thus, in themselves also history in the making. With Japan gaining the position that it now has in the world, his activities were perfectly suited to the times.

It is important in this case that this term "all sentient beings" no longer remains merely a vague concept but comes to mean "Westerners," and thus takes on a clear limitation appropriate to the era. Looking at it from another angle, in Dr. Suzuki's activities, Buddhism came to possess a forward-moving direction with a frontier spirit. Further, for him to have had a frontier spirit outside Japan means he had a frontier spirit within Japan as well. This involved shouldering the task of rethinking, restating, and redoing traditional Buddhism to transmit it to Westerners as well as Easterners, to truly and realistically create a world Buddhism. (And when Buddhism becomes a world Buddhism perhaps it will for the first time be brought back to life in the hearts of the Japanese people of the present and future.) To accomplish this task it is necessary to be deeply engrossed in the tradition, and at the same time to grasp the longing and the way of thinking within the hearts of Westerners. From there, new possibilities should open up in the study of the Buddhist Dharma which have yet to be found in Buddhist history. And this is

"Going in search of Awakening" in its true sense, in which one stands firmly in the historical reality.

If one is not really "Going in search of Awakening," then even though one says he is transmitting Buddhism to the West, he is only selling an exported sham. It will never lead to "Returning to save all sentient beings." Likewise, if "Returning to save all sentient beings" is not perfectly suited to the times, then "Going in search of Awakening" will end up being something merely of interest to old-fashioned traditionalists. Either way, this unlimited task will not endure.

Up to now this new Buddhist path has been blazed almost single-handedly by Dr. Suzuki. He did it on behalf of the whole Buddhist world. And with his passing the whole Buddhist world must step in and fill his shoes. To do this, Buddhists must realize, more than anything else, the horizon of this historical "world" which is right underfoot. It is necessary to reform that antiquated consciousness which, with its face turned only toward our own country, has been locked up within our religious institutions. Next, people of a similar mind must work together open-mindedly. Then there must be systematic planning for the education of young people to continue Dr. Suzuki's work.

Dr. Suzuki's passing is a cause for grief; but if we merely remember him, even for a very long time, that will not truly be mourning him. If that is all we do, then his soul would not rest in peace. It might sound wrong to say that, but if we merely mourn Dr. Suzuki, who, in his restful nirvana, "has left home, yet is not on the way"[3] he will give us a sardonic smile. As Rinzai says, "Don't make the one out to be Wei-mojie (Vimalakirti) and the other to be Fu Daishi."[4] Nor should we make one out to be Daisetz Suzuki.

Included in the eighteenth volume of *Daisetz Suzuki's Complete Works*[5] are two rather unique writings, *Various Problems of Zen* and *The Primary Meaning of Zen.* The former was published in 1941 with the following included in the preface: "This is a collection of slightly scholarly writings about Zen which I wrote over the past ten years." The latter was published in 1914 and is a very early piece. Between these two writings is a period of almost thirty years, and yet there are essential features common to both. First of all, he emphasized in both works that the primary meaning or essence of Zen cannot be realized without the actual experience, without one's own living fact of real mastery, of real Awakening. He took a psychological approach to elucidate this. Secondly, he rejected all logic, considered science and also philosophy as the standpoint of the discriminating intellect and, concerning the primary meaning of Zen, he emphasized that religion and philosophy are completely unrelated to each other. Thirdly, he showed that Zen is not just Buddhism but the consummation of all religion, and that living religious faiths such as the (Pure Land) *nembutsu*[6] and also Christianity culminate in the Zen Awakening, provided they are thoroughgoing. To show this universality of Zen he took up the mystical religious experience and often made special reference to the affinity between Zen and Western mysticism.

Among these common features: the standpoint of that experience directly underfoot which is prior to the distinction of subject and object; the psychological approach connected with this; empathy for a mysticism which originates from this standpoint; and the desire to seek out the point where the various religions are one, all can be found as well in *A Study of Good*, the earliest work of Nishida philosophy. (There are also places in Dr. Suzuki's works where the term "immediate experience" occurs.)[7] But there was probably no direct influence between them on these matters. Because the standpoint of *A Study of Good* is also basically connected with Zen Awakening, the similarity is not surprising. Further, there was a common intention which motivated both of them in their work. And that was to find within the essence of the Oriental mind or spirit represented by Zen something of profound significance for the modern world; to remove that which is significant from its traditional framework and revive it for modern man. From out of this motivation they established a common basis which may have been found already at work in the close friendship of classmates during their youth in Kanazawa.

Dr. Suzuki's two writings mentioned above are strongly critical of the philosophical approach to Zen, and he must have had good reason for such criticism. In the beginning of *The Primary Meaning of Zen* he spoke of "the numerous publications on Zen that have been popping up recently like bamboo shoots after the rain," thus expressing his indignation at those who spoke about Zen Awakening without actually having practiced it, but merely from within the sphere of discriminating intellect. I do not know what the situation was like at the time (i.e., around 1914) but there must have been some kind of "Zen boom" in Japan. I can only vaguely remember it. In "Introductory Remarks Concerning the Essence of Zen"—the opening chapter of *Various Problems of Zen* (1941)—he states that most scholars of contemporary Japan do not clearly know the difference between the actual Awakening of Zen and Zen theory or Zen philosophy, and that the interpretations of these scholars often miss the mark. Proceeding to the main text of *Various Problems of Zen*, the first section is entitled "Philosophy of Zen" and begins with this:

QUESTION: What is the philosophy of Zen?
ANSWER: An Egg is square, *tofu* [bean curd, which is usually square] is round.
Without this kind of *mondo* [question-and-answer] the matter will never be settled.

How like Dr. Suzuki—unique and interesting.

In considering what Dr. Suzuki's motive for writing this might have been, Dr. Hajime Tanabe's *My Philosophical Perspective on the Shobogenzo*, which came out a few years earlier (1939), comes to mind.[8] Come to think of it, there are many stimulating statements in Dr. Suzuki's works to back this thought up. For example, he states:

If you begin by intellectually fabricating some philosophical system, you cannot then pull Zen out of it. You have to do it the other way around.

If Dr. Suzuki wrote this with Dr. Tanabe's above-mentioned work in mind, I must say it fits Dr. Suzuki's style. I think Dr. Suzuki already had "The Philosophy of the Shobogenzo" in mind when he penned the title, "The Philosophy of Zen." This guess may not be correct, but the "matter" at issue referred to by Dr. Suzuki above, is precisely the problem dealt with in the books of both Dr. Suzuki and Dr. Tanabe.

Dr. Tanabe confronted the standpoint of Zen (especially Rinzai Zen) as found in Dr. Nishida and Dr. Suzuki, as well as in Dr. Shin'ichi Hisamatsu,[9] from before Dr. Tanabe's book was published until long after. During this time I was sometimes made by Dr. Tanabe to play the opponent's role so to speak, to take a beating for them. And whenever I would go to visit Dr. Tanabe, we ended up discussing these problems, such as the relation between Zen and philosophy. From this fact, and also from the fact that when Dr. Nishida and Dr. Suzuki met, Dr. Tanabe's thought was often the subject of conversation, I tend to think that this formed the background for Dr. Suzuki's writing *Various Problems of Zen.*

Dr. Suzuki's criticism pierces right to the heart of the fundamental problem involved in Dr. Tanabe's standpoint as regards Zen. Until the end, Dr. Tanabe had a tough time mediating Zen and philosophy, but I feel that when he used the term "mediation," Zen had already been squeezed into philosophy and the profound significance that the "experiential fact" has in Zen was not sufficiently recognized. At the same time, however, his concept of mediation was not that simple. For example, Dr. Tanabe has said:

Self power exhausts itself and comes to its own end. There, aiding *mu* [Nothingness] to become present, I participate.[10]

In such a struggle, philosophy must exhaust itself for itself.[11]

From the standpoint of philosophy mediated by religion, there is mediation; but from the standpoint of religion itself, there is no mediation. In this relation of "is and is not" "is not and is," philosophy must completely accord with religion. Mediation must be without mediation.[12]

In this aspect of no-mediation Zen is recognized as an experiential fact. Reasoning such as Dr. Tanabe's is rather complicated and perhaps Dr. Suzuki, thinking it cumbersome, refused to swallow it. This might also be why Dr. Suzuki cut philosophy off from Zen so completely.

At any rate, this problem of Zen and philosophy seemed to have remained unsettled between the two men. On the contrary, it remains even now to be settled. It is, after all, the task remaining at the core of the spiritual and cultural encounter between East and West.

Dr. Suzuki's approach to Zen, however, later changed and was no longer simply psychological. He became concerned with the problem of the logic of the Zen standpoint and of the philosophical formation of

Zen thought. Thus he developed his "logic of *sokuhi* [is and is not]."
Already in the first section of *Zen Thought*, now in Volume 13 of his
complete works and originally published two years later (1943) than
Various Problems of Zen, Dr. Suzuki speaks of "the knowing of not-
knowing," and "the discrimination of non-discrimination." Such ideas
were definitely influenced by the "absolutely contradictory Self-identity
of the "logic of place" in Nishida's philosophy. While Dr. Suzuki spoke
of the above-mentioned elimination of philosophy, if the thought of
the Prajnaparamita School and Kegon School are considered, then he
thought something might already exist that can be called Zen philosophy. This approach could be considered to have been developed by
Dr. Suzuki later on. He also came to include a negative view of Zen's
affinity with mysticism, and thus was not simply in agreement with
Christianity, but rather strengthened his critical attitude toward it.

In any event, the two works mentioned above, namely, Dr. Suzuki's
Various Problems of Zen and Dr. Tanabe's *My Philosophical Perspective
on the Shobogenzo* take into account the basic problem of modern Japan,
the confrontation of Eastern and Western culture. Further, the background of the relationship between representative thinkers of modern
Japan, such as Suzuki, Nishida, and Tanabe is also of interest for this
reason. Interest in the content of the books themselves need not even
be mentioned. Even in the earliest work, *The Primary Meaning of Zen*, I
was deeply impressed with the penetrating, refreshing, and outstanding
elucidation.

At about six in the morning on the day that Dr. Suzuki passed away,
I received a telephone call from a newspaper office in Tokyo; that was
how I first heard of his passing. It was rather unexpected and I was struck
dumb for an instant.

A little later I received word from someone connected with Otani
University that at about noon Dr. Suzuki's body would be returned
to Matsugaoka from the hospital, so I caught a train out of Kyoto early
that afternoon.[13] I arrived in Kamakura after four in the afternoon and
found almost no one on the temple grounds of Tokeiji. Matsugaoka too
was deserted, showing only the vivid color of the red and white flowers.
His home also was closed up. I then learned that the return of his body

had been delayed until the following day, and so his private secretary, Mihoko Okamura, had returned alone from the hospital to Matsugaoka, where she was resting. I decided to visit again later, went to pay my respects to the memory of Kitaro Nishida at one of his burial spots nearby, and then called on Shokin Furuta[14] at the Shoden'an on the temple grounds of Engakuji, where I rested.[15] Mr. Furuta seemed busy preparing obituaries and making telephone calls.

In the evening, when it began to get dark, I returned to Matsugaoka. Mihoko was already awake. Besides her, there were only a house-maid and two young men—Mr. Sato and Mr. Nitta. The two men had graduated from Kyoto University and Tokyo University respectively; Mr. Sato had been a student of mine, after which, under the guidance of Dr. Suzuki, he was doing research on Saichi Asahara (1850–1932).[16]

Whenever I had gone there the hill was quiet, but that evening there was an especially profound stillness. The house felt somehow barren without Dr. Suzuki; even our hushed voices seemed to echo. Standing on the veranda I looked out at the garden on the flattened top of the hill; it was not very wide and there was only a flower garden without any tall trees growing. The view was open, the sky expansive. Across the valley was a rather low range of mountains almost surrounding it and framing the view. From the space where the ravine below, thick with trees, stuck out like a border around the garden, only the temple roof of Tokeiji was visible; not a house was in sight. I felt that below the wide open sky lay a completely separate earth. Before long the remaining evening light was gone and the top of the hill began gradually sinking into darkness. There was a feeling of collapse, as if some significant presence had been lost, and a strange stillness filled the air. The surrounding hill and trees sinking in the dusk, the shadow of a bird in flight—all slipping out of "time," as if clothed in the countenance of stillness. Here I could feel his "death" running through all things.

That evening I planned to spend the night at Mr. Torataro Shimomura's[17] home in Zushi, but when I tried to take my leave, Miss O-kamura urged me to stay. She said she could not bear being alone that evening. And so, together with Mr. Sato and Mr. Nitta, four of us spent the evening preparing for the following day and watching a memorial program for Dr. Suzuki on television. When it got late we had a light meal and, together with the housemaid, sat around the dinner table chatting; but heartfelt words which innocently fell from Miss Okamura's lips were deeply impressed on my mind. At the hospital, she was at his bedside; he had already breathed his last. At that time she thought that though his body was lying there motionless it was as if his life continued. She said she did not feel any great change occurred between him alive and him in death.

When I heard this I recalled the incident between Feng Chichuan and Dahui.[18] Once when I was reading *The Wind and Moon on the River and Lake Collection*, I had found it in the commentary, and since then it had laid buried in my memory. Feng Chichuan (1107–53) called himself Layman Putong, and was a minister of state, so he was also called Minister Feng. His name is well-known in the annals of Zen history. Dogen quotes a poem of his in the "Bendowa" chapter of *Shobo Genzo*.[19] When Minister Feng met Dahui, the minister was passing the summer retreat on Mt. Jing [Mt. Ching], where he made the following skeleton verse while practicing under Dahui:

> Here is the skeleton,
> But where is the person?
> Thus we know the soul
> Does not belong to the sack of flesh
> [i.e., the body].

Seeing this, Dahui rebuked him, saying:

> Why do you maintain such an understanding?

And continued with his own verse:

> That very skeleton
> Is the person himself!
> The one-soul-sack-of-flesh,
> Sack-of-flesh-one-soul.

In an annotation of *The Wind and Moon on the River and Lake Collection*, this continues with another famous incident concerning the three Zen masters, Xiangyan, Shishuang and Caoshan.[20] The same incident is also mentioned in the verse of the second case of the *Blue Cliff Record*:

The skull has no more consciousness,
and how could emotions be stirred?
In the dry forest the dragon bellows;
the trees are not dead yet.[21]

That is what happened to Miss Okamura, who had accompanied Dr. Suzuki over the years as the shadow accompanies the form. It is not strange that she had felt somehow within his everyday life something that transcended life-and-death. The reverberation of that dragon in the dry forest must always have been pliantly resounding in his daily life. It seems only natural then that Miss Okamura would not sense much of a change tending his body as it lay there silent and steady just after he passed away. Over the years, as they became close, perhaps that is how deeply the fragrance of the man himself had sunk in.

When it was decided that the discontinued *Eastern Buddhist* journal, which Dr. Suzuki had started forty-five years earlier, was to be reissued, I, together with a number of others, was left in charge of the work, and in the fall of 1965 the first issue of the new series came out. Dr. Suzuki had planned an English translation of the *Blue Cliff Record* with the reissuing of the journal, and the first case was included in this first issue. Shortly before he passed away, and in the midst of a tremendous amount of work, he managed to complete a translation of the second case. As mentioned above, the second case includes the following mondo:

As you know, Kyogen [Xiangyan] was once asked by a monk, "What is the Way (*Dao*)?" Kyogen answered, "In the dry forest the dragon bellows." The monk asked, "What is a man of the Way?" The master answered, "The eyes are glittering in the skull."

The second case also includes the critique by Shishuang and Caoshan of this mondo.

When I heard Miss Okamura's words, I immediately recalled the incident involving Dahui which by association brought me back to the incident concerning Xiangyan and the others, then to Dr. Suzuki's translation work, and then again to Miss Okamura. This was what lay behind the profound impact her words had on me.

When I awoke the following morning, it was clear and bright. Standing on the veranda and looking at the view, it no longer felt like Matsugaoka was another world as it had the previous night—like the shadow of death, like the feeling of collapse after one has lost one's master. A calm pervaded it now that differed from the profound loneliness and desolate stillness of the previous night. With a mildly warm and peaceful landscape before my eyes, the following passage, also from the second case of the *Blue Cliff Record* came to mind:

"In the sky, the sun rises, the moon sets;
Before the railings, the mountain stands high, the water
[flowing below] is cold."

Later the coffin was brought in, many people came one after another and it got increasingly lively. After nightfall, feeling I should get to Zushi, I descended the hill and was given a ride by a friend.

Postscript

Afterwards, while reading the issue of *The Great Dharma Wheel* journal (September, 1966), which was dedicated to the memory of Dr. Suzuki, I learned that the verse of Xuedou[22] quoted above, "In the sky, the sun rises, the moon sets; / Before the railings, the mountain stands high, the water / [flowing below] is cold" had been written down by Dr. Suzuki to be engraved on a stone monument at a spot in Usui pass. He had himself, the year before, stopped by that stone monument. Of course he had gone through Karuizawa every summer for many years, so that is probably how such a plan arose. But I had no idea of this when that passage came to me while standing on the veranda at Matsugaoka Library or even when I wrote the above. Thus when I read the journal article which mentioned this, I was struck by the strange coincidence. But then again it is not without reason.

Perhaps during or just after his English translation of the second case of the *Blue Cliff Record*, he recalled that there was a phrase most fitting for Usui pass. I had read the English translation before, and so I remembered it that morning. Nevertheless, that the same passage should occur to me just after he passed away, and also that he had it written for this stone monument just prior to his passing, was, more than just a mere coincidence, something which profoundly affected me.

15

Mihoko Okamura
"Wondrous Activity"

1

THE FIRST TIME I MET SENSEI was more than fifteen years ago. I was living with my parents in New York at the time. From two years after our first meeting, until the twelfth of July, 1966, I was fortunate to be able to remain always at his side.

When I am asked about my memories of him, I find it hard to reply. He was always so near at hand that his whole being, everything about him, is for me a memory, and I don't see how I can pluck out one instance or event to share. The sight of him drinking his tea, or lost in his research in his study; the soft words he may have spoken to the flowers blooming in the garden or the cat playing on his lap; these recollections fill and occupy my whole heart, and among them I cannot choose. All I can do is to relate the images that come to me as I recollect, and that is what I offer here.

Above all, Sensei was a sound man, in mind and body alike. About him there was nothing of the stuffy scholar or the mystic monk. He lived a life as natural and effortless as a flowing stream; at the same time he was quite independent. While Sensei's life and thought were marked by a great rationality, he also transcended mere rationality and moved in a realm of complete freedom. For me the most difficult thing to fathom about his character was the way in which he managed to combine within himself such discipline and gentleness, without the slightest contradiction.

The French proverb "To know all is to forgive all" was a favorite of Sensei. "To understand that," he often said, "is all that you need to know." And he certainly did.

I was still unused to life in Japan. I would grow lonely or angry for some reason, and many times I was reduced to sobbing noisily, not to be comforted. When Sensei came upon me in such a state he looked at me with great pity and sympathy and said "Strike me, as hard as you can," offering himself as a way for me to vent the frustrations and hurt inside me. But when I contemplated hurting him with my own willfulness and selfishness, the knot in my breast evaporated. As I half-playfully drummed my fists on Sensei's chest, my frustrations already spent, he responded with a pained grimace and cries of "Ouch, ouch!" A short while afterward he remarked ruefully, "Thank heaven you didn't really strike me."

It was then that I truly understood, with my whole being, Sensei's motto "To know all is to forgive all." I felt an indefinable something, an unquestioning acceptance of everything that is, whether it is good or bad, whether it hurts or it doesn't. I was awed, somehow, and humbled.

In his last years, I used to give Sensei nightly injections of vitamin supplements and take his blood pressure. After that we had a chance to talk pleasantly together until he began to feel sleepy. One night we had the following conversation.

"Sensei, the world is a frightening place, isn't it?" (I said this in reference to something that had happened that day.) Sensei looked into my eyes for a few moments, without saying anything. In those eyes that I cannot describe, so intense and kind, I saw tears welling up. "So you understand?" he said. "That's good. Now I can die in peace."

He understood only too well how frightening a place our world is. Knowing it, he did not run from it, but placed himself firmly in the midst of the tempest and set about his work. While he placed great trust in people, he was dependent on no one, and he kept to himself something that he did not give to anyone. Even I, who took care of his daily needs, felt this unapproachable aspect of Sensei. Afterward I learned that the great energy that Sensei devoted to his work was based on this unshakeable center.

⌁   ⌁   ⌁

One morning the housemaid came to me to say that a bit more money was needed for household expenses. I went up to the second floor, where Sensei was, to tell him this. "It seems we need a bit more money for the daily budget," I ventured.

Sensei laughed and said brightly "Here you are. Take it."

"I wonder if there is anyone else in the world who is so cheerful to part with his money," I teased.

"To me, tissue papers in this room that you are so eager to throw out are worth more, you can be sure."

"I wouldn't be surprised." I gently waved the ten-thousand-yen note I had received from Sensei before his face. "This wouldn't be much use for blowing your nose, after all." And that set him into peals of laughter.

Sensei was always saving things like paper and string. He was conscious of any sort of waste. Not only did he keep paper napkins, scrap paper, tissue, and stationery, but he would use old envelopes—he wrote on the backs—as paper for his manuscripts. He stuffed these treasures randomly in every drawer and box in his study, and a tremendous commotion always ensued when it came time to search for something. This bothered me, and the study looked a mess; I asked him on several occasions to permit me to throw away at least a part of this collection. But he always refused: "No. Just leave things as they are." To be sure, there would come a time when something he had saved would come in handy, and then he'd turn his teasing gaze on me and declare with joking superiority, "I told you so."

One day—when was it?—Sensei was speaking of the brevity of the time left to him. "I hope you don't mind, but I have every intention of following you wherever you go, you know," I said. For a moment he looked troubled; then: "That's fine with me. Come along." And thus he comforted me. But now indeed he has left me behind. Wherever I look, however long I wait, he is not to be found. This emptiness I feel— for an instant it was dispelled, by the cry of a crow a moment ago, as it flew off into the dawn.

2

The nasty appearance of cockroaches as the weather gets warmer calls up for me a fond recollection.

Whenever Daisetz Sensei found bugs or insects in the house he would say "You fellows would be much better off outside," and, picking them up with the long chopstick-like tongs used for placing coals in the brazier, open a window and send them gently back outdoors. But with cockroaches it was a different story. When Sensei spotted one his eyes would take on a determined glint and he would whip off one slipper and begin to chase the cockroach about the room slapping here and there, right and left. More often than not, the cockroach would get the better of him and Sensei would return panting to his seat with a rueful look.

I was amused to discover that even Daisetz Sensei had an enemy, and I couldn't resist the temptation to do a little "preaching to the Buddha," as it were. "But Sensei, don't all living things have the buddha nature?..." "No, I draw the line at cockroaches. They eat the glue of my books. But they're just so fast, I don't stand a chance." This he delivered with the tragic air of someone who had just lost a bitter struggle with his greatest rival. The man Daisetz and the bug cockroach—two sentient beings. When bothered, both bothered with all their might. No room here for any feelings of superiority.

All sorts of things could bother Daisetz the man. Once in a train station a handicapped person happened to walk past us. Sensei's gaze grew sad and introspective. "What a terrible shame. But it's the responsibility of all of us, Mihoko-san. Well, we can't just stand here. We must get to work, to work!" When I first heard these words I wondered to myself why that unknown person's disability was our responsibility, but gradually I feel as if I have come to fully understand Sensei's feelings and his thoughts.

Sensei was always looking at the entity of all living beings, and he understood and interpreted each individual as one part of that entity. From that point of view, the sum total of human activity cannot be divorced from our individual actions. Whatever is done, whatever we do, each of us, as someone who has been born in this world as a human being, has a responsibility toward all humanity. For Sensei, to live was for each of us to do what we were meant to do with all our strength, all our heart.

Sensei's belief concerning the individual was reflected in every aspect of his daily life. Whenever he asked something of me, whether it was to sew on a button that had come off or to type one of his manuscripts, he was always grateful when the finished work was brought to him. I received the impression at those times of not merely gratitude to me as an individual, but rather a gesture of obeisance to all sentient beings. His gratitude did not stop with the single individual before his eyes; somehow his gaze was directed to a more removed world, and to that realm he proclaimed his thanks. His voice at these times had a resonance that seemed to transcend the human state. It was as if all existence were bowing in thanks to all existence. The lovely reverberations of that sound linger with me yet, and show no trace of disappearing.

Many people were drawn to this quality in Sensei and came to speak to him of their problems. Sensei would sit for hours, his hand cupped to his slightly deaf ear, listening to the sufferings and problems of these people in deepest sympathy, punctuating their accounts with "Well . . . yes . . . I see." His posture was always completely free of tension. In the quiet light of his eyes one felt a gentleness that would give audience to anything, and his deliberate, well-savored "yes" was a balm that soothed the hearts of those who came to him.

And when the story had come to an end and the speaker turned to Sensei with the question "Sensei, what should I do?" his answer was almost always: "Well . . . I don't know." Listening nearby, I at first thought this was a cold and heartless way to respond. I puzzled over the matter in various ways: "Why does he say he doesn't know when he very well does?" . . . or, sometimes, "He's just tired, and he's saying he doesn't know to put an end to this." But upon hearing Sensei's "I don't know" time and time again, I began to realize the great meaning that was enclosed in that simple utterance.

If you listened closely, you could hear the following echoing within Sensei's "I don't know": the individual's problem is not merely the individual's problem. If the problem could be treated that way, as the problem of one person cut off from all others, his answer would no doubt be "I know." But Sensei was looking at the individual from a much wider perspective. That's why his answer was "I don't know." Though a person might come to Sensei with a very particular individual problem, Sensei saw it as a universal problem, one of the entire human race. And he saw it as his own problem, too. In his eyes, each individual also reflected the whole of existence while preserving his or her own uniqueness, each was irreplaceable, and for that reason unfathomable, infinitely novel. And thus for Sensei each individual was endlessly fascinating, and for each he was endlessly grateful.

⚓   ⚓   ⚓

I was always struck by Daisetz Sensei's great kindness. Once we had guests to dinner, and I had put on my Japanese dress for the occasion. Everyone was at the table, and as I began to serve the food Sensei appeared at my side and lifted the long sleeves of my kimono so that they would not be in the way as I served. Without worrying in the least about what the others thought, he continued to hold up my sleeves until I had finished.

One night I was sewing curtains late at night. Sensei, who had already gone to bed, got up and sat opposite me at the sewing machine, pulling the long pieces of cloth to help me with my work. From the night-clothes-clad form of Sensei, so cheerfully willing to help, I feel I learned a great many things that night.

The first time I encountered Sensei's realm of complete freedom, loosed from the bounds of the individual, was when he stayed for a time at my home in New York. One night I was washing his back in the bath and he began to relate in a casual way, "There was once a Zen master called Daito Kokushi . . . "

"One day he realized that the day of his death had come. One of his legs was bad, and he couldn't bend it. But on that day he said to his leg, 'I have put up with you all my life and let you do as you liked; but today I'm going to have my way'.

"And he gripped the unbending leg and folded it under himself with a snap, sat in the *zazen* posture, and peacefully entered nirvana, they say. People in the old days were pretty strong-willed indeed. . . ."

"Yes, he sounds like a true Stoic. And Sensei, what about you?" I asked.

With that he immediately stuck one of his legs out of the bath water and declared, "I prefer to let nature take its course."

I remember as if it were yesterday Sensei's strong and healthy leg sticking out of the bath water right before my eyes, and the way I nearly fell over from laughing at the sight of it. That one wet leg will remain sticking out in front of me forever, pointing the way to the world of the unobstructed, the realm of eternity.

3

I first heard of Daisetz Sensei when I was fifteen or sixteen, a first-year high school student in New York. "An important professor of Buddhism has come from Japan. You should go listen to him speak," I was told. Of course at that time I knew nothing of Zen or Daisetz Sensei's great work or reputation.

I was at an age when I was beginning to feel doubts about the adult world as well as to question the nature of my own existence, exactly midway in the growth from child to adult.

Following the suggestion I had been given, I made my way to the large auditorium in the Lowe Library of Columbia University to hear Sensei's lecture, stealthily finding a place for myself among the large number of students and professors who were there. Maybe it was because I had skipped school to attend. For some reason I felt a bit intimidated and, trying to be inconspicuous, I waited for the arrival of Sensei.

Finally, the side door of the auditorium opened with force and Sensei marched in with long, vigorous strides. In one arm he hugged a dark brown *furoshiki*, as he walked up to the podium. He presented to me an extremely striking figure, and for a moment I thought he was a young man.

He rose to the high lectern and looked at his watch. The auditorium grew quieter and then completely still. The students around me were leaning forward in their seats with expectant looks directed toward the front of the room. The face of Sensei's watch was strapped to the inside of his wrist, and he held it close to his nearsighted eyes. Perhaps the numbers on the dial were small. For an instant, he squinted, and those famous long eyebrows changed their direction. Perhaps it was only my imagination, but it was as if a butterfly were moving his antennae. And his wrist, perhaps because it was relaxed, hung down like a monkey's paw. His eyes, peering out from under his eyebrows were like those of a wise elephant, and seemed to be filled with a deep, embracing compassion. I was struck suddenly by the feeling that I had traveled back in time . . . a strong sense of déjà vu. But, strangely, I also felt that all of those features were proclaiming the immediate and very real presence of Daisetz Sensei.

Sensei carefully opened the *furoshiki* and took out two Chinese-style books. Now he removed his glasses and began to flip through the pages. The movement of his hand seemed to be the activity of some other creature, of some being that knew no falsehood.

Was he aware of our presence or not? It was hard to say which, and it could have been either. This only added to the ineffable atmosphere that clung to him. Yet as we watched these gestures, we were somehow put at ease. One professor at Columbia remarked "When I am listening to Dr. Suzuki's lectures, everything seems alright and certain; but when the lecture is over and I leave, the old confusion returns." How true that was.

When Sensei had found the right page, he began to speak in a soft voice. I was taken aback by his refined and accomplished English. But not only that. While Sensei was clearly speaking to the audience before him, there was also, somewhere in his attitude, the feeling of a monologue unfolding. It was as if instead of preaching to others he was affirming for himself the truth he knew.

Only much, much later did I realize that Daisetz Sensei did not as a rule make a distinction between self and others. I came to know how true that was as, contemplating his words, I saw that suddenly, effortlessly, self became others and others grew linked to self. He had attained the realm in which that boundary no longer existed. When listening to the troubles of others he would exclaim "Ah, how painful that must have been!" or "What a shame!" with an expression as if he felt the pain himself. This was not simply sympathy for others, nor putting oneself in another's place. Sensei lived in a world in which he could become the other. Nor was his ability to transform himself restricted to human beings. It was the same when he felt for animals and plants. Sensei traveled freely back and forth from self to other, and testified in his life and experience to the fundamental identity of the two.

One day Sensei, gazing at his own hand, began to speak to me in his usual, inimitable manner, as if he were talking to himself. "How strange," he said. "When I think of this as my own hand, there is no doubt that it is. But if I think that it is not my own hand, it seems as if it no longer is. Do you see? I didn't come into this world of my own choosing. I had parents. My parents had parents and their parents had parents. If we follow that all the way back to the beginning, we come to the God who created this world. God surely knew that I would eventually come to be. If I were to claim everything I do is not my responsibility but God's, it would be hard to deny.

"But this hand. Just because it is not mine doesn't mean I can place it in the fire without regrets. How about it? (He took my hand and moved it near the space heater in front of us.) Hot, isn't it? . . . There is, after all, someone or something that looks after it. We can't think of it as simply another's hand. It's neither mine nor not-mine. . . . Just this—"

And Sensei let his hands dance in the air.

"It moves freely. . . . I call this 'wondrous' (*myo*). This is the 'wondrous activity'."

I was afraid for a moment in this conversation that my hand might be placed too near the fire of the nearby space heater, but fortunately, Daisetz Sensei had no trouble distinguishing my hand from his.

⤐   ⤐   ⤐

I have another recollection of Sensei that has to do with hands. It took place on my third visit to him. He was eighty-two at the time, and he was living in Butler Hall, a residential hotel belonging to Columbia University. His apartment was on the sixteenth floor, facing north. When I rang the bell I heard the sound of steps on the carpet and the door opened. Above the well-starched shirt and a smartly fastened necktie was a face that looked for all the world like the Okina mask in Noh. He greeted me kindly, hung my coat up for me in the closet, and led me to the living room.

The first thing that caught my eye was a giant mandala in scarlet and green that hung on the right wall. It was nearly a meter and one-half on each side, brightly colored, and full of Buddhas, large and small. When I looked at them I suddenly thought "They look like human beings. . . yet somehow they're different." And I was momentarily lost in curious thoughts.

In the room were a sofa and a desk together with a large leather armchair. Every other space was piled with books, so many that one could hardly find a place to step. Not just Japanese and English books, but Greek and Hebrew dictionaries, Sanskrit and Chinese texts as well. And all of them were very obviously being used. One sight that I will never forget is Sensei bent over a Chinese woodblock-printed book that looked to be four or five hundred years old, blithely writing notes in the margin.

Near the windows of the room an African violet was sweetly blooming toward the light. The sight of the typewriter and telephone on his desk, and Sensei's impeccable dress and fluent English, left me with the immensely appealing impression of a harmonious blending of different eras. "I can't trust people any more. Life seems empty to me."

He listened to the plea of that girl in pigtails and answered only: "Well." I thought at the time that he neither affirmed nor denied what I had said. But now I realize afresh that the resonance I heard behind those words lent my straying heart a new life. Sensei took my hand and opened it, palm upward.

"What a pretty hand. Look carefully at it. This is the Buddha's hand." His eyes shone as he spoke.

And so our talk ended that time. That was the atmosphere in which I began to receive help in solving my problems while I assisted Sensei with his work.

When Sensei's lecture in the auditorium began, I took out a pen and notebook and decided to stretch a net of will, as it were, to catch what I could. But as I bent forward to listen I began to realize that this was quite different from the usual lecture. It had the depth and range of a great ocean, and the taste of its water, too.

No matter that I cast my net—it was a small and frail thing, not up to the task. The title of the lecture was "Huayan Philosophy," and there was little reason to suspect I would comprehend it. Since my net was of no use, all I could do was listen with my whole being, and that I did.

Sensei would direct his gaze somewhere, search for the right words, and try to communicate them to us. "Wait a minute now. Was it before or after? Or was it in the middle? Never mind. It doesn't matter. It most certainly happened. And since it happened . . ." And while thus tormenting his listeners, he would pursue some point of focus that was visible only to him. His strength of purpose never failed to impress his listeners. Even though he might wander or falter here or there, he never lost the trust of his listeners, a power of his that baffled me.

Of course, some pointed to the vagueness of some of his statements and criticized him: "Suzuki Daisetz is not a scholar!" That may have been true. On the other hand, it may not. Daisetz Sensei would not have cared. To me he often said: "The path is still long. Instead of standing about here, we must move ahead." And: "The essential thing is not to be found in academic study itself. Study is to make clearer a basic peace of mind. If it can do that, that's more than enough."

Sensei was, without a doubt, making a plea for something important and essential. I did not grasp it as I sat listening to his lecture. Yet the voice I heard made me feel that there was something. When he spoke it was like a lion roaring, the breath coming up from the very tips of his toes and leaving his mouth together with his words. The voice of truth, I thought. A man who thinks with his whole body and mind. And a man who does not speak of what he does not know.

For me, who did not comprehend the content of the lecture that Sensei was delivering, Sensei's very presence was a Great Sermon delivered through his entire being, and it was to this I clung.

In the fifteen years I was with him after that, he never once betrayed that first impression.

Daisetz the Death-Man

Reminiscing about Sensei after his death means, I suppose, looking for him as he was in life, digging up old memories and looking through the traces he left behind: the things, the writings, the photographs.

But what I really feel is that he left no such traces at all, perhaps like a person who had never existed from the start.

The day he died I returned to Mastsugaoka Bunko, his residence in Kamakura, and entered the room where he had been only a few hours before. I tried somehow to discover the shadow of his presence in the objects there: the articles of clothing, the photographs, and the books. By touching them, I hoped to bring myself to some kind of personal acceptance of this sudden change. But no matter what I looked at or what I touched, I felt Sensei's presence not in the least. Instead, strangely, my efforts to recapture him only drove him farther and farther away. And so I passed several comfortless, futile hours.

As Sensei grew more and more advanced in years, I tried, of course, to prepare myself for the time when we would have to part. But preparation is preparation. When the day finally came and he disappeared from before my eyes, all that preparation was transformed in an instant to distress.

Searching for something somewhere that would bring me comfort, I went into his study and looked at the desk where he sat working every day. For a moment, I seemed to see his figure there—but in the next instant, I knew that it was nothing, and I realized that this ghost hunt would never bring me what I sought. I suddenly felt a desire to go outside.

The garden was unchanged, as if nothing had happened. I saw spread before me a world which did not allow for my pursuit of Sensei's traces. Yet, somehow, it felt so familiar. Thinking of nothing in particular, I headed back toward the entranceway of the house, where I stopped. At that moment a branch of the nearby pine tree swayed in the wind, and I knew: "So, this was it . . . here he is . . . Sensei . . ." I felt that at last I had found "him" again. Ever since then, whenever I am quiet, everything about me "is" him. The only problem is that I so much liked to see him as he was and to feel the gentle warmth of his hand. And though I might find Sensei in this pine tree I see now, it remains a pine tree. Where is his face, and where his hand? But these are things I am not likely to understand until I, too, have become the pine tree.

Once quite some years ago, I asked Sensei what death was.

"Death?" he replied. "This is death."

And with that he fell back on the couch, stuck out his tongue, rolled his eyes to the ceiling, and expired: "Goodbye, John!"

Sensei was not normally one for imitations or other tricks of that sort, but this spontaneous, dramatization of a corpse in response to my very serious question was as hilarious as it was unexpected, and I broke into laughter. He got up and joined me, half laughing too, but also slightly challenging.

"So, do you see?"

"Bravo!" And I applauded. But I also know that I had been shown something very important, as I sensed Sensei's eyes moving over my face with his intense gaze. He seemed to be saying that living and dying, coming or going, this world or that world, were spontaneous activities —no need to theorize about it. So his whole being spoke to me then, and when I looked at his face in its long sleep, I sensed he was right, for it was the same face I had known. He was already, even long ago, a dead man—one who had abandoned all that can be abandoned. When he at last assumed the appearance of a dead man as well, there was no real difference: nothing would begin because of his death, and nothing would end.

I remember once when a famous parapsychologist came to visit Daisetz Sensei. He spoke to Sensei of many events that would usually be considered supernatural. But when Sensei didn't seem particularly impressed by these stories, the parapsychologist was a bit put off, and asked whether Sensei didn't wonder what would happen to him after death. As if speaking to himself, Sensei replied, "But what about the here, the now? Won't it be too late after death?"

I had believed from the start that this sort of thing was nonsense, and later I openly expressed my pleasure with Sensei's remark. Sensei, however, scolded me in no uncertain terms: "There are many things in this world that we don't understand. It's a mistake to dismiss such things so lightly, as you do."

On the night of his ninety-fourth birthday he said to me, "I just don't feel like dying yet. There are so many things that I still want to write, and I can't do that if I'm dead. To come to understand things you didn't understand—it's fascinating. There are lots of reasons that people have to live long. You live long, too, Mihoko-san." Thoughtfully stroking his forehead, he said in a teasing tone, "It would be so interesting to see wrinkles gradually appearing on your forehead. I'd like to live to see that."

I still hear in all the different words of Sensei the echoes of our finite world and the infinite realm, free from contradiction, as natural as rain falling from heaven to earth. Rain falls because it is rain. People try, for a moment, to separate life from death because they are people. But what we learn when we finally come to understand is that divorced from the here-and-now, there is nothing at all we can speak of. Sensei seemed to have grasped that better than anyone. He was, in his way, an incarnation of that here and now.

Above, opposite, and previous page: Matsugaoka Bunko, October 1963.

At the Fourth East-West Philosophers'
Conference, Honolulu, Hawaii, 1964.

At Diamond Sangha Kokoan, Honolulu, 1964. *From left to right:* D.T. Suzuki, Eido Tai Shimano, the abbot of the Dai Bosatsu Zendo (The Zen Studies Society) in New York, and Robert Aitken.

Diamond Sangha, 1964.

Honolulu, 196

Kojirin, a public meditation hall attached to Engakuji.

Tombstone of D.T. Suzuki and his wife, Beatrice Lane
Suzuki, in the Tokeiji temple grounds, 1966.

16

Shokin Furuta

Daisetz T. Suzuki

T HE *Shobo Genzo*, THE MOST CELEBRATED work of the priest
Dogen (1200–53), founder of the Soto sect of Zen Buddhism,
has a strange fascination. The ideas which it expounds cannot
be understood by any normal logical processes, yet despite this it has
some undefinable, compelling quality. Without a doubt it has its own
unique philosophy.

To talk of a philosophy in a Zen context is inevitably to call to mind
Daisetz T. Suzuki. The history of Zen thought in Japan affords few
examples of men who had an explicit philosophy, much less a systematic
one. In fact, if one were to search history for a man to rank alongside
Dogen, Daisetz would be one of the few to come to mind.

Zen, with its rejection of reliance on the written word and doctrine,
might seem to deny any explicit philosophy from the start, but this is
not so. Indeed, as we shall see later, a Zen deprived of philosophy would
lose its creativity.

The main purpose here is not to make a comparison of Dogen and
Daisetz; the disparities between the Kamakura period (1192–1336),
when Dogen lived, and the present age, make any such comparison
pointless. One thing that the two men certainly had in common was
the acute sensitivity of their thought-processes. However, they were of
basically differing temperaments, and their characters were in many
ways complementary. If Dogen by nature was sensitive to the point of

being highly strung, Daisetz might well be described as unconcerned about things to the point of being callous.

In talking of their common qualities and their differences I am, perhaps, making comparisons of a kind after all; either way, it is also interesting to note that Dogen went to China to study the Zen of Southern Song, while Daisetz went to America, where he studied Western philosophy. Though what they learned was different, they were alike in being exposed to unfamiliar ideas. They were alike, too, in absorbing what they learned while at the same time retaining their critical faculty unimpaired. The present age is far more complex than the Kamakura period. One cannot tell whether Daisetz will ever come to occupy a place in the history of ideas similar to that of Dogen. Even so, and despite the relative unimportance of philosophy and religion on the surface of history today compared with, say, politics or economics, it seems unlikely that Daisetz's name will ever fall into oblivion. The roots of the ideas he formulated run deep, and such roots do not easily wither even when the sprouts they put forth above the soil are trampled underfoot.

I would liken Daisetz's philosophy to a common weed. The simile, which I will explain in a moment, is borrowed from Dogen, and I feel it appropriate, in considering Daisetz, to refer to the writings of one whose name must always call up that of his twentieth-century successor.

To anyone who would object to the simile, I would say that the humble weed is not to be scorned. Most weeds have a robust lifeforce which belies the frailty of their appearance. Their very robustness can often, in fact, be a source of annoyance—but that is no part of our simile here.

In the "Genjo Koan" of the *Shobo Genzo*, Dogen says, "Flowers fall amidst regrets; weeds live long on neglect." The point here is in the "live long": flowers (he refers here, of course, to the cherry blossom) are beautiful, but have little of the power of survival without which even the loveliest things are doomed to vanish. It is not that Daisetz's philosophy had none of the flower's beauty, but that comparison with a flower gives a wrong idea of its real quality—even though in some respects it was literary and poetic in its modes of expression. The word "neglect," on the other hand, has an unpleasant ring, yet the fact remains that academic study is not something which can be achieved in the face of too much flattering attention. To be shunned by others actually helps a scholar to devote himself to his work. In his later years

Daisetz showed a marked change, becoming almost sociable, but twenty or thirty years previously he was in no sense a good mixer. He stood aloof from others, both personally and in his studies.

An old proverb says, "the hated child prospers long." It often seems to happen, indeed, that those who are generally loved are not long in this world, whereas those who are unpopular live long and prosper greatly. So, too, it is popularly believed that the beautiful woman is destined to die young. It is an odd quirk of the human affections that time spent with what is loved should seem to pass all too soon, whereas every moment spent with an object of dislike drags unbearably. Regret for something that is no more is associated with brevity, with swiftness, whereas dislike is always associated with lengthiness and tardiness. This does not mean, conversely, that the long-lasting and the slow necessarily imply a feeling of dislike, but it does mean that what is long-lasting or slow can never inspire us with that nostalgic sense of time's rapid passage. In their robustness and strength, the weeds that wax so fat on neglect lack poignancy. Daisetz lived—and lived strong and healthy— to the ripe old age of 96. His death, though it may remind us of the fleeting nature of human life considered in terms of eternity, scarcely brought the same poignant regret one feels for the cherry blossom scattered by a single night's rain. If one hesitates to say that he "thrived on neglect," then one is at liberty to substitute "love," but this expression, too, somehow misses the man's essential robustness. As I see him, Daisetz was a man who thrived on—who positively enjoyed—neglect, and who lived life with determination for just as long as he could.

Dogen died in 1253 at the age of fifty-three. Daisetz lived more than forty years longer. Dogen's death, perhaps, was the proverbial early death of those whom the gods especially favor. The same can hardly be said of a man who lived as long as Daisetz.

In comparing Daisetz's philosophy with the humble weed I had something else in mind, too. It was two famous poems from the *Shin Kokinshu*—a famous court anthology of *waka* (31-syllable verse)—which Rikyu (1521–91), the great master of the tea ceremony, quotes in his *Namboroku*. One of them, by Fujiwara Sadaie, reads: "As far as the eye could see / No cherry blossom, no maple / At the thatched hut by the bay / That autumn twilight." The second, by Fujiwara Ietaka, runs: "To those who long only / For the cherry blossom / I would show spring / In the mountain villages / With the grass poking through the snow."

Rikyu considered Sadaie's poem as a perfect expression of the Buddhist concept of Nothingness and as embodying the essential spirit of the tea ceremony. The Ietaka poem he sees as an expression of the need, as the next stage, for Nothingness to produce something out of itself—for some differentiated function, as it were, to make itself apparent within the non-differentiated. The twilight autumn scene at the thatched hut— the bleak bay devoid of blossoms, maple leaves, or any color—is blanketed in time with snow, thus expressing still more perfectly the state of Nothingness, of non-differentiation. Yet eventually, with the first rays of the spring sun, the snow will begin to vanish, and from beneath it the first shoots of grass will appear. For Rikyu, this grass poking through the snow was the perfect expression of the mysterious workings of the Void, an understanding of which is necessary if one is to grasp the true spirit of the tea ceremony.

Daisetz's philosophy is, in a sense, like the humble weeds poking through the snow. It exists beyond the blossom and the autumn leaves. It is a philosophy of the Void which recalls that "autumn twilight at the thatched hut by the bay." This philosophy of the Void derives originally from his experience of Zen meditation when he was at the prime of life, but his outlook was broadened by his subsequent studies of Buddhism. Still later, he came to concentrate on Zen and on the teachings of Pure Land Buddhism, which added—especially the Zen— a new depth to the breadth he had already acquired. The philosophy of the Void was expressed in various ways—as the doctrine of "no-mind," as the idea of "nonconceptual conceptualization," and as "the logic of negation." "No-mind" indicates a state of mind which has transcended the need to work in intellectual concepts—which is another way of expressing the "nonconceptual conceptualization." The "logic of negation" refers to the belief that the affirmation "A is A" only has any real truth when it is reached via the assertion that "A is non-A." That "A is A" is a judgment based on ordinary conceptualization. The statement that "A is non-A" represents a transcending of those ordinary conceptual processes, while the reaffirmation of A that follows this is "nonconceptualized conceptualization." This latter idea has sometimes been referred to as "divine intuition," a word which Daisetz used frequently around the years 1944–46.

A work published in 1939 which sums up Daisetz's views on the "no-mind" is *Mushin to iu Koto* (On no-mind). It is significant that in this work he refers to the "activity of the no-mind."

Daisetz's theories of no-mind, nonconceptualized conceptualization, the logic of negation, and the like are, of course, not original, and clearly owe a great deal to the philosophy of Zen classics and the sutras of *prajnaparamita* (Hannya gyo) one of the philosophical cornerstones of Mahayana Buddhism. What gives his ideas on the Void their characteristic quality is his attempt to systematize the idea of Void on the basis of his own thinking and his experience of Zen. Moreover, he was aided, in his attempt to elucidate the special nature of the peculiarly Oriental concept of the Void, by the knowledge of Western ideas which he acquired during his stay in America. In this respect, his treatment of the idea of the Void differs greatly from that of Oriental classicists of the past.

For Daisetz, the quintessence of the "Void" was not the white snow, but the new shoots pushing their way up through it. When one considers how he always considered Oriental thought in relation to Western thought, one might see the grass as itself corresponding to Western thought. In Daisetz's works, thus, the idea of the Void, essentially Oriental though it is, also has some affinities with the ideas of the West. The large number of Western readers which his works have attracted is not a result of the excellence of his English alone.

Let us return, though, to our original theme—"weeds thrive long on neglect." Few Japanese intellectuals in modern times can have poured out so many works in their later years as Daisetz. A list of his works shows that he was particularly prolific in the years between 1934, when he was 64, and 1948, when he was 79. Surprisingly, no fewer than nine works were published in the last of those years, 1948. More surprisingly still, the same period saw publication of nine volumes in English as well. Even the weeds could scarcely be more prolific. Even after this he continued to publish new works from year to year, and the whole series of his works—ending with *Toyo no Kokoro* (The mind of the East), published in August, 1965, the year before he died—totaled more than one hundred volumes in Japanese and more than thirty in English. To turn out too many works is not necessarily admirable, of course—some philosophers have produced not a single volume—yet in Daisetz's case there were many people who would have liked him if possible to turn out still more. He lived on through three eras—Meiji, Taisho, and Sho-wa—and every stage was significant in his history; indeed, his position as a figure who went on developing steadily throughout these three eras is remarkable, whether he is considered as a Japanese or a citizen of the world. In this he was different from most other intellectuals. The intellectual, it is believed in Japan, tends to collapse at the first sign of resistance, but Daisetz, despite his small physical stature, had a surprising inner strength and determination. The weed, even for a weed, had its roots particularly deep in the ground.

The ordinary weed bears seeds, scatters them about, and spreads in no time. The shoots that Daisetz put up through the snow will in due time, as spring gives way to summer and summer to autumn, bear their fruit and proliferate. Daisetz himself is no longer of this world, but the seeds which he sowed—weeds though some may call them—will put out shoots in the most unlikely places, in Japan and in the West as well.

Though one talks of "Zen thought," the fact remains that Zen stresses its independence of the written word and of doctrine, and the question arises of how Daisetz could have a "Zen philosophy." A word is necessary here to correct a common misunderstanding of Zen. A refusal to depend on the written word and doctrine is not the same as saying that the latter are without their uses. It means, ultimately, that one should not attempt to understand in terms of intellectual concepts—that one should not, to put it more crudely, try to understand with one's head. It means that one should experience things directly, without conceptualization—experience them, that is, with one's whole being, and not simply with one's intellect. Zen "thought," one might say, is the outcome of thinking without conceptualization. In the many works which Daisetz published, he discusses the nature of "nonconceptualized thought" and how it developed within the Zen tradition in the course of history. One might, in fact, sum up Daisetz's Zen philosophy as the attempt to apply, as far as possible, the principle of "nonconceptualized thought" in an investigation of those Zen teachings which lie outside doctrine and the written word.

Zen as an organized religion tends to carry this nonreliance on written word and doctrine to the point of rejecting all philosophizing as an unnecessary hindrance, but in fact Zen without philosophy would be no more than a lifeless corpse. Zen practice bereft of ideas would deteriorate into a kind of asceticism, a purely physical discipline. Few people can have stressed as strongly as Daisetz that nonreliance on words does not mean that words are useless. All the written works on which he spent his whole life were, in this respect, devoted to the philosophical justification of the idea of a truth incommunicable through written word and doctrine. It is quite certain that it is thanks to Daisetz rather than the Zen church that so much interest in Zen is being shown today throughout the world.

Despite its proclaimed independence of the scriptures and doctrine, Zen has produced more literature than any other Buddhist sect. What is more, this literature is still widely read today. For example, the *Hekiganshu*, compiled in the Song Dynasty, has been read as the most important work of the Zen sect ever since ancient times by countless readers. However, the Zen classics are too difficult to make popular reading today. So it comes about that the works of Daisetz are read and enjoyed by large numbers of people today. The large number of books produced by Zen is a tangible proof that it does not hold the written word to be useless, and Daisetz's works are a continuation of the same tradition.

As I have said, it seems inappropriate to compare Daisetz and his philosophy with the cherry blossom, somewhat irreverent though the simile of the weeds may seem. It is not that people do not regret his passing, but that he and his ideas just cannot fall and vanish overnight. His physical presence may be no more, but he will certainly live on as an inspiration in men's minds, while his ideas will survive and, in time, spread far and wide throughout the world. That is why I have compared him to the tough, prolific grass and weeds. For all the apparent neglect, the Zen he taught is spreading even among other religions. A considerable interest is being shown in Zen among Christians, for example, despite a certain amount of resistance.

Daisetz departed this earth suddenly on July 12, 1966. I was reminded of a Zen saying: "The flaming clouds of June dispel the white snow"—referring to the way true enlightenment drives out ordinary conceptual understanding. On that hot, humid summer morning the accumulated snow suddenly shifted and fell, crushing the shoots already pushing up through it. At this moment, Daisetz ended his earthly activities. Yet even crushed beneath the snow, the roots of the grass still extend deep into the ground. With the thaw, the grass will put forth new, different shoots.

One final word: some people claim that Daisetz's Zen was the Zen of the Rinzai sect. It is true that quite a few of his works deal with Rinzai philosophy, but this does not mean it should be taken as Rinzai Zen in the sectarian sense. His ideas are unrelated to any particular Zen sect, whether it be Rinzai, Soto, or Obaku. It is this fact which gives his Zen its unique character, and it will elude any attempt to fit it into a sectarian framework.

17

Akihisa Kondo

The Stone Bridge of Joshu

I N T H E *Hekiganshu,* O N E O F T H E M O S T important writings of
Zen literature, there is a passage as follows:

A monk asked Joshu, "The stone bridge of Joshu is famous. But what
I see is just a log bridge. Why?" Joshu answered, "You see only the
log bridge, but cannot see the stone bridge." The monk asked, "What
is then the stone bridge?" Joshu answered, "That which lets the asses
and horses pass."

The stone bridge of Joshu represents the ever-functioning dynamic
spirit of Zen—Zen in action—which has been transmitted, from mind
to mind, from generation to generation, in the history of Zen.

Throughout his long life of ninety-five years, Dr. Daisetz Teitaro
Suzuki lived a life of the stone bridge in the exact sense Joshu meant.

It is a well-known fact that he exerted his effort in expounding the
meaning of the enlightenment experience, satori, and the importance
of *prajna* (wisdom) in Zen. Satori, in other words, means awakening
to *prajna.*

Thanks to his effort no one doubts today the importance of the enlightenment experience in Zen. Therefore, it is quite understandable
that, given this importance, the attainment of enlightenment is apt to
be taken as the ultimate goal of Zen practice.

However, if one simply aims at the attainment of enlightenment and is gratified with it, he does not really understand the full purport of the meaning of satori experience.

As Dr. Suzuki so correctly pointed out, enlightenment is important, but its importance lies in the fact that it is not merely the moment of fulfilment of one's long cherished aspiration but it is the moment of his rebirth, the beginning of his spiritual life as a new being, to live not for himself but with other sentient and insentient beings, to share their sufferings and sorrows with them, and to help them become enlightened so that they too can liberate themselves from the bondage of troubles and pains, their anxieties and their feeling of meaninglessness. In other words, with his awakening to *prajna*, his new life with and for the people begins in direct response to the irresistible urge of *karuna* (compassion), the immediate self-expression of *prajna*. This kind of life is called the life of the Bodhisattva, which Joshu, in his plain but graphically concrete Zen term, calls his "stone bridge."

In this sense, after his enlightenment experience, Dr. Suzuki walked the way of the Bodhisattva throughout his life with his undaunted, tireless spirit. By virtue of his version of Joshu's stone bridge, not only asses and horses but people in the West as well as in the East, irrespective of the difference of nationality, color, race, class, culture, language, intelligence, age, sex, profession, richness and other worldly values, were able to deliver themselves from the shore of ignorance to the other shore of truth.

In the East, around the time he began to write about Zen, it was a fact that Zen was just for practicing. Any intellectual elucidation or noetic approach was considered somewhat blasphemous or at least useless and obstructive.

Of course, so far as Zen experience is concerned, as long as it is something to be experienced, practice is important. But if no noetic elucidation is allowed, there is a danger, in Zen practice, of falling into a kind of seemingly mystical state of self-complacency, a Zen sickness, which is a far more harmful obstacle to real *prajna* awakening.

Since even intellection—*vijnana* in Buddhistic terms—is one of the functions of *prajna*, it ceases to be a hindrance, if it does not assert its conceited claim for supremacy and is operated in its legitimate function by a person who has achieved its mastery by awakening to *prajna*. On the contrary, intellection will serve as one of the most efficient tools to discern the nature of enlightenment experience and promote the correct understanding of Zen practice.

It is true that you cannot make a horse drink water, but you can at least lead him to the water. Any effort, therefore, to contrive means or ways—*upaya*—to take him to the water is meaningful because it will give him a chance to drink when he wants it. It this sense Dr. Suzuki's elucidation of Zen through his voluminous writings was illuminating and helpful for those who were in need of guidance and instruction. His style of writing in Japanese was extremely plain, clear, and readable. Without using difficult Buddhistic terms unnecessarily, his works were permeated with profound wisdom. He wrote with a touch of warmth, which was a reflection of his personality, so that people could feel themselves closer and more intimate with the spirit of Zen which had been existing intrinsically in their veins but which they had erroneously taken as something mysterious and incomprehensible that belonged entirely to the possession of a selected few.

His noetic approach was more appealing and instructive to the younger Japanese who, being brought up in the rationalistic Western way of education, did not feel so syntonic with the traditional authoritative atmosphere of Zen, even though they respected its value.

Generally speaking, his books not only stimulated those in the temple, but also helped common people appreciate Zen as a traditional asset benefiting their own lives. His contribution in this regard is quite significant in view of the present state of Japanese culture which is being "modernized" under the strong influence of the West, because any change could not be successfully accomplished in any country not attuned to its basic cultural assets embedded in the hearts of its people.

To the West, where analytical, intellectual ways of thinking had traditionally prevailed, his analytical way of elucidation was not nearly as strange as it was to the East. However, the subject he introduced to the West was not something with which Western minds were familiar. Therefore, it was quite understandable that people in the West at first took what he talked about as just another esoteric product of the mysterious East.

It seems a strange but interesting coincidence that in the year of 1900, when he published in the United States his first book in English about

Zen, *Açvaghosha's Discourse on the Awakening of Faith in the Mahayana,*
Freud published his first book on psychoanalysis, *The Interpretation of
Dreams.*

But perhaps this is not so strange or accidental. Because, though they
did not know each other at all and were not aware what they had in
common, they had started on the same mission, the criticism of the path-
ology of modern Western culture, especially of the supremacy of reason,
to which both offered remedies in their own way. Freud stressed the
meaning of the unconscious, the forces of emotion, as opposed to the
conscious, the power of reason, and their conflict as the source of neu-
rosis. Suzuki specifically clarified the dichotomous and discriminating
nature of reason at the source of human suffering.

Because of Freud's audacious and ruthless exposure of the problem,
Western minds began to open their eyes to the alienation of man from
his wholeness as a human being as revealed in the form of numerous
cases of psychic disturbances. The forerunners of Freud, Nietzsche,
Marx, and Kierkegaard had forseen the phenomenon even though it
had been well covered by the glory of the materialistic achievements
called progress.

Freud's approach to the solution of the problem was by means of
psychoanalysis. It was guided by the principle of bringing the unconscious into consciousness, the unreasonable into the realm of reason,
that is, according to his phrasing, "Where there was *id*—there shall be
ego."

In that sense he was still in the traditional rationalistic cultural pattern
of the West. With all his colossal laborious works in psychoanalysis,
however, he came to a pessimistic conclusion about the future of human
civilization because he found by his critical observation the existence of
the self-destructive tendency which he believed intrinsic in human
nature. He concluded also, by his rationalistic thinking, that religion is
an illusion and a sort of infantilism.

Suzuki's contribution in this regard was, of course, the way of Zen.
He stressed the importance of awakening, and he used the word
"conscious" as Freud used it. However, in his case, what he means by
conscious is different from Freud's notion of bringing the libidinal
unconscious into consciousness. Suzuki's term means to become conscious of "the Cosmic Unconsciousness," which is achieved by awakening to *prajna.*

As Buddhism essentially originated from the realistic observation and understanding of the state of mankind as suffering, it can agree with Freud in the respect that man's state of existence is pessimistic at present as well as in the future so long as man is driven by his self-destructive tendency which is ultimately rooted in his ignorance.

According to Buddhistic understanding, man's existential state of suffering comes out of two kinds of ignorance, both of which are inseparably related. One is the ignorance of the fact that he is alienated from the Buddha Nature, and the other is the ignorance of the truth of the existence of the Buddha Nature in every human being. In short, man is ignorant of his ignorance of the Buddha Nature he is bestowed with. And just because of this ignorance, he surrenders himself blindly to the instinctual impulses which are governed by the principles, in Freud's terms, of pleasure and death. The more he is driven by these impulses and pursues their fulfilment, even with the resistance of reason by way of repression, the more he is alienated from his real self. The way by which man can liberate himself from his self-alienation, according to Zen Buddhism, is not by repression or sublimation through reason, but by breaking through his ignorance and realizing the Buddha Nature through his experience of awakening to *prajna*. In this sense, even though Zen, as a school of Buddhism, shares the same view of the existential state of mankind with Freud, it begins to develop its own doctrine of liberation from the very point where Freud ended with pessimism. It helps man to see his original face, according to its expression, to have a rebirth as a whole human being and to enable him to attain a new spiritual life beyond the death and pleasure principles, transcending the dichotomy of reason at the same time. To experience this and live in it, helping others to get enlightened, is the religious life of Zen. For Suzuki, the religion he believed in and practiced is not an illusion or infantilism. Religion is for him the way of maturity and realism in the sense that one can live his life fully with it as a new whole being helping his fellow men to restore their wholeness.

At that time when the West was beginning to be colored by the rosy notion of progress based on the belief in the supremacy of reason, it was most opportune that a message was conveyed from the East. Zen stated that by becoming aware of his state of self-estrangement resulting from the supremacy of reason, man is able to free himself from his ignorance so that he can realize his Buddha Nature. In that sense it is

nothing to be afraid of to be exposed to the emptiness and meaninglessness of his existential state, for it is to be taken as the turning point that
opens the way for his ultimate awakening to *prajna* as prepared in Zen.
This was the message conveyed by Suzuki in person to the world—a
message for the resurrection of man himself.

Perhaps more than any other group, those engaged in the treatment
of the mentally disturbed became keenly sensitive to the sickness of
Western civilization as a direct result of their observations in their offices.
While Freudian therapists were more or less negativistic and skeptical
or indifferent toward Zen because of their libidinal orientation, other
psychiatrists or psychotherapists whose minds were not limited by
theories but more open to psychic reality, showed their interest in what
Suzuki talked about. Among them Jung was the first one who recognized and appreciated the meaning of Zen experience. In his foreword
to Suzuki's *Introduction to Zen Buddhism*, he stated, "The only movement
inside of our civilization which has, or should have, some understanding
of these endeavors is psychotherapy." He compared Zen experience with
the mystic experiences of Meister Eckhart and John Ruysbroeck and
interpreted it as a process of individuation, his term for "becoming
whole." However, he made an understandable reservation by stating
that "Great as is the value of Zen Buddhism for understanding the
religious transformation process, its use among Western people is problematic." Whether its use among Western people is problematic or not
is a question to be answered in the future. But if Suzuki did not feel the
value of its use for the West in respect to "becoming whole," what
would be the meaning of his lifework dedicated to Zen's transmission
to the West? Personally I would rather like to stress another statement
of Jung's, "I have no doubt that the satori experience does occur also
in the West." Because I believe, so far as the Cosmic Unconscious is
concerned in which satori takes place, it is all-embracing and boundless
beyond the differences of culture. Even though he is conditioned by
culture, man has the intrinsic potentiality to make a leap and free himself
from his attachment to cultural prejudices, the product of discrimination,
by becoming conscious of the Cosmic Unconscious which is universal.
Following Jung, Karen Horney, through her personal contact and discussions with Suzuki, became very much interested in Zen. Her holistic
approach to man himself and her basic concept of the real self with her
stress on the importance of intuition in therapy, all urged her to study

and absorb eagerly what Zen had consummated. In her trip to Japan with Suzuki, the memory of which is still vivid in my mind, she met and exchanged opinions with quite a number of Zen masters. Even though she had been considered as one of the leaders of the culturists group, she, as a person, was much greater than her theory. As she felt herself congenial and had so much in common with Zen, she was anxious to develop her ideas by thought-stimulation experiences in Japan. Unfortunately due to her sudden death, what she got from this trip became unavailable to us. After her death, Suzuki had a series of lectures and discussions with her group that was led by Harold Kelman.

In 1957, Suzuki was invited to a conference in Mexico by Erich Fromm. Their encounter resulted in the publication of a book, *Zen Buddhism and Psychoanalysis.* It was quite a meaningful event, because while originating in different cultures and at different times, Zen and psychoanalysis had been sharing the same function of restoring man as a whole being in this modern age of split personality and anxiety, and they were brought into direct contact for collaboration to confirm mutually their common end.

Thus, his incessant activities for elucidation and transmitting Zen in the East and West began to bear fruit during the latter part of his life. It is a most outstanding fact that all through the long years of his pioneering activities, he worked practically single-handed. In that sense, he was alone and independent, although he had the helpful assistance and personal care of Miss Mihoko Okamura until his death. The way he opened was followed and cultivated by many others including R.H. Blyth, Alan Watts, Richard DeMartino, and Philip Kapleau.

One evening, when I was staying with him in Ipswich, near Boston, I happened to ask him, while we were seated talking, "What is Hyaku-jo's 'Sitting alone on the summit of Mt. Daxiong [Ta-hsiung]'?" As a reply, he suddenly raised himself with tremendous agility, and sat cross-legged in the chair. I can never forget my experience that his whole body suddenly looked grander and radiated an enormously overwhelming power at that moment. There I witnessed the forcefulness and dignity of his aloneness.

In 1952, he was still chiefly stressing the importance of *prajna* in his lectures. But in my view, he was actually teaching us *karuna* by his daily conduct. One evening I was telling him of my experience with a patient who had made a radical breakthrough after painful effort and suffering.

I was dumbfounded to find him in tears. After a while, he said, "How grateful I feel for what you have done!" Here I felt his great concern with human suffering. From the depth of his heart, he could not help feeling grateful for any help in liberating people from their sufferings. Hence his utterance of gratitude on behalf of my patient who, for him, was not a stranger at all, but a kinsman in the sense that he was also a human being anxiously struggling for the realization of his Buddha Nature. I was strongly moved at that moment by the effusion of his sincere desire—the expression of *karuna*—to free people from their suffering as well as their ignorance. His words penetrated deep into my heart, and his voice is still ringing in my ears awakening me to the real meaning of my work as a doctor.

In the later days of his life, he became more and more explicit in expressing the significance of *karuna* in his lectures and writings. Especially after working on the English translation of *Kyo, Gyo, Shin, Sho* (Teaching, Act, Faith, Enlightenment) by Shinran, one of the most important texts of Pure Land Buddhism, he stressed the meaning of the Great Act, a dynamic expression of *karuna* which is really the actual functioning of *prajna* to enable man to attain rebirth as a whole being.

The words he left on his death bed were, "Don't worry!" "Thank you!" "Thank you!" To the last moment in his life, he did not wish to make people suffer for his sake despite the extreme pains he was suffering from his disease, and he never ceased to feel grateful for everything that is given, even death. In that sense, he himself was the example of what he taught us throughout his life, compassion and grand affirmation.

He closed his life here in this world. But, look! For those who can see it, the stone bridge of Joshu is ever present.

18

Alan Watts

The "Mind-less" Scholar

I HAVE NEVER HAD a formal teacher (guru or *roshi*) in the spiritual life—only an exemplar, whose example I have not really followed because no sensitive person likes to be mimicked. That exemplar was Suzuki Daisetz—at once the subtlest and the simplest person I have known. His intellectual and spiritual mood or atmosphere (風) I found wholly congenial, although I never knew him really initmately and although I myself am an entirely different kind of person. Suzuki introduced me to Zen when I first read his *Essays in Zen Buddhism* in mid-adolescence, and in the years that followed I read everything he wrote with fascination and delight. For what he said was always unexpected and open-ended. He did not travel in the well-worn ruts of philosophical and religious thought. He rambled, he digressed, he dropped hints, he left you suspended in midair, he astonished you with his learning (which was prodigious) and yet charmed you with scholarship handled so lightly and unpretentiously. For I found in the engagingly disorganized maze of his writings the passage to a Garden of Reconciled Opposites.

He showed why Zen is immensely difficult and perfectly easy, why it is at once impenetrable and obvious, why the infinite and eternal is exactly the same as your own nose at this moment, why morals are both essential and irrelevant to the spiritual life, and why *jiriki* (the way of personal effort) comes finally to the same point as *tariki* (the way of liberation through pure faith). The trick in following Suzuki was never

189

to "stay put," as if you had at last got his point and were on firm ground —for the next moment he would show you that you had missed it altogether.

Suzuki was also outside the ordinary ruts in that, without any show of eccentricity, he did not present himself in the stereotype of the usual "Zen personality" which one finds among Japanese monks. Anyone visiting him for the first time, expecting to find an old gentleman with flashing eyes, sitting in a bare *shibui*-type room, and ready to engage you in swift and vigorous repartee, would have been very much surprised. For Suzuki, with his miraculous eyebrows, was more like a Chinese Daoist scholar—a sort of bookish Laozi—gifted, as all good Daoists are, with what can only be called metaphysical humor. Every so often his eyes twinkled as if he had seen the Ultimate Joke, and as if, out of compassion for those who had not, he were refraining from laughing out loud.

He lived in the Western-style section of his home in Kamakura completely surrounded with piles of books and papers. This scholarly disarray was spread through several rooms, in each of which he was writing a separate book, or separate chapters of one book. He could thus move from room to room without having to clear away all his reference materials when feeling inclined to work upon one project rather than another, but somehow his admirable secretary Miss Okamura (who was actually an *apsara* sent down from the Western Paradise to take care of him in his old age) seemed to know where everything was.

Suzuki spoke slowly, deliberately, and gently in excellent English with a slight and, to our ears, very pleasing Japanese accent. In conversation, he almost always explained himself with the aid of pen and paper, drawing diagrams to illustrate his points and Chinese characters to identify his terms. Though a man of wonderful patience, he had a genius for deflating windy argument or academic pedantry without giving offense. I remember a lecture where a member of the audience asked him, "Dr. Suzuki, when you use the word 'reality,' are you referring to the relative reality of the physical world, or to the absolute reality of the transcendental world?" He closed his eyes and went into that characteristic attitude which some of his students call "doing a Suzuki," for no one could tell whether he was in deep meditation or fast asleep. After about a minute's silence, though it seemed longer, he opened his eyes and said, "Yes."

During a class on the basic principles of Buddhism: "This morning we come to Fourth Noble Truth. . . called Noble Eightfold Path. First step of Noble Eightfold Path is called *sho ken*. *Sho ken* means Right View. All Buddhism is really summed up in Right View, because Right View is having no special view, no fixed view. Second step of Noble Eightfold Path. . . (and here there was a long pause). Oh, I forget second step. You look it up in the book." In the same vein, I remember his address to the final meeting of the 1936 World Congress of Faiths at the old Queen's Hall in London. The theme was "The Supreme Spiritual Ideal," and after several speakers had delivered themselves of volumes of hot air, Suzuki's turn came to take the platform. "When I was first asked," he said, "to talk about the Supreme Spiritual Ideal I did not exactly know what to answer. Firstly, I am just a simple-minded countryman from a far away corner of the world suddenly thrust into the midst of this hustling city of London, and I am bewildered and my mind refuses to work in the same way that it does when I am in my own land. Secondly, how can a humble person like myself talk about such a grand thing as the Supreme Spiritual Ideal? . . . Really I do not know what Spiritual is, what Ideal is, and what Supreme Spiritual Ideal is." Whereupon he devoted the rest of his speech to a description of his house and garden in Japan, contrasting it with the life of a great city. This from the translator of the *Lankavatara Sutra*! And the audience gave him a standing ovation.

Being well aware of the relativity and inadequacy of all opinions, he would never argue. When a student tried to provoke him into a discussion of certain points upon which the celebrated Buddhist scholar Junjiro Takakusu differed from him, his only comment was, "This is very big world; plenty of room in it for both Professor Takakusu and myself." Well, perhaps there was one argument—when the Chinese scholar Hu Shi accused him of obscurantism (in asserting that Zen could not be expressed in rational language) and of lacking a sense of history. But in the course of a very courteous reply Suzuki said, "The Zen master, generally speaking, despises those who indulge in word- or idea-mongering, and in this respect Hu Shi and myself are great sinners, murderers of Buddhas and patriarchs; we are both destined for hell."

I have never known a great scholar and intellectual so devoid of conceit. When I first met Suzuki, I was flabbergasted that he asked me (aged 20) how to prepare a certain article, and that when I was brash enough to give my advice he followed it. Academic pomposity and testiness were simply not in him. Thus certain American sinologists, who make a fine art of demolishing one another with acrimonious footnotes, are apt to go into a huff about his rather casual use of documentation and "critical apparatus," and speak of him as a mere "popularizer." They do not realize that he genuinely loved scholarship and thus made no show of "being a scholar." He had no interest in using bibliography as a gimmick for boosting his personality.

Perhaps the real spirit of Suzuki could never be caught from his writings alone; one had to know the man. Many readers complain that his work is so un-Zen-like—verbose, discursive, obscure, and cluttered with technicalities. A Zen monk once explained to me that the attitude of *mushin* (the Zen style of unselfconsciousness) was like the Japanese carpenter who can build a house without a blue-print. I asked, "What about the man who draws a blue-print without making a plan for it?" This was, I believe, Suzuki's attitude in scholarship: he thought, he intellectualized, he pored over manuscripts and dictionaries as any Zen monk might sweep floors in the spirit of *mushin*. In his own words, "Man is a thinking reed but his great works are done when he is not calculating and thinking. 'Childlikeness' has to be restored with long years of training in the art of self-forgetfulness. When this is attained, man thinks yet he does not think. He thinks like showers coming down from the sky; he thinks like the waves rolling on the ocean; he thinks like the stars illuminating the nightly heavens; he thinks like the green foliage shooting forth in the relaxing spring breeze. Indeed, he is the showers, the ocean, the stars, the foliage."

19

Richard DeMartino

On My First Coming to Meet Dr. D.T. Suzuki

I T MAY ON OCCASION HAPPEN in one's life that a particular person, or a particular meeting with a particular person, becomes instrumental in bringing about a radical change in the whole course of that life. In my life, Dr. Daisetz T. Suzuki was just such a person, and my initial meeting with him in March of 1947 was just such a meeting.

I had originally come to know the name Daisetz Teitaro Suzuki two years prior to that, in the spring of 1945. At that time serving with the American Navy at Pearl Harbor, I was, in my off-hours, auditing a course on Oriental Philosophy at the University of Hawaii in Honolulu. This course was being given in the Philosophy Department by the department chairman, Professor Charles A. Moore. The text Dr. Moore was using for the course was a book published the year before that he had edited entitled *Philosophy—East and West.* It was a collection of all of the papers presented at the First East-West Philosophers' Conference held at the University of Hawaii during the summer of 1939.

Although Dr. Suzuki had been invited to this 1939 conference, because of the illness of his wife, Beatrice Lane Suzuki, who died later that year, he did not attend. He did, nevertheless, submit a paper. It was that paper, "An Interpretation of Zen-Experience," contained in the volume *Philosophy—East and West* that was my incipient exposure to Dr. Suzuki—and to Zen.

This exposure, I must confess, did not influence me very much. For the essay was completely beyond me. Had my contact with Dr. Suzuki—and with Zen—been limited to this writing alone, the net effect would most likely have been quite negligible.

With the termination of World War II in August, 1945, I was ordered to Japan. Learning of this when I bade him farewell on the eve of my departure, Dr. Moore said to me, "When you get to Japan, please give my best regards to Dr. Suzuki, if you should ever meet him." I replied that I most assuredly would—if I should ever meet him.

I knew that Dr. Suzuki's home was in Kyoto, and that he had taught at Otani University. My own duty in Japan from September, 1945 to February, 1946 was, however, in the southern island of Kyushu. So it was not until March of 1946 that I could manage to get to Kyoto, but then merely to pass through it briefly en route to Tokyo preparatory to my return to the United States.

In Tokyo, while awaiting transportation back to America, I came, instead, to accept from the United States Government a civilian position as historical consultant to the defense panel of the International Military Tribunal for the Far East. This was the tribunal before which the former Japanese premier Tojo and twenty-seven other top-ranking Japanese leaders were being tried as war criminals.

The demands of my new position were such that the thought of trying to contact Dr. Suzuki faded temporarily into the background. But it never totally disappeared, and was unexpectedly to spring prominently into the foreground one Monday morning in February of the next year, 1947.

Riding to work that morning in the special Tokyo bus that ran from the Daiichi Hotel to the International Military Tribunal, I happened to overhear the then United States Naval Commander Denzel Carr, head of the International Prosecution's Translation Division at the Tribunal, mention to someone that he had, the previous day, visited Dr. D.T. Suzuki. I immediately went to the rear of the bus where Commander Carr was sitting and asked where in Kyoto Dr. Suzuki was living. To my joyous surprise, Commander Carr said that Dr. Suzuki was no longer residing in Kyoto. Rather, he was currently living in Kita Kamakura, about an hour's train ride from Tokyo, in a little house in the famous Engakuji Zen monastery-temple compound. In that moment I knew that it would not now be too far off when I would at last meet Dr. Suzuki to convey Dr. Moore's greetings.

Several days later, before I had been able to make the actual arrangements for a visit to Engakuji, I was asked by my very good friend Philip Kapleau, then also with the International Military Tribunal, to join him as weekend guests of a Japanese friend of his. I accepted gladly. But not until the three of us boarded a train in the Tokyo station did I learn that our Japanese host lived in Kamakura.

Instantly, there crossed my mind the possibility of including in the two-day itinerary a side trip to Kita (i.e., North) Kamakura. Not knowing, though, if to suggest this would in any way offend my Japanese host (whom I had only met) I thought it better for the time being not to say anything.

When the train on which the three of us were riding pulled out of the Ofuna station and veered onto a trunk line leaving the Tokaido main line, the Japanese (whose name, unfortunately, I have forgotten) abruptly said to Phil Kapleau and to me that he would like us to get off with him at the next station—which was not quite Kamakura—because there was a man living nearby whom he wished us to meet. Getting off at the ensuing station, I soon realized that it was Kita Kamakura.

While I kept looking around trying to familiarize myself with the surroundings for any possible future need, the young Japanese led us, walking single file, along a dirt and cinder path paralleling the railroad tracks, and then, making a right-angle turn away from the tracks, up a flight of stone steps leading to a large temple gate. Upon approaching and entering the gate, I saw a carved wooden signboard that read, in Japanese, "Engakuji."

I still did not know whom we were to meet, but at that point I felt that in any event it would not be impolite to mention the matter of Dr. Suzuki. When I did, it was difficult to determine who was the more startled, the Japanese or myself. For the person whose acquaintance he wished us to make was none other than Daisetz T. Suzuki.

Walking through the temple grounds of Engakuji toward Shoden' an, the specific dwelling that was our destination, I quickly briefed my friend Philip Kapleau on what I knew of Dr. Suzuki. As I did so, I was trying to imagine to myself the kind of person he would be. Predictably—or, perhaps, oddly—I pictured a tall man with a long, flowing white beard and an inscrutable, unworldly appearance who would be, in some strange, albeit undefined manner, extremely "Oriental."

After we had walked for an appreciable distance, our Japanese friend led us this time up a shorter set of stone steps, through a low wooden fence-gate, and around a simple garden in front of a small house. When we passed the garden and turned toward the house, all at once, from behind a glass panelled shoji sliding door of a modest study, there came into full view, sitting on his knees Japanese fashion before a Western typewriter, on which he was pecking away with the index finger of either hand, a little, clean-shaven old man in a black kimono wearing, down over his eyeglasses, a Western-style green bookkeeper's eyeshade.

Hearing and then seeing us approach, he stopped his typing, arose—standing barely over five feet—and came forth to receive us. With an outstretched right hand, he welcomed Phil Kapleau and myself without hesitation in English even before our Japanese friend had fully concluded his own courtesies, explanations, and introductions in Japanese. On being formally introduced (after the foregoing impromptu greeting), I proceeded to convey Dr. Moore's salutations. Dr. Suzuki was a trifle astonished—but most pleased—to hear of this, and was solicitous, in turn, concerning Dr. Moore.

Although he kept urging us to come in, we felt that since we had made our call unannounced, we ought not to impose any further. So with Dr. Suzuki standing above on the veranda-like *roka* and the three of us on the ground below, we all stood and chatted for no more than a few minutes. But in those few moments, I definitely knew that even though I had executed my "mission" and had delivered Dr. Moore's "message," I very much wanted to return for another visit with this extremely enchanting individual. I asked him if this would be possible. He most cordially and gracefully invited me to do so. The three of us then left.

My naive and fanciful romantic image had been shattered. Still, replaced by the kindly, warm, unpretentious figure of this charming little man in a Japanese kimono wearing a green Western office-worker's eyeshade and speaking an engagingly fluent English, the result was not only all positive but strangely magnetic. I knew practically nothing of Zen—or, indeed, of Buddhism. The short chat had not really touched upon those subjects. Nonetheless, even from this rather truncated meeting I carried away the irresistible feeling that whatever it was about this alluring person, there was something here that I greatly desired to pursue further.

So I returned to visit Dr. Suzuki for a second time, and then a third, and then a fourth, until I started to call upon him regularly, in the beginning once a week, and then, in 1948, twice a week—on the weekends. For I eventually became a personal student of his, and entered into an association with him that was to extend for almost twenty years—that is, until his death on July 12, 1966.

From this long association, there especially stand out for me six other images or vignettes of Dr. Suzuki that I either witnessed or was told about. Five of these go back to the early 1950's when he was living and teaching in America.

The earliest took place in the spring of 1950 in Claremont, California, where Dr. Suzuki was a Visiting Professor at the Claremont Graduate School. One evening he told me at dinner of an exchange he had that afternoon with a reporter from one of the Los Angeles Japanese language newspapers. The reporter, apparently given the assignment of obtaining for the Los Angeles Japanese community a comprehensive interview with this visiting luminary from Japan, initiated his inquiry by asking, understandably, "What is Zen?" To this, Dr. Suzuki said he replied, "Zen is Zen." A bit nonplussed, but evidently undaunted, the reporter valiantly tried again and asked, "Well, when did it begin?" Dr. Suzuki said his reponse this time was, "In the beginningless past." Then, turning to face me fully, his face aglow with his soft, remotely impish—but aways ingratiating—smile, he said, "I just felt that way."

The second was etched a few months later at Columbia University, where Dr. Suzuki was, again, a Visiting Professor. A woman psychiatrist, a relative of a member of Dr. Suzuki's class, had come especially that day to attend his lecture. During the question period that followed the lecture, the woman began to query Dr. Suzuki on the relationship between Zen and the various clairvoyant powers. Not too well pleased with his general negative attitude toward these questions, she then demanded to know, a bit belligerently, did not he himself have clairvoyant powers. He answered that he did not. This notwithstanding, the lady remained obdurate and kept insisting that, despite his open disavowal, certainly he must be able to know the mind of another. With the faintest trace of admonishment—rather than exasperation or irritation—Dr. Suzuki turned to her and said, "What's the use of knowing the mind of another? The important thing is to know your own mind."

The third—in a sense perhaps the most uniquely characteristic "vignette" or "tableau" of all—occurred the succeeding year on a cold, snowy, and icy New York March evening. A number of Japanese had taken Dr. Suzuki to dinner at the famous old Miyako Japanese Restaurant in midtown Manhattan. One of those Japanese subsequently gave me the following account.

With the snow thinly falling in a subfreezing temperature that night, the outside flight of brownstone steps leading up to the entrance of the Miyako Restaurant, one floor above the pavement, was treacherously slippery underfoot. The Japanese hosts, consequently, were most apprehensive and careful in helping Dr. Suzuki, then eighty-one, up the steps, and even more apprehensive, later in the evening when the dinner was over, helping him down.

As the rest of the assemblage stood conversing and taking their farewells on the sidewalk after the descent, attention momentarily shifted away from Dr. Suzuki, who happened to notice a small cat dart by and go scooting up the steps. At the top of the landing, however, the restaurant door was closed, and the cat, unable to open it, could not get in. While the others were still busily engaged in talking and taking leave of each other, Dr. Suzuki quietly slipped away, gingerly ascended the icy steps, opened the door for the cat, and then began to descend again as the group below, suddenly aware of what had happened, rushed to his side in great consternation. Dr. Suzuki's only reaction was his large, captivating smile.

Almost exactly a year after that, on the evening of March 19, 1952, Dr. Suzuki was a guest of Dr. Karen Horney, the Neo-Freudian Dean of the New York-based American Institute for Psychoanalysis, at a Town Hall symposium that she and her associates were conducting on the issue of the malleability or changeability of human nature. The formal panel of speakers included Dr. Horney herself, two other lecturers from her Institute, Drs. Harold Kelman and Frederick Weiss, and Dr. Paul Tillich, who was then teaching at Union Theological Seminary. Dr. Suzuki was sitting in the front row in an aisle seat. Having had to arrive at the hall late, I was up in the balcony.

At the conclusion of between three and four hours of a spirited discussion and debate that did not end in any overall unanimity of opinion on the possible extent—if any—of the malleability or changeability of human nature, Dr. Horney announced that sitting in the audience was the renowned exponent of Zen Buddhism, Dr. Daisetz T. Suzuki. She then turned to Dr. Suzuki, sitting directly below her, and asked if he would perhaps like to comment on the evening's topic: what did he think, can human nature change.

When a portable microphone from the stage was carried down to him, Dr. Suzuki, continuing to hold his overcoat folded over his knees, half arose in his seat, arched slightly into the microphone, and said, "The question is not, can human nature change. Human nature must change. Thank you very much." He then slid back into his seat. A lingering pause on the part of an audience for whom the retort was obviously entirely unexpected gradually became transformed into a loud round of applause.

Approximately another year or so subsequent to this Town Hall symposium, Dr. Suzuki was among the late Sunday morning guests of Dr. and Mrs. Paul Tillich in their McGiffert Hall apartment at Union Theological Seminary. Earlier that morning Dr. Tillich had delivered a sermon in the Seminary's chapel on the theme, "By What Authority?" He and his wife were now holding a small reception for some of their many friends.

As he moved around the room welcoming his guests, Dr. Tillich spotted Dr. Suzuki and went up to him. After a mutual exchange of greetings and cordialities, Dr. Tillich asked Dr. Suzuki what he would say, where does religious authority ultimately reside. Dr. Suzuki, a good deal smaller than his host, raised up on his toes, tilted forward facing Dr. Tillich, pointed his right index finger at the latter's chest—actually touching it gently for emphasis—and said, "You, Dr. Paul Tillich, are the authority." Dr. Tillich stood for a moment with a pensive look on his face and then said, "Yes, yes. I thought you would say something like that."

The closing "vignette" or "tableau" unfolded a little more than ten years later, during the summer of 1964, at the University of Hawaii. In connection with the Fourth East-West Philosophers' Conference, then being held at the University, Dr. Suzuki was scheduled to give a public talk in the large John F. Kennedy Auditorium at the East-West Center on the campus.

Word began to circulate from mid-afternoon that day that the evening's proceedings were to be televised, and that if one wished to secure a seat, one had better not procrastinate. So although the presentation was scheduled for 8 P.M., I decided to try to get there around 7 P.M. In spite of this, when I arrived, every seat in the auditorium was already filled, and I had to settle for a place on the carpeted steps.

Upon being introduced by Dr. Charles A. Moore (who was the Director of this Fourth Conference—as he had also been of the other three), Dr. Suzuki launched into a number of reflections on an item that seemed not to be in his written text. It rather appeared to me to be a sort of a carry-over from a conversation that he was probably having with the professor who drove him to the auditorium. In any case, it was not until close to fifteen or twenty minutes thereafter that he turned to his actual manuscript.

Because of this, when it got to be about a quarter of nine, Dr. Moore wrote a note and passed it to Dr. Suzuki. Dr. Suzuki stopped speaking, read the note carefully, and, as the audience kept waiting, he slowly flipped through the remaining pages of his prepared paper. Arriving at the final sheets, he spoke briefly about the Chinese Zen master Ju Zhi (Chu Chih; or, in Japanese, Gutei), who tended to respond to any question regarding Zen by raising one finger. Next, he spoke briefly about the Zen master Kwasan, who liked to play a drum and so, on his part, tended to respond to any question regarding Zen with an onomato-poetic utterance that resembled the sound of his beloved drum, "don-doko-don."

The time was now but a couple of minutes before nine. Clearly, Dr. Moore's note had been to remind Dr. Suzuki that since the talk was being televised, it had to end promptly at nine. Dr. Suzuki then conjec-tured aloud, as if talking to himself, that the audience may just be wondering why this old man (he was almost ninety-four) had traveled so far from across the Pacific Ocean to come there and speak such non-sense. Well, he continued, he may just reply (and here he began to rap the lectern softly with his closed right hand to accentuate the rhythmic cadence of his words), "*Don-doko-don.*"

The effect was electrifying. In fact, the talk became one of the major local topics of conversation for days. Among the many reactions it elicited was that of a senior member of the Conference, an American professor of Western philosophy, who remarked that Dr. Suzuki in his own masterful, unassuming, and unintentional manner had "played the audience like an accordion."

But strong and unforgettable as these and other images and memories are and shall ever remain, the most memorable and the most indelible will always be the very first sight I ever had of Dr. Suzuki—there in

Shoden' an, deftly sitting on his knees, leaning over and pecking away at a typewriter, wearing a black kimono and a green eyeshade.

> What is Zen?
> Zen is Zen.
> When did it begin?
> In the beginningless past.
> Why such nonsense?
> *Don-doko-don.*

20

Philip Kapleau

Reminiscences of Dr. Suzuki

IN HIS FOREWORD to *The Three Pillars of Zen* Huston Smith (quoting historian Lynn White, Jr.) wrote: "It may well be that the publication of D.T. Suzuki's *First Essays in Zen Buddhism* in 1927 will seem to future generations as great an intellectual event as William Moerbeke's Latin translation of Aristotle in the thirteenth century, or Marsiglio Ficino's of Plato in the fifteenth." Lynn White, Jr.'s statement appeared in his book *Frontiers of Knowledge in the Study of Man*, published in 1956, and it is clear that his prediction has already come true. General semantics, linguistics, psychology, psychiatry, philosophy —even Western art and literature—have all been influenced, I think it is fair to say, to one degree or another by Zen Buddhism. And it is mainly the writings of Dr. Suzuki that have shaped the West's intellectual understanding of Zen.

This intellectual understanding is a vital first step in the "journey of a thousand miles" that constitutes Zen training and awakening. For just as it is said that an elephant will not walk over an unknown surface until it has first tested it to be sure it will bear its weight, so the ordinary person cannot be persuaded to undertake serious Zen training until his intellect is satisfied of its value and feasibility. That there are today Zen training centers in the United States, Canada, Europe, Mexico, and South America is a tribute to the comprehensive and illuminating works of Dr. Suzuki. And that there is scarcely an educated person in the West today who has not heard of Zen or who hasn't some acquaintance with its tenets is also due to the prodigious labors of this man who, at the age of eighty, came to America to explicate its arcane philosophy. In this he evokes the spirit of the redoubtable Bodhidharma. Tradition tells us that this first partiarch of Zen in China in the later years of his life turned his back on his native India and went forth to China to plant the seed of a Buddhism later to be known as Zen. Like Bodhidharma, Dr. Suzuki must have been possessed of a strong determination and a deep sense of mission, for it was no mean feat to go to America at a time when embers of anti-Japanese feelings stemming from World War II were still glowing in the United States to propagate a form of Buddhism identified in the minds of many with Japanese militarism. And although Sensei, as his students called him, did not suffer the fate of poisoning, as did Bodhidharma, he nevertheless had to cope with many hostile audiences.

One such encounter is still vivid in my mind even after 30 years. It took place in 1951 at Yale University, where Sensei had gone to give a talk on Zen. His audience, consisting of students, professors, and townspeople, was a large and rabid one. After the talk there was a question period, and the first question came from a man with a large shock of white hair and a professorial air. As he rose to ask his question he wrathfully shook his head and brandished his fist.

"Isn't it true," he asked, "that warlords like General Tojo meditated in the Zen monasteries of Japan?"

"Yes." The answer came slowly and softly.

"How compassionate a religion is Zen Buddhism when it allows warlords of his ilk into its temples?"

Dr. Suzuki paused for what seemed like an eternity as the tension mounted among the audience. The silence was thundering. The answer came slowly:

"Don't you think that a soldier, who has to face death many times, needs the solace of religion even more than a civilian?"

And he might have added, "Were Generals Eisenhower and Patton barred from churches because they were soldiers?"

This sparseness of language was characteristic of Dr. Suzuki's speech, as it was indeed of most Japanese of his generation. Writer Robert Ozaki called it "the language of Ah-ness"—a sort of Morse code of dots of conversation interspersed with dashes of silence. Dr. Suzuki had an all-pervading silence about him. When he talked he spoke quietly, slowly, and succinctly, without rhetorical flourishes. There was silence in his speech and speech in his silence. Well did he understand that speech and silence are relative concepts belonging to the ephemeral sphere, that the preaching of the Dharma is at one and the same time both vocal and silent. Sensei's writings, on the other hand, were profuse and discursive, for he was a prolific writer. His titles in Japanese alone number over 100, and in English more than a score. Sensei loved the written word, and the longer the better. He was constantly dredging up sesquipedalian expressions, words that sent those of use who were privileged to edit his English scurrying to our Websters to be sure Sensei did not use them incorrectly. He seldom did. At the same time his writings had an uncommon clarity, vigor, and warmth. No one could describe them as dusty philosophy.

My acquaintance with Sensei dates back to 1947, when he was living in a small house in the compound of Engaku monastery, in Kamakura, and I was on the staff of the International Military Tribunal for the Far East in Tokyo. One day a Japanese friend, an interpreter at the Tribunal, asked if I would like to meet one of Japan's most renowned philosophers, Dr. D.T. Suzuki; if so, he could arrange a meeting. I told him I'd be honored. And so on a Saturday afternoon the two of us traveled to Kita Kamakura, where the monastery is located. Engakuji (Temple of Full Enlightenment) is one of the largest Rinzai mother-temples in the Kanto area, with numerous sub-temples throughout Japan. It is situated on some five hundred acres of wooded land, flowing streams, and giant cryptomeria trees. Tucked away in an out-of-the-way corner of the compound was Sensei's small dwelling. Having read the romantic novels *The Lost Horizon* and *The Razor's Edge*, I expected to be greeted by a sage with long white hair and beard, flowing robes, and crooked walking stick. Instead I came upon a short, clean-shaven, almost bald Japanese who looked for all the world like an editor. His book-lined study, the visor shading his eyes, and his one-finger typing at an old Underwood all strengthened this impression. Dr. Suzuki was most cordial. He spoke of his American wife, Beatrice Lane Suzuki, and of his years in the United States with Dr. Paul Carus. Before we left he invited me to return whenever I wished. Later Richard DeMartino, another member of the Tribunal staff and a student of philosophy, joined me in these visits.

It so happened that the Tribunal judge from the Netherlands had a brother who had studied with Dr. Suzuki, and he was eager to meet the renowned philosopher. The judge from India also expressed a wish to meet Dr. Suzuki. And so one day the two judges approached Richard and me to ask whether we could arrange a meeting between them and Dr. Suzuki at his place in the Engakuji compound. The meeting, they emphasized, was to be a private one, with only themselves, their clerks, and the two of us.

Sensei, when we spoke with him about it, said he would be happy to receive the distinguished judges. But no one had counted on the awesome Tribunal grapevine. The meeting was the best kept open secret. Some twenty-five to thirty persons converged on Sensei's small dwelling at the appointed time. Shades of the confrontation between Manjushri and Vimilakirti, when eight thousand sons of devas with Manjushri crowded into Vimilakirti's ten-foot-square room!

The judges were visibly embarrassed. Not Sensei, though. With a faint smile he calmly surveyed the group of uninvited guests, some of whom were perched on windows, others crowding the doorway, and still others lounging on the grass outside. Myself, I had brought several notebooks, prepared to impale for future generations the words of wisdom I felt sure would fall from the mouths of Sensei and the learned judges. After a long awkward silence the Indian judge spoke:

"Dr. Suzuki, I understand that General Tojo (on trial as an alleged war criminal) had been a student of yours at the University? Is that true?"

"Yes."

"What did you think of him as a student?"

The rapt audience edged forward expectantly. Pause—a long pause. Then:

"Not much."

The audience tittered as the two judges squirmed in mild discomfort. Sensei, with no change of expression, sat quietly, attentively. Were the judges weighing the chances for further meaningful dialogue? Or had they decided that discretion was the better part of valor in the face of this unlooked-for audience? No one could say for sure. The subsequent conversation, if it could be called that, quickly lapsed into banalities and soon the judges departed in the private car in which they had come. The others quickly dispersed and went their own ways.

In the United States Sensei lived a simple and unpretentious life. Making allowances for the fact that he was a scholar and not a monk, it was in the best Zen tradition. Undoubtedly it was this example that inspired many young Americans later to enter monasteries in Japan for practical training in Zen Buddhism. Many of these people later became teachers and began the arduous task of propagating this unique teaching in the West.

21

Gary Snyder

On The Road with D.T. Suzuki

I CLEARLY REMEMBER when I first read a book by D.T. Suzuki; it was September of 1951, and I was standing by the roadside in the vast desert of eastern Nevada hitchhiking the old Route 40. I had found his book a few days earlier in a "metaphysical" bookshop in San Francisco. I was on my way to enter graduate school in Indiana, and here by the highway in the long wait for another ride I opened my new book. The size of the space and the paucity of cars gave me much time to read *Essays in Zen*, First Series. It catapulted me into an even larger space; and though I didn't know it at the moment, that was the end of my career as an anthropologist. It took a semester to finish up affairs at Indiana. Back on the West Coast in the spring, I found a few others who had been touched by D.T., including Alan Watts, and we shared our discovery with yet others.

The ground was already prepared. I moved in circles that were acutely critical of the direction of American politics and economics, but were also painfully leaving the hope of an ideal Socialist world behind. We were post-Stalin, and found some inspiration in the relict Syndicalist-Anarchist traditions of the Finnish and Italian workingmen's societies of San Francisco, and the teachings and example of Gandhi. As working poets and artists we were repelled by the neo-conservatism in fashion in the academies then. We got our poetics from William Carlos Williams, Ezra Pound, D.H. Lawrence, Gertrude Stein, Wallace Stevens,

William Blake, and folksongs. Most of us were reading the Chinese poetry translations of Arthur Waley, Witter Bynner, Florence Ayscough, and of course Pound. We were exploring haiku and further Zen through the books of R.H. Blyth. We were people of the Far West, loving our continent for its great wild beauty, feeling no ties to Europe. Our politics and aesthetics were one. Dr. Suzuki's exposition of Zen gave us an idea of a religion and an all-embracing view of nature to augment that of scientific Ecology, which had already begun to instruct us.

We took Dr. Suzuki as our own, and didn't realize at the time how unique he was: a Japanese man thoroughly at home in English, writing with a full cosmopolitan command of the Occidental intellectual tradition, and presenting a compelling, creative picture of a school of Buddhism that barely knew what he was up to. And moreover, a school considered moribund by many Japanese and actively disliked by some leading Japanese intellectuals! All that came later.

For us, in our energy of the fifties, early Buddhism, Laozi, Gandhi, Thoreau, Kropotkin, and Zen were all one teaching. We stood for original human nature and the spontaneous creative spirit. Dr. Suzuki's Zen presentation of the "original life force," the "life-impulse," "the enlivening spirit of the Buddha"—the emphasis on personal direct experience, seemed to lead in the same direction. Some of my colleagues of those days took all this to mean no constraints at all, even in matters of form and manners. Fellow poets Lew Welch, Philip Whalen, and myself read in Zen the call for commitment and discipline, at least up to a point. For some of us, the Berkeley Shinshu Church's study group— hosted by the gracious and wise team of Rev. Kanmo and Jane Imamura, gave us our first taste of the living Buddhist tradition. That and further reading in D.T. Suzuki led me to re-enter graduate school in Far Eastern languages and take courses in Chinese and Japanese so that I could travel to Japan and try traditional *zazen* practice.

The daily realities of a Rinzai Zen sodo came as something of a shock, but I survived and worked out ways to stay with my teacher. I had playful thoughts about how Dr. Suzuki had led me into this, but absolutely no regrets. What hurt worst was the incomprehension of Japanese poets of my own generation with whom I could share a few hours' comradely talk until the subject of Zen came up, and then I lost them. Eventually I came to understand that many Japanese identify Zen with authoritarianism, feudalism, and militarism, and why. I also came to see that Dr. Suzuki's presentation of Zen is in many ways a creative leap out of the medieval mentality that brought Zen to that point, a personal way of pointing Zen in a fresh, liberating direction, without even saying so. D.T. Suzuki gave me the push of my life and I can never be too grateful. Now, living again in America, I see evidence of his strong, subtle effect in many arts and fields, as well as in the communities of Americans now practicing Zen.

Finally I got to meet him: in April 1961, at a little dinner party at Ryoko'in, Kobori Roshi's temple in Daitokuji. I went along as one of Mrs. Ruth Sasaki's researchers. Burton Watson, Philip Yampolsky, Seizan Yanagida and Dr. Yoshitaka Iriya, leading Zen scholars, were also there. Miss Okamura was with him. He was small and quiet, responding politely to introductions and then returning to conversation with Kobori Osho. We ate the most elegant traditional Zen food, on tatami, in one of the tearooms. I took the opportunity to ask Dr. Iriya once more about the walking route over the mountains from Kyoto to the Japan Sea, a four-day trip. He had completed it as a young man on the occasion of deciding to make his life work Chinese literature. Dr. Iriya sketched some forks and passes for me. Then I got to bow my head to Dr. Suzuki and say a few stumbling things, and I almost wept. And I had to leave quite early, for before dawn I was starting on my walk to the Japan Sea. I carried that powerful face (and those eyebrows!) with me the whole trip.

22

Robert Aitken

Openness and Engagement: Memories of
Dr. D.T. Suzuki

I FIRST ENCOUNTERED Dr. Suzuki's name in R.H. Blyth's *Zen in English Literature and Oriental Classics*, which I read in an internment camp in Kobe, Japan, in the winter of 1942–43. Later on when our camps were combined, I met Professor Blyth in person, and he told me about his first conversation with Suzuki Sensei:

BLYTH: I have just come from Korea, where I studied Zen with Kayama Taigi Roshi of Myoshinji Betsuin.
SUZUKI: Is that so? Tell me, what is Zen?
BLYTH: As I understand it, there is no such thing.
SUZUKI: I can see you know something of Zen.

If there was challenge in Sensei's words, it was of the mildest sort. His fundamental purpose was to encourage. Many scholars and students of Zen can tell similar stories—I think especially of Richard DeMartino, Philip Kalpeau, and Zhongyuan Zhang [Chung-yuan Chang].

My own first meeting with Sensei was in 1949 at the Second East-West Philosophers' Conference at the University of Hawaii. That was a wonderful summer. There were many stars at the conference, particularly from India, but Sensei by his manner (for few could understand him), stole the show. It was just after F.S.C. Northrup had published

The Meeting of East and West. Everyone was uncomfortable with the conceptual formulations in this work, but no one could pinpoint the problem. Sensei could, however, and I remember the chuckles of amusement among the scholars when he remarked, "The trouble with the 'undifferentiated aesthetic continuum' is that it is too differentiated."

I was part of a clique of graduate students who attached themselves to Sensei, and we attended (or crashed) many dinners and receptions that were given for him by University of Hawaii dignitaries and by Japanese-American organizations in the Honolulu community. Richard De-Martino was his secretary and companion at that time, and had purchased a Model A Ford for their transportation. Those were the days when the Model A was just an old car, not a precious antique, and I remember the endearing sight of Sensei rattling up to distinguished addresses in that aged clunker, full of dignity and good humor.

I wanted to continue my study of Zen, and asked Sensei's advice: "Should I return to Los Angeles and study with Nyogen Senzaki, or should I go to Japan?"

"Go to Japan," he said, and he wrote the letters I needed for my visa. In the summer of 1951, I called at the Matsugaoka Library in Kita Kamakura, where Sensei had just returned from his two years in the United States. I was ill from the rigors of monastic living, and Sensei insisted that I stay with him and recuperate.

I remained with him for two weeks, as I recall. Sensei saw that I was well cared for by his staff, and he included me in all of the gatherings at the Library. I remember particularly a memorial service for Beatrice Lane Suzuki. He was inspired by his experiences at Columbia University, and I wish now that I had kept a record of his words about the scholars he had met. I do recall him saying that he felt more accord with anthropologists than with Protestant theologians.

Thereafter, down through the years until his death, we kept in touch. When he visited Hawaii, or when Anne Aitken and I visited Japan, we always had tea, or a meal together. Anne recalls a dinner we attended with him given by the Young Buddhist Association of Honolulu in 1959. We were standing around afterwards, waiting for the dishes to be cleared away, and she noticed Sensei browsing among the tables, and picking off parsley from the plates, and eating it. Catching her eye, he grinned like a little boy and said, "People don't eat their parsley, and it is so good for them." She was moved by his sensitive expression of responsibility to others, including the parsley which would otherwise be sacrificed for nothing.

Most memorable of those later meetings was on his last trip to Hawaii in the summer of 1964. He spoke to a packed house at the Kokoan zendo, and in the question period, a student asked, "Is *zazen* (meditation) necessary?"

Sensei replied, "*Zazen* is absolutely not necessary." This created quite a stir among the Kokoan members.

The next year, Professor Masao Abe visited the East-West Center, where I was on the staff. We met on the steps of Jefferson Hall and greeted each other.

"Mr. Aitken," said Professor Abe, "I hear that Suzuki Sensei spoke at Kokoan last year. Is that correct?"

"Yes," I said, "it is."

"I hear," continued Professor Abe, "he said *zazen* is not necessary. Is that correct?"

"Yes," I replied, "he said *zazen* is absolutely not necessary."

"Oh," said Professor Abe, "he meant *zazen* is relatively necessary."

Now that was very clever of Professor Abe, but it served to highlight Sensei's unorthodoxy. He knew very well, but seldom said, that *zazen* is relatively necessary. He did, however, criticize notions by Alan Watts and others that in the Tang period Zen people did not sit.

Comparing notes about our old teacher, Anne and I find that we both asked him, at different times, about the interpretation that Mr. Watts gave to a story about Nanyue [Nan-yüeh] and Mazu [Ma-tsu]. Nanyue found Mazu doing *zazen* and asked him what he was trying to do. Mazu said that he was trying to become a Buddha. Nanyue thereupon picked up a piece of roofing tile and began rubbing it with a stone. When Mazu asked him what he was doing, Nanyue said he was making a mirror out of the tile. "No matter how you rub that tile," said Mazu, it will never become a mirror." Nanyue then replied, "No matter how much you do *zazen*, you will never become a Buddha."

Mr Watts remarks somewhere in his books that this dialogue showed how Tang period Zen people disapproved of *zazen*. He did not know that rather it reflects disapproval of trying to become something you already are. The story is about motive, not about *zazen*. Dr. Suzuki said to both Anne and me, "I regret to say that Mr. Watts did not understand that story."

Still, Sensei hardly ever mentioned *zazen* in his writings. Even *The Training of the Zen Buddhist Monk* barely touches this fundamental aspect of Zen life. Now that I am more intimately involved in Zen practice, I would like to talk with him about *zazen* and other matters. It would be a long conversation. I would want to take up the nature of the koan, the place of *prajna* and the mind (are these just human conditions?), the function of words, and the writings of Dogen Zenji.

He would listen—he always did. The trouble is that people did not talk back to him, except Hu Shi who was on an altogether different wavelength.

Once, in a class at the University of Hawaii, I asked him about a version of Chiyoni's haiku, "The Morning Glory," which he had written on the blackboard. This verse is usually rendered: "*Asagao ni | tsurube torarete | morai mizu,*" and translated:

> The morning glory
> has taken the well-bucket;
> I must ask elsewhere for water.

However, Sensei had written "*Asagao ya. . .*" on the blackboard, and the difference between *ya*, a cutting word, and *ni*, a postposition, would make the translation:

> The morning glory!
> It has taken the well-bucket;
> I must ask elsewhere for water.

This changes a rather precious poem about someone who finds that the morning glory has entwined the bucket and does not want to disturb it, to a Zen-like poem about someone who is struck by the beauty of the morning glory, and can only exclaim, "The morning glory!" and then as an afterthought, consider borrowing water from the neighbors.

Anyway, I knew the conventional version, and I suspected that Sensei with his Zen attitude had inadvertently imposed his own revision. He listened to me, and wrote to scholars in Japan and learned that indeed there was some speculation that *ya* was the original particle in the first line. He did not stop there, but went on to discuss the matter in class, and then to write his cogent essay, "Morning Glory" (later published in *The Way* [Los Angeles: Higashi Hongwanji Y.B.A., 1950–51]). Incidentally, this essay contains Sensei's clearest presentation of a concern that preoccupied him during his later years, world peace. Clearly, he felt that people are not sensitive to flowers or to the sacrifice of parsley, and so we have nations threatening each other with nuclear weapons.

The development of that essay is an example of Sensei's creative process generally—openness and engagement. He would listen or read with an open mind, and then involve himself in considering the matter, and finally come forth with his own unique response.

Openness and engagement show in his face in these sensitive portraits by Francis Haar, the purity and wisdom of a very old man who has devoted his life to the Dao. They evoke his inspiring presence, and remind me that I need not wait for some kind of miraculous logistical arrangement for our conversation.

"Now, about the importance of *zazen*, Sensei. . ."

23

Masao Abe

Memories of Daisetz Suzuki Sensei

1

I T WAS ENTIRELY DUE to the thoughtfulness of Shin'ichi Hisamatsu Sensei that I was able to become acquainted with Daisetz Teitaro Suzuki Sensei.[1] During the winter of 1947 I was a teaching assistant in religious studies in the Department of Literature at Kyoto University. Hisamatsu Sensei, who was teaching religious studies, in addition to Buddhism, requested that I go in his place to pay a sick call on Suzuki Sensei, whom we had learned was resting in bed with a bad cold. It was quite an occasion for me as a novice to visit the sickbed of this eminent Buddhist scholar, with whom I previously had contact through the medium of his writings only. I felt tense as I entered the gate of his Western-style house, which was located just behind Otani University.

I was shown into Suzuki Sensei's sickroom on the second floor. The sunlight of the fading winter afternoon was being overtaken by shadows, and although the garden could still be seen from the window the room was already gloomy. In this room, which made me think of the bottom of a deep lake, Sensei was lying in his bed.

When I had conveyed Hisamatsu Sensei's message of condolence concerning the illness, Suzuki Sensei said, "Thank you for coming.

I'll be better again soon." Then he asked, "By the way, is Hisamatsu-san well?"[2]

Suzuki Sensei had been lying on his back, but when he asked me this question he turned in my direction. At that moment I sensed in him a certain comfortably quality, which immediately set me deeply at ease in body and mind. I was suffering at this point in my life with a seemingly insoluble problem of faith. I could not endure my own self, which despite all my efforts would not abandon calculations of its own egotistical advantage. Faith, itself, had become, almost without my knowledge, another pose of my ego. Caught in this personal dilemma, I was extremely sensitive at the time to the presence in others of this kind of egotistical pose in the guise of religion. But the special quality which now transmitted itself to me from the man lying in repose before me—transmitted itself from his voice, and his expression, and his whole body—was something deeper and vaster than even the prevailing sense in the room of being at the bottom of a deep lake. This special quality contained something of breadth and abundance, conveying no impression of being a pose, or of concealing the slightest calculation. It brought forth to my mind the Buddhist expression, "The myriad streams of water, on entering the sea, are all of one flavor." Aware as I was in those days that the root of egotism is buried even in the base of faith itself, in meeting Suzuki Sensei, I had the sensation for the first time that I had encountered something like this "one flavor" of the great sea.

When I went to excuse myself, thinking that I must not overstay my welcome, Sensei inquired whether I had a copy of *Bukkyo no Taii*[3] which had just been published. He explained that this work had been issued in a special commemorative edition on the occasion of his seventy-seventh birthday by a group of his friends and students. It contained a revised set of a series of lectures he had presented a year before to the emperor. I said that I did not have the book, and he told me to come by in a week or so to pick up a copy.

When I appeared at his house again somewhat more than a week afterwards to inquire about the book, a member of the household presented it to me. On reaching home I opened the book. Inside the cover, handwritten in vivid ink characters, was the inscription, "In daily affairs, not apart from No-mind, Daisetz."

2

I believe that the following occurred about a year later. Hisamatsu Sensei approached me with a request: "I have heard that Suzuki Sensei is leaving for America soon. And they say that he's going in order to lecture at universities, so he may be over there for the remainder of his life. But I think that Suzuki Sensei should stay in Japan and devote himself to doing more translations of Zen texts and more scholarship in English concerning Zen—that kind of work is something that no one else can do the way that he can, and it will also continue to be available for posterity. I want you to visit Suzuki Sensei for me and tell him what I have said." Several days later I visited Suzuki Sensei. I was shown immediately to the second floor and found myself in what appeared to be a study, which had been formed by connecting two rooms. The floor-to-ceiling shelves yawned emptily, most of the books having been removed. The task of packing for the trip to America seemed already well underway. I waited for a short while before Sensei entered from the adjoining room. He was dressed in the Japanese style, but set carelessly on his head, at an angle, was a sun visor with a pale green plastic brim and a thin white headband. The figure presented by the aged and traditionally-dressed Suzuki Sensei as he walked into the room, with that sun visor, of the type you would wear playing tennis, set obliquely on his head, was altogether incongruous to me. I was taken by complete surprise. Despite his outrageous get-up, there was a "lightness" about him that conveyed no sense of anything forced or deliberate. He had the air of a perfectly unconstrained man.

Suzuki Sensei sat down right next to me on the sofa where I had been sitting, as though entrusting himself to me. He listened quietly while I was conveying Hisamatsu's message to him.

"Hmm, so Hisamatsu-san said that?" he asked, in an energetic voice, after he had heard me out.

There was silence for a moment. Then Suzuki Sensei turned suddenly to peer into my face, the sun visor still perched on his head.

"Abe-san, would it be wrong for me to go to America?"

He addressed me with a warmth that made it almost seem as though he was talking to his own grandson. At the same time, there was a strong suggestion in his words that he was at a momentary loss as to what he should do about this matter. I had been able to gaze upon Suzuki Sensei's unguarded heart—his unbound, unfettered heart, and his truly guileless and natural attitude. Here was a man who undoubtedly lived authentically, without constraint, and from moment to moment, no matter the circumstance or individual he encountered. I was struck deeply by the character of this man. I could not help but ponder, as well, where does this unfettered innocence of each and every moment emerge from?

Just then, a woman of sixty or so came in by way of the same adjoining room from which Suzuki Sensei had entered.

"Sensei, I found this behind the books on one of the bookcases," she said, passing on to Suzuki Sensei something that looked like a short bamboo tube.

What Sensei now held in his hand was a bamboo incense holder from a famous Kyoto store called Kyukyodo. He immediately tried to take off the top of the bamboo tube, but the cover was closed and appeared difficult to remove. When he applied more force with his fingers though, the cover came free with a pop and some pellets of black incense scattered on the carpet in front of us. The surrounding air was momentarily filled with the fragrant scent of the incense.

The impression I received of Suzuki Sensei on that day is still recorded in my heart in all its sharpness, as is the smell of that incense.

✢   ✢   ✢

In those days I knew nothing about Zen. Or it would probably be more accurate to say that I viewed Zen through my own subjective reactions and prejudices. I was sticking hardheadedly to the path of Pure Land Buddhism and made no move to yield to anyone on religious matters. Now, even in reminiscing about Suzuki Sensei, I cannot help but think gratefully about Hisamatsu Sensei's thoughtfulness in having sent me twice, rigid as I was then, to meet Suzuki Sensei. Over the next twenty years I was blessed with the good fortune to meet repeatedly with Suzuki Sensei in the friendliest of circumstances in New York, Kyoto, and Kamakura.

Chronology

1870 Born October 18 as Teitaro Suzuki in Kanazawa, Ishikawa Prefecture, Japan, the youngest of five children.

1875 Age 5. Entered Hondamachi Primary School. Death of his father Ryojun on November 16.

1883 Age 13. Entered Middle School attached to Ishikawa Semmon Gakko.

1885 Age 15. Published, with others, the magazine *Meiji Yoteki*, and became its editor.

1887 Age 17. Advanced to Upper Middle School. Met Kitaro Nishida. Forced to leave school soon afterwards because of financial difficulties at home.

1889 Age 19. Traveled to Noto Peninsula to teach English at Iida Primary School.

1890 Age 20. Taught English at Mikawa Primary School in Ishikawa. Death of his mother Masu on April 8.

1891 Age 21. Entered Tokyo Semmon Gakko (the Waseda University of today). Later this year, persuaded by Kitaro Nishida, entered Tokyo Imperial University as a special student. Met Yakichi Ataka. Introduced to Imagita Kosen, abbot and Zen master of Engakuji in Kamakura. Spare time is spent in this monastery as a novice.

1892 Age 22. Death of Imagita Kosen. Zen studies continued under Shaku Soen, Kosen Roshi's successor.

1893 Age 23. Translated into English the address delivered by Shaku

Soen at the Parliament of Religions during Chicago World's Fair.

1895 Age 25. Paul Carus's *The Gospel of Buddha* (*Butsuda no Fukuin*) translated and published.

1896 Age 26. "Essay on Emerson" and *Shin Shukyo Ron* published.

1897 Age 27. Joined Paul Carus in La Salle, Illinois, to assist in translating Chinese texts into English. Stayed to work on the editorial staff of the Open Court Publishing Company.

1900 Age 30. *Açvaghosha's Discourse on the Awakening of Faith in the Mahayana* published.

1905 Age 35. Served as interpreter for Shaku Soen during his tour of the United States. Talks given by Shaku Soen were later compiled to form *The Sermons of a Buddhist Abbot.*

1906 Age 36. *T'ai-Shang Kan-Ying P'ien, Yin Chin Wen,* and *Amida Butsu* published.

1907 Age 37. Series of articles published in the *Monist* on ancient Chinese history. In Maine, gave his first lectures on Buddhism which were compiled to form his first book in English, *Outlines of Mahayana Buddhism,* published in London.

1908 Age 38. Departed from La Salle for New York, and soon after, for Europe. Much time spent at the Bibliothèque Nationale copying, photographing, and researching on The Dunhuang manuscripts, especially *The Gandavyuha.* Journeyed through Germany and back to London where he was invited by the Swedenborg Society to translate *Heaven and Hell* into Japanese. December and January, 1909, spent intensively on this task.

1909 Age 39. Arrived back in Japan in April. Became lecturer of English at Gakushuin (Peers' School) in August, and at Tokyo Imperial University in October.

1910 Age 40. Appointed professor at Gakushuin. Remained in this capacity until 1921. Began serving as editor of the magazine *Zendo. Tengai to Jigoku* published. Translated into English *Principal Teachings of the True Sect of the Pure Land* (*Shinshu Kyogi*) and other writings from the Jodo Shinshu.

1911 Age 41. First thesis on the Pure Land sect, *Jiriki to Tariki* (Self-power and other-power) published. Marriage to Miss Beatrice Erskine Lane, on December 12 in Yokohama.

1912 Age 42. To England, on second invitation from the Swedenborg Society to translate *The Divine Love and the Divine Wisdom, The New Jerusalem,* and *The Divine Providence* into Japanese. Returned to Japan in two months.

1913 Age 43. *Swedenborugu* and *Zengaku Taiyo* published.

1914   Age 44. Retired as lecturer at Tokyo Imperial University. Series of articles on Zen Buddhism published in the magazine *The New East*, edited by Robertson Scott. *Zen no Dai Ichigi* and *A Brief History of Early Chinese Philosophy* published.

1915   Age 45. *Kojo no Tettsui* published.

1916   Age 46. Appointed dormitory master of Gakushuin. Led a group of Gakushuin students on a tour of China. Alan Masaru adopted. *Zen no Kenkyu* and *Zen no Tachiba Kara* published.

1919   Age 49. Death of Shaku Soen on November 1.

1921   Age 51. Began the publication of *The Eastern Buddhist* with Mrs. Suzuki as coeditor. In May, moved to Kyoto to take the chair of Professor of Buddhist Philosophy at Otani University.

1925   Age 55. *Hyaku Shu Sen Setsu* published.

1927   Age 57. *Essays in Zen Buddhism, First Series*, and *Zuihitsu: Zen* published.

1929   Age 59. With Mrs. Suzuki founded Jihien, animal shelter, in Kita Kamakura.

1930   Age 60. *Studies in the Lankavatara Sutra* and *Zen to wa Nanzoya* published.

1932   Age 62. *The Lankavatara Sutra*, and reproduction of *Jinne Roku* published.

1933   Age 63. D. Litt. (Bungaku Hakushi) degree received from Otani University. *Essays, Second Series*, and *Index Verborum to the Lankavatara Sutra* published.

1934   Age 64. May and June, traveled in Korea, Manchuria, and China. *Essays, Third Series*, *The Training of the Zen Buddhist Monk*, *An Introduction to Zen Buddhism*, *The Gandavyuha Sutra*, *Shina Bukkyo Insho Ki*, *Rokuso Dangyo* (two versions), *Jinne Roku* manuscripts and enlarged edition of *Index Verborum* published.

1935   Age 65. *Manual of Zen Buddhism*, *Godo Zen*, and *Zen to Nihonjin no Kishitsu* published. Reproduction of Bodhidharma's *Shoshitsu Issho* also appeared.

1936   Age 66. In April, attended The World Congress of Faiths in London headed by Sir Francis Younghusband. Under the auspices of the Japanese Foreign Ministry, lectured on Zen Buddhism and Japanese culture at Oxford, Cambridge, Durham, Edinburgh, and London universities. During the fall months, traveled through the United States lecturing on the same subject at several central and eastern universities. *Buddhist Philosophy and Its Effects on the Life and Thought of the Japanese People*, and a critical dissertation of Bodhidharma's *Shoshitsu Issho* published.

1937   Age 67. Returned to Japan on January 7. *Sukoshi Shukyo o Toku* published.

1938   Age 68. Mrs. Suzuki taken seriously ill in the spring. *Zen Buddhism and Its Influence on Japanese Culture*, and *Zen no Shomondai* published.

1939   Age 69. Death of Mrs. Suzuki on July 16. *Mushin to iu Koto* published.

1940   Age 70. Ichio Suzuki adopted. *Zendo no Kyoiku, Bankei no Fusho zen, Rokusoshi Dangyo* (Daijoji edition) published.

1941   Age 71. *Zen e no Michi, Zen Mondo to Satori, Bukkyo no Kakushin, Bankei Zenji Goroku, Ichi Shinjitsu no Sekai*, and *Zen no Mikata to Okonai Kata* published.

1942   Age 72. *Toyoteki Ichi, Jodokei Shiso Ron*, and *Bankei zen no Kenkyu*, published; *Bukka Hekigan* critically edited.

1943   Age 73. *Bunka to Shukyo, Ichi Zensha no Shisaku, Shukyo Keiken no Jijitsu, Zen Shiso Shi Kenkyu, I., Zen no Shiso, Bankei Zenji Seppo, Zen Hyaku Dai*, and *Bassui Zenji Hogo* published.

1944   Age 74. *Nihonteki Reisei, Daito Hyakunijussoku*, and *Gettan Osho Hogo* published.

1945   Age 75. Death of Kitaro Nishida on June 7. Edited *Zekkan Ron*.

1946   Age 76. Founded Matsugaoka Bunko (Pine Hill Library), a depository of ancient and modern works on Zen Buddhism, as well as the Suzukis' personal collection of books. With R. H. Blyth as coeditor, began the publication of the magazine *The Cultural East. Imagita Kosen, Reiseiteki Nihon no Kensetsu*, and *Nihonteki Reiseiteki Jikaku* published.

1947   Age 77. Lectured on Buddhism to His Majesty the Emperor. *Jishuteki ni Kangaeru, Shimpi Shugi to Zen, Shukyo to Seikatsu*, and *Bukkyo no Taii* published.

1948   Age 78. *Myokonin, Toyo to Seiyo, Shukyo to kindai Jin, Zen Issatsu, Shukyo to Bunka*, and *Seinen ni Atau* published.

1949   Age 79. Elected member of Japan Academy (January). Attended the Second East-West Philosophers' Conference in Honolulu (June). Stayed on to lecture on Zen Buddhism at University of Hawaii (September to February, 1950). Decorated *in absentia* with the Cultural Medal by the emperor of Japan in November. Presented with the festschrift *Zen no Ronko*, commemorating his seventy-ninth birthday. *The Zen Doctrine of No-Mind, A Miscellany on the Shin Teaching of Buddhism, Living by Zen, Bukkyo to Kirisutokyo* and *Rinzai no Kihon Shiso* published.

1950   Age 80. Lectured on Japanese culture and Buddhism at Claremont

College, February to June. Moved to New York in September to lecture at Princeton, Columbia, Harvard, Chicago, Yale, Cornell, Northwestern, and Wesleyan universities on the subject of "Oriental Culture and Thought" sponsored by the Rockefeller Foundation.

1951   Age 81. Lectured at Columbia University on Kegon philosophy from February to June. Spent the summer in Japan. From September to February, 1952, lectured once more at Claremont. *Zen Shisoshi Kenkyu, II* published.

1952   Age 82. At Columbia University as visiting professor lecturing on Zen Buddhist philosophy in the Department of Religion. Summer months spent in Japan accompanied by Karen Horney, Cornelius Crane, Richard DeMartino, and others. *Shukyo Nyumon, Shukyo no Konpon Giten ni Tsuite*, and *Shukyo Ronshu* published.

1953   Age 83. Continued lecturing at Columbia. June to August spent attending the Eranos Conference in Switzerland, and touring and lecturing in Paris, London, Zurich, Munich, Rome, Brussels, and other places in Europe. Met Carl Jung, Martin Heidegger and Karl Jaspers.

1954   Age 84. Continued lecturing at Columbia. The summer months at Eranos Conference, and lecturing and touring in London, Paris, Cologne, Marburg, Stuttgart, Munich, Vienna, Rome, Assisi. Met Arnold Toynbee, Gabriel Marcel, Arthur Waley, Friedrich Heiler, and others. In September, departed for Japan for a stay of four months.

1955   Age 85. Received the Asahi Cultural Award (January). Left Japan for New York again to lecture at Columbia University on "Philosophy and Religion of Zen Buddhism" in the Department of Philosophy. *Studies in Zen* published.

1956   Age 86. Continued lecturing at Columbia. Summer spent in Mexico City lecturing at Mexico City College and to private groups.

1957   Age 87. Retired from Columbia in June. Summer months with Erich Fromm in Cuernavaca, Mexico, lecturing at the conference on Zen and psychoanalysis. Talks given at the University of Mexico. In September, attended Paul Carus Memorial Symposium, Peru, Illinois. Moved to Cambridge, Massachusetts, for the following seven months to join Shin'ichi Hisamatsu. Lectures given at Harvard, M.I.T, Wellesley, Brandeis, Radcliffe, and Amherst. *Mysticism: Christian and Buddhist*, and *Nihon Bukkyo* published.

1958   Age 88. Attended the Belgian World's Fair in May to represent the Far East in giving a talk on the subject of "Spirituality." Toured Dublin, Edinburgh, Lisbon, Avila, Seville, Madrid. Lectured in Brussels, and in London at the London Buddhist Society. Returned to Japan by late November. *Zen and Japanese Buddhism* and *Shukyo to Gendai Seikatsu* published.

1959   Age 89. Participated in the Third East-West Philosophers' Conference in June. Conferred Honorary Doctor of Law degree by University of Hawaii. *Zen and Japanese Culture* published.

1960   Age 90. Presented with the festschrift *Buddhism and Culture* in celebration of his ninetieth birthday. In December, took a four week tour of India as a state guest. *Zen Buddhism and Psychoanalysis* published.

1961   Age 91. Finished a draft translation of Shinran Shonin's *Kyogyoshinsho*. Wrote the commentaries for the catalogue of Sengai drawings in preparation for European exhibitions.

1963   Age 93. *Toyoteki na Mikata* published.

1964   Age 94. Awarded The Rabindranath Tagore Birth-Centenary Medal from the Asiatic Society, India. In July, spent two weeks in New York, meeting Fr. Thomas Merton and other friends, and attended the Fourth East-West Philosophers' Conference in Honolulu. *Shinran no Sekai* and *Joshu Zenji Goroku* published.

1965   Age 95. Reassumed editorship of the New Series of *The Eastern Buddhist*. *Toyo no Kokoro* published.

1966   Age 95 and 9 months. Died at St. Luke's Hospital, Tokyo, July 12 at 5:05 A.M. The Senior Grade of the Third Court rank (正三位) was granted him posthumously. *Daisetz Tsurezure Gusa, Ningen Ikani Iku Bekika,* and *Myokonin Asahara Saichishu* were posthumously published.

Notes

CHAPTER 1

1. Kanazawa is the capital of the Ishikawa Prefecture in the middle of the West coast. For three hundred years it was under the jurisdiction of the feudal clan of Maeda, and Dr. Suzuki's ancestors were physicians to the Lord Maeda's court.

2. *Hekigan Roku*, usually translated "The Blue Cliff Record." One of the most important textbooks of Zen. See *The Blue Cliff Record*, trans. Dr. R.D.M. Shaw (Michael Joseph, 1961). [See also Cleary, chapter 8, note 9.]

3. The Greek Orthodox Church.

4. Imagita Kosen Roshi was the predecessor of Soen Shaku Roshi at Engakuji, Kamakura, where he is buried. Dr. Suzuki has written a biography in Japanese.

5. *Orategama*, "My Little Iron Kettle," is a collection of letters written by Hakuin Zenji (1685–1769) to his disciples. See *The Embossed Tea-kettle*, trans. Dr. R. D. M. Shaw. (Allen and Unwin, 1963.)

6. The roshi is the master of the Zen monastery who takes pupils in *sanzen*, personal interviews and supervises their *Zen* meditation.

7. From Tokyo to Kamakura is thirty miles.

8. Daruma is the Japanese name for Bodhidharma (Sk.) or Tamo (Chin.), the first Patriarch of Chan, or Zen, Buddhism who arrived in China from India in A.D. 520

9. A koan is a word or phrase which cannot be "solved" by the intellect. It is given by a roshi to his pupil to help him gain insight into reality, which lies beyond the reach of dualistic thought.

10. Muso Kokushi's last words may be found in Suzuki, *Manual of Zen Buddhism*, 1st ed., 182.

11. A daikon is a very long and large white radish. A popular vegetable in Japan.

12. Shaku Soen is known to the West by the name of Soyen Shaku [or Soen Shaku] as the author of *Sermons of a Buddhist Abbot* (Chicago, 1906). He was the favorite disciple of Imagita Kosen (see n.4), and was only twenty-five when he received his master's "seal" (*inka*). In 1893 he attended the World's Parliament of Religions in Chicago. He later traveled in Europe.

13. Hojo Tokimune was the regent who in 1282 founded Engakuji, the Zen monastery north of Kamakura where Dr. Suzuki lived for many years in the sub-temple building, Shoden'an.

14. The Shariden building in Engakuji (see n.13), is the only surviving example of Song dynasty temple architecture. It is quite small and severely plain. Although damaged in the great earthquake in 1923, it was later restored.

15. Kitaro Nishida (1870–1945). The great modern Japanese philosopher and an intimate friend of Dr. Suzuki's since early youth. [See also chapter 2, n. 7.]

16. *Sesshin.* A period of intense sitting meditation lasting one week.

17. *Rohatsu sesshin. Ro* refers to the month of December, and *hatsu* or *hachi* means the eighth. December 8 is traditionally regarded as the date of Buddha's enlightenment. Everyone makes a special effort

at this sesshin, which begins December 1 and ends early at dawn on December 8, to become enlightened. Usually they go without sleep the whole time in their earnest endeavor.

18. This would be the *rohatsu sesshin* of 1896.

19. *Kensho.* "Seeing into the Self-nature." Can be described as the first glimpse of satori or enlightenment.

CHAPTER 2

1. Rennyo (1415–99) was an eighth-generation descendent of Shinran, the founder of Pure Land Shin Buddhism. He achieved great reknown as a powerful reformer of that sect.

2. Eiheiji Temple is one of the two principal temples of the Soto sect of Zen and was established by Dogen (1200–53) in 1244. Sojiji Temple, established by Keizan Jokin (1266–1325), is the other principal temple of the Soto sect.

3. East and West Honganji are the two leading branches of Pure Land Shin Buddhism. The former was established in 1602, the latter in 1591.

4. *Hijibomon* is considered by Pure Land Shin Buddhist orthodoxy as a heretical form of Pure Land Shin Buddhism. It is characterized by a secret transmission of faith through the mercy of Amida, occurring at

meetings frequently held in the middle of the night or in a darkened warehouse.

5. In Sanskrit, Acala, a Buddhist deity believed to have the power to foil the snares of devils and cure diseases.

6. Daitokuji Temple is the seat of a subdivision of the Rinzai School of Zen and is one of the most powerful Zen temples in Kyoto. It was established by the National Teacher Daito (1282–1338) in 1323.

7. Kitaro Nishida was a lifelong friend of Suzuki, their relationship continuing uninterruptedly from their Upper Middle School days. Nishida later became the foremost philosopher of modern Japan and created a unique philosophical system which attempted a synthesis of Buddhist and Western philosophies.

8. Kusunoki Masashige (1294–1336) defended the emperor Go-Daigo against the powerful Hojo clan which eventually succeeded in forcing the emperor into exile. Masashige has since that time been revered as the prototype of loyalty and devotion to the imperial dynasty.

9. Kosen Imagita (1826–92) was one of the outstanding Zen masters of the Meiji era. Suzuki practiced Zen under Kosen during the last year of the latter's life.

10. *Teisho* is the Dharma talk given by Zen masters.

11. Soseki Natsume (1867–1916)

is esteemed as one of the most eminent writers of modern Japan. Suzuki here resolves two long-standing questions in Japan: What was Natsume's relationship with Suzuki during their days at Engakuji Temple, and what was the extent of Natsume's involvement in the translation of Shaku Soen's address given at the World's Parliament of Religions in 1893.

12. Yukichi Fukuzawa (1835–1901) was a leader of the "civilization and enlightenment" movement during the early Meiji era and the founder of Keio Gijuku University, one of the leading private universities in Japan.

13. Hegeler was the owner of a zinc company in Illinois. He managed the Open Court Publishing Company together with his son-in-law, Dr. Paul Carus.

14. Tenshin Okakura (1861–1913) was a critic and scholar in the field of Japanese Fine Arts and served as curator of the Oriental Arts section of the Boston Museum of Fine Arts.

15. Robertson Scott was the editor of the journal *New East*, which was published in Japan during World War I.

16. Tai Hsu (1890–1949). A leader of the Buddhist revival movement in modern China.

17. Yin Kwang Sheng Liong (1862–1941). One of the most eminent Pure Land Buddhist monks of modern China, celebrated for his

practices of both *nembutsu* and charity.

CHAPTER 3

1. It was Ummon (雲門) who made his staff turn into a dragon and made the dragon swallow up the entire universe.

2. *Vinaya* in Sanskrit means "rules of moral discipline," forming one of the three departments of the Buddhist teaching: sutras are Buddha's personal discourses; *vinaya*, rules laid down by Buddha for his disciples of various grades; and *abhidharma*, philosophical treatises dealing with Buddhist thought.

3. From *Essentials of the Abrupt Awakening* (頓悟要門論), by Daishu Yekai.

4. "To utter a word," or simply "to say [something]," is Zen's technical way of expressing a view, either in words or in action, proper to the occasion.

5. He is the founder of Zen in China. But he is frequently made use of symbolically and stands for Buddha, Buddha-nature, the Absolute, etc. In Gensha's sermon here, Daruma (i.e., Bodhidharma) is quite alive and no abstraction whatever.

6. There is no "year of the ass" in the calendar formerly in use in China and Japan. "Until the year of the ass" therefore means "until doomsday."

7. *Hossu* was originally used in India for driving mosquitos away.

It is a kind of duster with a long tuft of horse's or yak's tail. Now it is a religious implement.

CHAPTER 4

1. In the title and throughout the article the author uses the term "Dr. Daisetz." In this translation it is replaced by "D. T. Suzuki," the name by which he is known in the West.

2. The term "Awakening," is used here and throughout the article to translate *keiken* and *taiken* ("experience") when used in reference to Zen. This is done to avoid misunderstanding Zen Awakening as an experience, psychological or otherwise.

3. The term "Mind" is used here and throughout the article to translate *shinri* ("mentality") and *shinrigaku* ("psychology") when used in reference to Zen. This is done to avoid misunderstanding Zen Mind as something psychological.

4. Color prints of "the floating world" popularized in the Tokugawa period (1615–1867).

5. Shortly after the Meiji Restoration (1887), the Japanese government, under the banner of "Western civilization and enlightenment," tried to modernize and Westernize Japanese society, which had been hitherto controlled by the feudal system.

6. *Kaitai Shinsho,* (*A Primer on Anatomy*) (1774), is a rendering of

Western anatomy by Genpaku Sugita (1732–1817), the first systematic study of modern Western science by Japanese.

7. This refers to the well-known incident of Shakyamuni silently holding up a flower rather than giving a talk before the assembly. No one understood except Kashyapa, who smiled. It is taken up as a koan for Zen study in Case Six of the Chinese Zen classic, *Mumonkan*. See Zenkei Shibayama's *Zen Comments on the Mumonkan* (Harper and Row), 1974, 58ff.

8. See n.3 above.

CHAPTER 5

1. See Christmas Humphreys, ed., *A Buddhist Student's Manual* (London: The Buddhist Society, 1956).

CHAPTER 7

1. For a detailed account of the effects of this seminal event, see my article, "Historical and Philosophical Implications of the 1893 Chicago World's Parliament of Religions," *The Eastern Buddhist*, n.s., 15 (Spring 1982): 122–45.

2. W. T. Stace, *Mysticism and Philosophy* (New York: J. B. Lippincott, 1960), 175.

3. Thomas Merton, *Zen and the Birds of Appetite* (New York: New Directions, 1968).

4. Charles A. Moore, "Suzuki:

The Man and the Scholar," *The Eastern Buddhist*, n.s., 2 (August 1967): 16–17.

5. Mrs. Rhys Davids, *A Manual of Buddhism* (London: Sheldon Press, 1932), 33.

6. Edward Conze, *Thirty Years of Buddhist Studies: Selected Essays* (Columbia, S.C.: University of South Carolina Press, 1968), 27.

7. Arthur Koestler, *The Lotus and the Robot* (New York: Hutchinson and Co., 1960), 233. For a more complete account of Koestler's respones to Suzuki as well as a defense of Suzuki's position, see my article "Arthur Koestler's Critique of D. T. Suzuki's Interpretation of Zen," *The Eastern Buddhist*, n.s., 13 (Autumn 1980): 46–72.

8. D.T. Suzuki, *Die Grosse Befriung: Einfurung in den Zen-Buddhismus* (Leipzig: Curt Weller, 1939).

9. Gerhard Adler, *C. G. Jung: Letters*, Bollingen Series, vol. 1, no. 95 (Princeton, N. J.: Princeton University Press, 1971), 128.

10. Ibid., 441.

11. Ibid., 556.

12. Richard Wilhelm and C. G. Jung, *The Secret of the Golden Flower*, trans. C. F. Baynes (New York: Harcourt, Brace and World, 1962), 84.

13. Carl Gustav Jung, *Psychology and Religion: East and West*, 2nd ed., trans. R. F. C. Hull, vol. 11, no. 20 of *The Collected Works of C. G. Jung* (Princeton, N.J.: Princeton University Press, 1970), 548.

14. Ibid., 545.

15. Erich Fromm, D. T. Suzuki, and Richard DeMartino, *Zen Buddhism and Psychoanalysis* (New York: Harper and Row, 1960).

16. Ibid., vii.

17. Erich Fromm, "Memories of D. T. Suzuki," *The Eastern Buddhist*, n.s. 2 (August 1967): 87.

18. Much of the information on Horney has been gathered from personal conversations with Dr. Jack Rubins and the "Biography" section of his work on Horney's thought entitled *Developments in Horney Psychoanalysis* (Huntington, N.Y.: Krieger, 1972).

19. Karen Horney, "The Paucity of Inner Experiences," *The American Journal of Psychoanalysis*, 12 (1952): 4.

20. Ibid., 5.

21. Personal communication to the author.

22. D. T. Suzuki, *Zen Buddhism and Its Influence on Japanese Culture* (Kyoto, Japan: The Eastern Buddhist Society, 1938); later published as *Zen and Japanese Culture*, Bollingen Series, vol. 64 (Princeton, N.J.: Princeton University Press 1959,).

23. Richard Kostelanetz, ed., *John Cage* (New York: R. K. Editions 1970), 129.

24. John Cage, *Silence* (Middletown, Ct.: Wesleyan University Press, 1961), xi.

25. Personal correspondence to the author, February 2, 1976.

26. Christmas Humphreys, *Sixty Years of Buddhism in England* (London: The Buddhist Society, 1968), 41.

27. Ibid., 78–9.

28. Christmas Humphreys, *Zen Comes West* (London: George Allen and Unwin, 1960), 29.

29. Alan Watts, "The 'Mind-less' Scholar," *The Eastern Buddhist*, n.s., 2 (August 1967): 124.

30. Watts, *In My Own Way: An Autobiography* (New York: Pantheon Books, 1972), 113.

31. Watts, *The Spirit of Zen* (New York: Grove Press, 1958), 12.

32. Watts, *In My Own Way*, 78.

33. Ibid., 119.

34. Ibid., 298.

35. Personal correspondence to the author, May 7, 1976.

36. D.T. Suzuki, "Zen in the Modern World," *Japan Quarterly*, 5 (October–December, 1958): 454.

37. Ibid., 452.

CHAPTER 8

1. *The Gandavyuha Sutra*, critically edited in collaboration with H. Idzumi, 1934–36. See also "From Zen to the Gandavyuha," "The Gandavyuha, the Bodhisattva-Ideal and the Buddha," and "The Bodhisattva's Abode," in *Essays in Zen Buddhism*, 3d. ser. 1953. (For more detailed information on books listed in notes 1–4, 7, and 8, see the bibliography at the end of the book.)

2. *Jodo Kei Shiso Ron* (Studies in Pure Land Thought), 1954; *Myokonin* (The Wondrously Excellent

Ones), 1952; *A Miscellany on the Shin Teaching of Buddhism*, 1949; *Myokonin Asahara Saichi Shu* (Collection of Verses by Saichi), 1967; *Shin Buddhism*, 1970; translation of Shinran, *The Kyogyoshinsho* (The Collection of Passages Expounding the True Teaching, Living, Faith, and Realization of the Pure Land), 1973; and *Collected Writings on Shin Buddhism*, 1973.

3. *Buddhist Philosophy and Its Effects on the Life and Thought of the Japanese People*, 1936, revised edition with the title *Buddhism in the Life and Thought of Japan*, 1937; *Zen Buddhism and Its Influence on Japanese Culture*, 1938; *Zen und die Kultur Japans*, trans. Otto Fischer, 1941. Revised and enlarged edition with the title, *Zen and Japanese Culture*, 1959; *Japanese Spirituality*, 1969.

4. *Mysticism: Christian and Buddhist*, 1957. See also "Wisdom in Emptiness," in Thomas Merton, *Zen and the Birds of Appetite*, 1968, and "Eckhart and Zen Buddhism" in D. T. Suzuki, *The Field of Zen*, 1969.

5. Paul Carus, a German-born thinker who lived most of his life in La Salle, Illinois. The author of *The Gospel of Buddha*, Carus published the quarterly magazine, *The Monist*, from his own publishing company, Open Court. D. T. Suzuki worked for him from 1897 through 1909, translating Laozi's [Lao-Tzu] *The Canon of Reason and Virtue* (*Tao Te Ching*) [*Tao Teh King*] (1898), Açvaghosha's *Discourse on the Awakening of Faith in the Mahayana* (1900), *Daishang Kanyin Pien* [*T'ai-Shang Kan-Ying* P'ien] (1906), *Yin Jin Wen* [Yin Chin Wen] (1906) and others. See Shojun Bando, "D. T. Suzuki's Life in La Salle," *The Eastern Buddhist*, n.s., vol. 2, no. 1, (August 1967): 137–46.

6. Nearly ninety titles originally published in Japanese have been compiled in *Suzuki Daisetz Zenshu* (The Complete Works of Suzuki Daisetz), thirty-two volumes published by Iwanami Shoten, Tokyo, 1968–70.

7. *Tonko Shutsudo Kataku Jinne Zenji Goroku* 燉煌出土荷澤神會禪師語錄, 1932; *Tonko Shutsudo Rokuso Dangyo* 燉煌出土六祖壇經, 1934; *Kokan Shoshitsu Issho Oyobi Kaisetsu*, 校刊少室逸書及解說, 1936.

8. *Inshu Sokeizan Rokusoshi Dankyo*, 韶州曹溪山六祖師壇經, 1940; *Bankei Zenji Goroku*, 盤珪禪師語錄, 1941; *Bukka Hekigan Hakan Gekisetsu*, 佛果碧巖破關擊節, 1942; *Bankei Zenji Seppo*, 盤珪禪師說法, 1943; *Bassui Zenji Hogo*, 拔隊禪師法語, 1943; *Daito Hyakunijussoku*, 大燈百二十則, 1944; *Gettan Osho Hogo*, 月菴和尚法語, 1944; *Zekkan Ron*, 絕觀論, 1945; *Roankyo*, 驢鞍橋, 1948; *Joshu Zenji Goroku*, 趙州禪師語錄, 1964.

9. The reference to Kwasan (He Shan or Ho Shan, in Chinese) is from a Zen koan which appears as Case Fourty-four in the collection *The Blue Cliff Record*. See Thomas and J. C. Cleary, trans., *The Blue Cliff Record*, 2 (Boulder, Colo.: Shambala, 1977), 312–17. See also

D. T. Suzuki *Essays in Zen Buddhism,*
1st. ser., 281.

CHAPTER 13

1. A Zen question-and-answer
exchange.
2. See cf. 禪宗頌古聯珠通集 Chin.,
Chan Zong Songgu Lianzhu Tongji,
Jap., *Zen Shu Juko Renju Tsushu,*
vol. 2 compiled by Faying 法應
(Jap., Ho-o), b. 1175, Song dynasty;
禪宗正脈 Chin., *Chan Zong Zheng Mo,*
Jap. *Zen Shu Sho Myaku,* vol. 1;
五燈會元 Chin., *Wu Deng Huiyuan,*
Jap., *Go To Egen,* vol. 1.
3. 香嚴智閑 Hsiang-yen chih-hsien,
or Jap., Kyogen Chikan.
4. 道吾宗智 Tao-wu Tsung-chih.
Jap., Dogo Shuchi.
5. 漸源仲興 Chen-yuan chung-
hsing. Jap., Zengen Chuko.
6. 大隋法眞 Ta-sui Fa-Chen. Jap.,
Taizui Hoshin.

CHAPTER 14

1. Kitaro Nishida [See also chapter
1, n. 15; and chapter 2., n. 7.]
2. The Four Great Vows are:

All beings without limit
   I vow to save,
The passions inexhaustible
   I vow to destroy,
The numberless Dharma
   gates I vow to enter,
The supreme Buddha Way
   I vow to complete.

3. The author alludes to Rinzai's
utterance:

One man is endlessly on the
way, yet has never left home.
Another has left home, yet
is not on the way. Which one
deserves the offerings of men
and devas? (*The Record of
Lin-chi,* trans. Ruth F. Sasaki,
[San Francisco: Heian In-
ternational, 1975], 5.)

In this quotation "one man [who]
is endlessly on the way, yet has never
left home," refers to living in the
world of differentiation (*samsara*),
while never apart from awakening
to the world of equality (nirvana);
"another [who] has left home, yet
is not on the way," refers to non-
attachment even to the world of
equality (nirvana) without being
confined by the world of differentiation (*samsara*).
4. The author again alludes to
Rinzai's words:

The man on the summit of a
solitary peak has no path by
which to leave. The man at
the busy crossroads has neither front nor back. Which
one is before, which one is
after? Don't make the one
out to be Weimojie [Wei-
mo-chieh] [Vimalakirti] and
the other to be Fu Dashi
[Fu Ta-shih]. (*The Record of
Lin-chi,* 5).

Between the man atop the solitary

peak and the man at the busy cross-road there appears to be a difference. From Rinzai's authentic Zen Awakening, however, there is, in fact, no difference between the two. Vimalakirti (Jap., Yuimakitsu) and Fu Dashi (Jap., Fu Daishi, 497–569) are two outstanding laymen in the Mahayana Buddhist tradition famous for their penetrating and profound understanding of Buddha Dharma and for their selfless service to all sentient beings. The author places D. T. Suzuki on a par with Vimalakirti and Fu Dashi.

5. *Daisetz Suzuki's Complete Works* (in Japanese) consists of thirty-two volumes, published by Iwanami Shoten, Tokyo, 1968–71.

6. *Nembutsu*, or reciting the name of the Amidha Buddha, in Pure Land Buddhism.

7. The central concept of Nishida's *A Study of Good* is "pure experience." Nishitani is drawing a parallel between this concept and Suzuki's use of the term "immediate experience."

8. Hajime Tanabe (1885–1962) was an outstanding philosopher of modern Japan, who, during his era, was second in stature only to Nishida.

9. Shin'ichi Hisamatsu (1889–1980) and the author, Keiji Nishitani (1900–) are leading disciples of Nishida.

10. *Hajime Tanabe's Complete Works* (in Japanese) vol. 5., 457.

11. Ibid.

12. Ibid., 458.

13. Matsugaoka is a hill on the temple grounds of Tokeiji where Suzuki's private residence was located.

14. Shokin Furuta had been Suzuki's assistant and professor of Buddhism at Nihon University.

15. Engakuji is the head temple of the Engakuji School of the Rinzai Zen sect. [See also chapter 1, n. 13.]

16. Saichi Asahara is one of the *myokonin*, the "wondrous, good people" of the Shin Buddhist tradition. See D. T. Suzuki, *Mysticism: Christian and Buddhist*, 143–214.

17. Torataro Shimomura (1902–) is a disciple of Nishida and a friend of Suzuki. In his own right he is an outstanding philosophical thinker, especially in the field of the philosophy of mathematics and Western intellectual history.

18. Feng Chichuan [Chich'uan] (Jap., Hyosaisen, 1107–53), a lay disciple of Zen master Dahui Zonggao [Ta-hui Tsung-kao] (Jap. Daie Soko, 1089–1163).

19. See Dogen's *Bendowa*, trans. Norman Waddell and Masao Abe, *The Eastern Buddhist* 4, no. 1 (1971): 149–50.

20. Xiangyan Zhixian [Hsiang-yen Chih-hsien] (Jap., Kyogen Chi-kan, ninth century); Shishuang Chu-yuan [Shih-shuang Ch'u-yüan] (Jap., Sekiso Soen, 986–1039); Caoshan Benji [Ts'ao-shan Pen-chi] (Jap., Sozan Honjaku, 840–901).

21. Quotations from Case Two of the *Blue Cliff Record* are from

D. T. Suzuki's translation published in *The Eastern Buddhist* n.s., 1, no. 2 (September 1966): 12–20.

22. Xuedou Chongxian, or Hsüeh-tou Ch'ung-hsien (Jap., Setcho Juken, 980–1052).

CHAPTER 23

1. *Sensei*, the Japanese term for "teacher" or "master" in a discipline, is also used to address a university professor. As I feel it would be too formal to employ a title such as Doctor or Professor in referring to D. T. Suzuki in this context, and at the same time somehow insufficiently respectful were I to use no title at all, I will take the liberty of retaining the term *Sensei* here. I have also employed this term in reference to another teacher of mine,

Shin'ichi Hisamatsu. The association of the names of these two men with the word *Sensei* has become so familiar to me over the course of the years that no other word would fully express my feelings of affection and respect for them.

2. *San*, another common Japanese honorific title, has a broader application than *Sensei*. It can be used without reference to the person's gender or marital status, and it may be used to address both the senior and junior (in terms of social status), or older and younger, parties to a conversation.

3. Daisetz T. Suzuki, *Bukkyo no Taii*, (Kyoto: Hozokan, 1947, and Tokyo: Shunjusha, 1952). Suzuki's English translation of this work, *The Essence of Buddhism*, was published by The Buddhist Society, London, 1947.

Bibliography

This bibliography is complied from the bibliography that appeared in the memorial issue for D.T. Suzuki of *The Eastern Buddhist* (vol. 2, no. 1), and *Suzuki Daisetz Zenshu* (vol. 30). It also includes posthumous publications in book form, as well as articles that appeared in *The Eastern Buddhist*.

BOOKS

1895   佛陀の福音 *Butsuda no Fukuin* (The Gospel of Buddha). A Japanese translation of *The Gospel of Buddha* by Paul Carus. Tokyo: Morie Shoten.

1896   新宗教論 *Shin Shūkyō Ron* (A New Interpretation of Religion). Kyoto: Baiyō Shoin.

1898   *Lao-Tze's Tao-Teh King.* Translated in collaboration with Paul Carus. Chicago: The Open Court Publishing Co.

1900   靜坐のすすめ *Seiza no Susume* (An Invitation to Sitting). Written in collaboration with Shaku Sōen. Tokyo: Kōyūkan.

   Açvaghosha's Discourse on the Awakening of Faith in the Mahayana. A translation from the Chinese. Chicago: The Open Court Publishing Company.

1906   阿彌陀佛 *Amida Butsu.* A translation of *Amitabha* by Paul Carus. Tokyo: Heigosha.

   Sermons of a Buddhist Abbot. Translated from the Japanese manuscript of Shaku Sōen. Chicago: The Open Court Publishing Company.

T'ai-Shang Kan-Ying P'ien. Translated from the Chinese in collaboration with Paul Carus. Chicago: The Open Court Publishing Company.

Yin Chin Wen. Translated from the Chinese in collaboration with Paul Carus. Chicago: The Open Court Publishing Company.

1907   *Outlines of Mahayana Buddhism*. London: Luzac and Company; Chicago: The Open Court Publishing Company, 1908; New York: Schocken Books Inc., 1963.

1910   天界と地獄 *Tengai to Jigoku* (Heaven and Hell). A Japanese translation of *Heaven and Hell* by Emanuel Swedenborg. London: The Swedenborg Society; Tokyo: Yūrakusha.

1911   *The Life of the Shonin Shinran*. Translated in collaboration with Gessho Sasaki. Tokyo: The Buddhist Text Translation Society.

1913   スウェンボルグ *Suwedenborugu* (Swedenborg). Tokyo: Heigosha.

        禪學大要 *Zengaku Taiyō* (Outlines of Zen). Tokyo: Kōyūkan.

1914   新エレサレムとその教説 *Shin Eresaremu to Sono Kyōsetsu* (New Jerusalem and Its Doctrine). A Japanese translation of *The New Jerusalem* by Emanuel Swedenborg. London: The Swedenborg Society, 1912; Tokyo: Heigosha, 1914.

        神智と神愛 *Shinchi to Shin'ai* (Divine Wisdom and Divine Love). A Japanese translation of *The Divine Love and the Divine Wisdom* by Emanuel Swedenborg. London: The Swedenborg Society, 1912; Tokyo: Heigosha, 1914.

        禪の第一義 *Zen no Dai Ichigi* (Essence of Zen). Tokyo: Meiji Shoin; Heigosha, 1934, 1963 (世界教養全集 Series, pp. 359–476).

        A Brief History of Early Chinese Philosophy. London: Probsthain & Co.

1915   向上の鐵槌 *Kōjō no Tettsui* (The Incomparable Iron Hammer). Tokyo: Kōseikan Shoten.

        神慮論 *Shinryo Ron* (The Divine Providence). A Japanese translation of *The Divine Providence* by Emanuel Swedenborg. London: The Swedenborg Society, 1912; Tokyo: Heigosha, 1915.

1916   禪の研究 *Zen no Kenkyū* (Studies in Zen). Tokyo: Heigosha; Meiji Shoin, 1934.

        禪の立場から *Zen no Tachiba Kara* (From the Standpoint of Zen). Tokyo: Kōyūkan.

1921–   *The Eastern Buddhist* (May 1921–July 1939). A quarterly magazine
1939   devoted to the exposition of Mahayana Buddhism. Kyoto: Eastern Buddhist Publishing Society.

1925   百醜千拙 *Hyaku Shū Sen Setsu* (Hundred Uglinesses). Kyoto: Chūgai Shuppansha.

1927   随筆・禅 *Zuihitsu: Zen* (Zen: Short Essays). Tokyo: Daiyūkaku.

Essays in Zen Buddhism, First Series. London: Luzac and Company; Rider and Company, 1949, 1958; New York: Harper & Brothers, 1949, Grove Press, Inc., 1961; *Essais sur le Bouddhisme Zen. Premier volume* and *Deuxième volume*. Translated by Pierre Sauvageot and René Daumal. Neûchatel: Delachaux et Niestlé, 1941, 1944; Jean Herbert, Paris: Editions Albin Michel, 1940, 1943.

1929   *In Memoriam Emma Erskine Lasse Hahn*. Edited and published by D.T. Suzuki in Tokyo.

1930   *Studies in the Lankavatara Sutra*. London: George Routledge & Sons, Ltd., 1930, 1957.

宗教經驗に就きて *Shūkyō Keiken ni Tsukite* (On Religious Experience). Coauthor with Daiei Kaneko. Tokyo: Hakudōsha.

禅とは何ぞや *Zen to wa Nanzoya* (What is Zen?). Tokyo: Daiyūkaku; Daizō Shuppansha, 1946 (retitled *Zen to wa Nanika*); Sōgensha, 1953; Kadokawa Shobō, 1954; Shunjūsha, 1962.

1932   *The Lankavatara Sutra*. A translation from the original Sanskrit. London: George Routledge & Sons, Ltd., 1932, 1956, 1959.

燉煌出土荷澤神會禪師語錄 *Tonkō Shutsudo Kataku Jinne Zenji Goroku*. A facsimile reproduction of the Dunhuang manuscript of *The Sayings of Zen Master Jinne*. Private Circulation.

1933   *Essays in Zen Buddhism, Second Series*. London: Luzac and Company; Rider and Company, 1950, 1958; *Essais sur le Bouddhisme Zen, Troisième volume*, and *Quatrième volume*. Translated by René-Daumal. Neûchatel: Delachaux et Niestlé, 1944, 1946. *Der Wege zur Erleuchtung*, 1957. Translated by Fritz Kraus. Baden-Baden: Holle-Verlag, 1957.

An Index to the Lankavatara Sutra. With the Chinese and Tibetan equivalents. Kyoto: The Eastern Buddhist Society.

興聖寺本六祖檀經 *Kōshōji Bon Rokuso Dangyō*. A facsimile reproduction of the Kōshō temple edition of Sixth Patriarch's *Platform Sutra*. With commentary. Private Circulation.

1934   *Essays in Zen Buddhism, Third Series*. London: Luzac and Company; Rider and Company, 1953, 1958.

An Introduction to Zen Buddhism. Kyoto: The Eastern Buddhist Society. Republished with Foreword by C. G. Jung, London: Rider and Company, 1948; Arrow Books Ltd., 1959; *Die Grosse Befreiung, Einführung in den Zen-Buddhismus*. Translated by Felix

Schottlaender, Leipzig; Curt Weller & Co., 1939, 1947; Zurich, Rascher Verlag, 1958. *Introducion Al Budismo Zen*. Translated by William B. Moens. Buenos Aires: Ediciones Mundonuevo, 1960. Translated by Murile Nunes de Azevedo. Rio de Janeiro: Editora Civilizacão Brasileira, 1961.

The Training of the Zen Buddhist Monk. Kyoto: The Eastern Buddhist Society; New York: University Books, 1959.

An Index to the Lankavatara Sutra. Sanskrit-Chinese-Tibetan, Chinese-Sanskrit, and Tibetan-Sanskrit. Second, revised and enlarged edition. Kyoto. The Sanskrit Buddhist Texts Publishing Society.

The Gandavyuha Sutra (Four Parts). Critically edited with H. Idzumi. Kyoto: The Sanskrit Buddhist Text Publishing Society, 1934-36.

燉煌出土荷澤神會禪師語錄 *Tonkō Shutsudo Kataku Jinne Zenji Goroku* 燉煌出土六祖檀經 *Tonkō Shutsudo Rokuso Dangyō* 興聖寺本六祖檀經 *Kōshōji Bon Rokuso Dangyō*. Dunhuang manuscripts of *The Sayings of Jinne* and the Sixth Patriarch's *Platform Sutra*, Kōshō temple edition of the *Platform Sutra* critically edited and annotated in collaboration with Rentarō Kōda. Tokyo: Morie Shoten.

支那佛教印象記 *Shina Bukkyō Inshō Ki* (Impressions of Chinese Buddhism) Tokyo: Morie Shoten. 中國佛教印象記 (中國語譯) 張茂吉譯私家版 1936

1935   *Manual of Zen Buddhism*. Kyoto: The Eastern Buddhist Society; London: Rider and Company, 1950, 1956; New York: Grove Press Inc., 1960.

悟道禪 *Godō Zen* (Zen Enlightenment). Tokyo: Daiyūkaku.

少室逸書 *Shōshitsu Issho*. A facsimile reproduction of the Dunhuang manuscript ascribed to Bodhidharma. Private Circulation.

禪と日本人の氣質 *Zen to Nihonjin no Kishitsu* (Zen and Japanese Characteristics). Tokyo: Nihon Bunka Kyōkai.

1936   *Buddhist Philosophy and Its Effects on the Life and Thought of the Japanese People*. Tokyo: Kokusai Bunka Shinkōkai; revised and enlarged edition entitled *Buddhism in the Life and Thought of Japan*. The Buddhist Lodge, 1937.

校刊少室逸書及解説 *Kōkan Shōshitsu Issho Oyobi Kaisetsu*. Manuscripts ascribed to Bodhidharma and others, critically edited and annotated in Japanese. Osaka: Ataka Bukkyō Bunko.

1937   少し「宗教」を説く *Sukoshi Shūkyō o Toku.* (Talks on Religion). Tokyo: Kōyūkan.

禪と念佛の心理學的基礎 *Zen to Nembutsu no Shinrigakuteki Kiso* (Psychological Foundations of Zen and Nembutsu) Tokyo: Daitō Shuppansha.

1938 *Zen Buddhism and Its Influence on Japanese Culture.* Kyoto: The Eastern Buddhist Society; *Zen und die Kultur Japans.* Translated by Otto Fischer, Stuttgart: Deutsche Verlags-Anstalt, 1941.

禅の諸問題 *Zen no Shomondai* (The Problems of Zen). Tokyo: Daitō Shuppansha, 1938, 1941; Shunjūsha, 1956, 1961.

Japanese Buddhism. Tokyo: Board of Tourist Industry.

1939 無心といふこと *Mushin to iu Koto* (On "No-mind"). Tokyo: Daitō Shuppansha; Sōgensha, 1951; Shunjūsha, 1952, 1961; Kadokawa Shoten, 1955; Heibonsha, 1960 (世界教養全集 series, pp. 193–337).

1940 禅堂の教育 *Zendō no Kyōiku* (Training in the Zen Monastery). Tokyo: Sanyūsha.

禅學入門 *Zengaku Nyūmon* (Introduction to the Studies of Zen). Tokyo: Daitō Shuppansha.

禅と日本文化 *Zen to Nihonbunka* (Zen and Japanese Culture). Translated by Kitagawa Momoo. Tokyo: Iwanami Shoten.

韶州曹溪山六祖師壇經 *Inshū Sōkeizan Rokusoshi Dangyō.* The Daijō temple edition of Sixth Patriarch's *Platform Sutra* critically edited and annotated. With an index. Kyoto: Bonbun Butten Kankō-kai; Tokyo: Iwanami Shoten, 1942.

盤珪の不生禅 *Bankei no Fushō Zen* (Bankei on the "Unborn"). Tokyo: Kōbundō; Shunjūsha, 1952, 1961.

1941 禅への道 *Zen e no Michi* (The Way to Zen). Tokyo: Yūzankaku.

禅の見方と行ひ方 *Zen no Mikata to Okonai Kata* (Zen View and Zen Practice). Tokyo: Daitō Shuppansha; Shunjūsha (retitled *Zen no Mikata, Zen no Shugyō*), 1962.

禅問答と悟り *Zen Mondō to Satori* (Zen "Question and Answer" and Enlightenment). Tokyo: Kondō Shoten; Shunjūsha, 1952, 1960, 1961.

一眞實の世界 *Ichi Shinjitsu no Sekai* (The World of the Absolute). Tokyo: Kondō Shoten; Shunjūsha, 1952, 1960 (retitled *Zen no Sekai*), 1961.

盤珪禅師語録 *Bankei Zenji Goroku* (Sayings of Bankei). Edited and annotated. Tokyo: Iwanami Shoten.

佛教の核心 *Bukkyō no Kakushin* (The Heart of Buddhism). Kyoto: Kendō Shoin.

1942 淨土系思想論 *Jōdokei Shisō Ron* (Studies in the Pure Land Thought). Kyoto: Hōzōkan; Tokyo: Shunjūsha, 1954, 1961.

東洋的一 *Tōyōteki Ichi* (The Oriental "One"). Tokyo: Daitō Shuppansha.

盤珪禪の研究 *Bankei Zen no Kenkyū* (Studies on Bankei's Zen). Edited in collaboration with Shōkin Furuta. Tokyo: Sankibō Busshorin.

續禪と日本文化 *Zoku Zen to Nihonbunka* (Zen and Japanese Culture, second series). Translated by Kitagawa Momoo. Tokyo: Iwanami Shoten.

佛果碧巖破關擊節 (上下二冊) *Bukka Hekigan Hakan Gekisetsu.* Collection of critical examinations of 100 Zen "cases." Thirteenth-century manuscripts, critically edited and annotated. In two volumes. Tokyo: Iwanami Shoten.

1943   文化と宗教 *Bunka to Shūkyō* (Culture and Religion). Nagoya: Shindō Kaikan; Tokyo: Shimizu Shoten, 1947; Shunjūsha, 1953, 1961.

一禪者の思索 *Ichi Zensha no Shisaku* (The Thought of a Zen Buddhist). Tokyo: Ichijō Shobō; Sōgensha (vol. 14, *Gendai Zuihitsu Zenshū* series), 1954.

宗教經驗の事實 *Shūkyō Keiken no Jijitsu* (Facts of Religious Experience). Tokyo: Daitō Shuppansha; Shunjūsha, 1952, 1961.

禪思想史研究第一 *Zen Shisō Shi Kenkyū, I* (Studies in the History of Zen Thought, Vol. I) Tokyo: Iwanami Shoten.

禪の思想 *Zen no Shisō* (A Glimpse into Zen Thought). Tokyo: Nihon Hyōronsha; Shimizu Shoten, 1948; Shunjūsha, 1952, 1960, 1961.

禪百題 *Zen Hyaku Dai* (One Hundred Short Articles on Zen) Tokyo: Daitō Shuppansha; Shunjūsha, 1953, 1960, 1961.

盤珪禪師說法 *Bankei Zenji Seppō* (Sermons of Bankei). Edited in collaboration with Shōkin Furuta. Tokyo: Daitō Shuppansha.

拔隊禪師法語 *Bassui Zenji Hōgo* (Sermons of Bassui). Critically edited in collaboration with Shōkin Furuta. Private Circulation.

1944   日本的靈性 *Nihonteki Reisei* (Japanese Spirituality). Tokyo: Daitō Shuppansha; Shunjūsha, 1952, 1961.

大燈百二十則 *Daitō Hyakunijussoku* (One Hundred and Twenty Cases by Daitō). Text critically edited. Tokyo: Daitō Shuppansha.

月菴和尙法語 *Gettan Oshō Hōgo* (Sermons of Gettan). Edited in collaboration with Shōkin Furuta. Tokyo: Daitō Shuppansha.

1945   絕觀論 *Zekkan Ron* (An Essay on Transcendental Insights). Edited in collaboration with Shōkin Furuta. Tokyo: Kōbundō.

1946   *The Cultural East* (Journal). Joint editor with R. H. Blyth. Discontinued after two issues, July 1946 and August 1947. Kita Kamakura: The Culture of the East Society.

日本的靈性的自覺 *Nihonteki Reiseiteki Jikaku* (The Awakening of Japanese Spirituality). Kyoto: Ōtani Kyōgaku Kenkyūsho.

靈性的日本の建設 *Reiseiteki Nihon no Kensetsu* (The Building up of

Spiritual Japan). Tokyo: Daitō Shuppansha; Shunjūsha, 1953, 1961.

今北洪川 *Imagita Kōsen* (A Biography of Imagita Kōsen). Tokyo: Yūzankaku; Shunjūsha, 1963.

宗教について *Shūkyō ni Tsuite* (On Religion). A round-table talk with R. Mutai, K. Yanagida. Tokyo: Daitō Shuppansha.

宗教的信について *Shūkyōteki Shin ni Tsuite* (On Religious Faith). A round-table talk with S. Ono, R. Mutai, T. Shimomura. Tokyo: Daitō Shuppansha.

1947   *The Essence of Buddhism*. Translated by the author from the Imperial Lectures, *Bukkyō no Taii*. London: The Buddhist Society. Enlarged and revised edition, 1947, 1957; Kyoto: Hōzōkan, 1948; *L'essence du Bouddhisme*. Translated by Ivo Rens. Paris: Le Cercle du Livre, 1955.

佛教の大意 *Bukkyō no Taii* (Essence of Buddhism). Kyoto: Hōzōkan Tokyo: Shunjūsha, 1952, 1961.

日本の靈性化 *Nihon no Reiseika* (Spiritualizing Japan). Kyoto: Hōzōkan; Tokyo: Tenchisha, 1948.

神秘主義と禪 *Shimpi Shugi to Zen* (Mysticism and Zen). Tokyo: Taishōsha.

自主的に考へる *Jishuteki ni Kangaeru* (Self-reliance). Tokyo: Hidaka Shobō; Shunjūsha, 1952, 1961.

宗教と生活 *Shūkyō to Seikatsu* (Religion and Daily Life). Tokyo: Daizō Shuppansha; Shunjūsha, 1953, 1961.

1948   妙好人 *Myōkōnin* (The Wondrously Excellent Ones). Kyoto; Ōtani Shuppansha; Tokyo: Shunjūsha, 1952, 1961.

東洋と西洋 *Tōyō to Seiyō* (East and West). Tōkyō: Tōri Shoin; Shunjūsha (retitled *Shūkyō Ron Zoku Shū*), 1954, 1961.

宗教と近代人 *Shūkyō to Kindai Jin* (Religion and Modern Man). Tokyo: Tōri Shoin; Shunjūsha (retitled *Shūkyō Ron Zokū Shu*), 1954, 1961.

禪一撥 *Zen Issatsu* (Tidbits of Zen). Tokyo: Ryōginsha; Shunjūsha, 1953, 1961.

宗教と文化 *Shūkyō to Bunka* (Religion and Culture). Kyoto: Bukkyō Bunka Kyōkai.

青年に與ふ *Seinen ni Atau* (Dedicated to the Youth). Tokyo: Kōbundō; Shunjūsha, 1952, 1961.

驢鞍橋 *Roankyō* (On the "Donkey's Saddle"). Work by Shōsan Suzuki, critically edited and annotated. Tokyo: Iwanami Shoten.

242 BIBLIOGRAPHY

禪堂生活 *Zendō Seikatsu* (The Life in a Zen Meditation Hall) Tokyo: Daizō Shuppansha.

科學と宗教 *Kagaku to Shūkyō* (Science and Religion). A round-table talk with Y. Nishina, T. Shimomura, K. Nishitani. Tokyo: Kōbundō (Atene Bunko 25),

1949   *The Zen Doctrine of No-Mind. The Significance of the Sutra of Hui-Neng.* London: Rider and Company; *Le non-mental selon la pensée Zen.* Translated by Hubert Benoit. Paris: Le Cercle du Livre, 1952; *Die Zen-Lehre vom Nicht-Bewusstseim.* Translated by Emma von Pelet. Munich: Otto-Wilhelm-Barth-Verlag, 1957.

Living by Zen. Tokyo: Sanseido; London: Rider and Company, 1950; *Leben aus Zen.* Translated by Ursula von Mangoldt. Munich: Otto-Wilhelm-Barth-Verlag, 1955.) 禪による生活 *Zen ni yoru Seikatsu.* Translated by Momoo Kitagawa and Sōhaku Kobori. Tokyo: Shunjūsha, 1957, 1960.

A Miscellany on the Shin Teaching of Buddhism. Kyoto: Higashi-hongwanji.

佛教とキリスト教 *Bukkyō to Kirisutokyō* (Buddhism and Christianity). Kyoto: Hōzōkan; Tokyo: Shūnjusha (see under *Shūkyo Rōn Shū*), 1952, 1961.

臨濟の基本思想 *Rinzai no Kihon Shisō* (The Fundamental Thought of Rinzai). Tokyo: Chūōkōronsha; Shunjūsha, 1953, 1961.

1951   禪思想史研究第二 *Zen Shisōshi Kenkyū, II* (Studies in the History of Zen Thought, Vol. II). Tokyo: Iwanami Shoten.

1952   宗教入門 *Shūkyō Nyūmon* (An Introduction to Religion). Tokyo: Kōbundō.

宗教論集 *Shūkyō Ronshū* (A Collection of Essays on Religion). Edited by Shōkin Furuta. Tokyo: Shunjūsha.

1954   よみがえる東洋 *Yomigaeru Tōyō* (The Revival of the East). Tokyo: Yomiuri Shimbunsha.

宗教 *Shūkyō* (Religion). Edited papers by contemporary authors on various world religions. Tokyo: Mainichi Shimbunsha.

1955   *Studies in Zen.* London: Rider and Company; New York: Philosophical Library, 1955; (禪の研究 *Zen no Kenkyū.* Translated by Sōhaku Kobori. Tokyo: Shunjūsha, 1959)

1956   *Zen Buddhism.* Selected writings of D. T. Suzuki edited by William Barrett. New York: Doubleday and Company, Inc.; London: Hutchinson & Co., 1962.

1957   *Mysticism: Christian and Buddhist.* New York: Harper & Brothers;

Collier Books, 1962; London: Allen and Unwin, Ltd.; *Der Westliche und der Östliche Weg*. Edited by Ruth Nanda Anshen. Translated by Liselotte and Walter Hilsbescher. Frankfurt: Ullstein Taschenbücher-Verlag.

1958   *Zen and Japanese Buddhism*. Revised and enlarged edition of *Japanese Buddhism* (1938). Tokyo: Japan Travel Bureau.

宗教と現代生活 *Shūkyō to Gendai Seikatsu*. (Religion and Modern Life). Tokyo: Shunjūsha, 1958, 1961.

1959   *Zen and Japanese Culture* (Bollingen Series, vol. 66). Revised and enlarged edition of *Zen Buddhism and Its Influence on Japanese Culture* (1938). New York: Pantheon Books, Inc.; London: Routledge and Kegan Paul.

鈴木大拙集 *Suzuki Daisetsu Shū*. Selected writings of D. T. Suzuki edited by Ryūmin Akizuki. Tokyo: Nihon Shobō (Gendai Chisei Zenshū Series, vol. 29).

1960   *Zen Buddhism and Psychoanalysis*. In collaboration with Erich Fromm and Richard DeMartino. New York: Harper & Borthers; London: Allen and Unwin, Ltd., 1960; New York: Grove Press, Inc., 1963; Belgrade; Nolit, 1964.

The Sengai Calendar 1960–67. Translation with commentary on the ink drawings of Zen master Sengai. Tokyo: Idemitsu Kōsan, Co., Ltd.

1961   Catalogue to the Sengai Exhibition (November 1961–July 1964) Tokyo: Kokusai Bunka Shinkōkai.

1962   *The Essentials of Zen Buddhism*. Selected writings of D. T. Suzuki edited by Bernard Phillips. New York: E. P. Dutton & Co., Inc.

1963   東洋的な見方 *Tōyōteki na Mikata* (The Oriental Outlook). Tokyo: Shunjūsha.

1964   趙州禪師語錄 *Jōshū Zenji Goroku* (Sayings of Jōshū). The original Chinese text critically edited and annotated in Japanese. In collaboration with Ryūmin Akizuki. Kamakura: Matsugaoka Bunko.

親鸞の世界 *Shinran no Sekai* (The World of Shinran). Coauthor with Ryōjin Soga, Daiei Kaneko, Keiji Nishitani. Kyoto: Higashi Hongwanji Shuppanbu.

1965   東洋の心 *Tōyō no Kokoro* (The Mind) of the East. Tokyo: Shunjūsha.

1966   大拙つれづれ草 *Daisetsu Tsurezuregusa* (Gleanings from Daisetz). Tokyo: Yomiuri Shimbunsha.

1967   人間いかに生くべきか *Ningen Ikani Iku Bekika* (How Ought We to

Live?). Records of conversation with Kōson Fukuda, E. O. Reischauer, H. Dumoulin, *et al*. Tokyo: Shakai Shisōsha.

妙好人浅原才市集 *Myōkōnin Asahara Saichi Shū* (Collection of Verses by Saichi). Tokyo: Shunjūsha.

1968   鈴木大拙全集 *Suzuki Daisetz Zenshū* (Collected Works of Suzuki Daisetz) Thirty-two volumes. Tokyo: Iwanami Shoten 1968-70.

1969   *The Field of Zen*. London: The Buddhist Society.

1970   *Shin Buddhism*. New York: Harper & Row, Publishers, Inc.

1971   *What is Zen?* London: The Buddhist Society.

1973   *Sengai, The Zen Master*. London: Faber & Faber. *The Kyōgyōshin-shō*—The Collection of Passages Expounding the True Teaching, Living, Faith, and Realization of Pure Land. Kyoto: Shinshū Ōtaniha. *Collected Writings in Shin Buddhism*. Kyoto: Shinshū Ōtaniha.

ESSAYS IN *The Eastern Buddhist*

OLD SERIES

1921   "Zen Buddhism as Purifier and Liberation of Life." 1, (no. 1). "The Avatamsaka Sutra, epitomized." (Parts 1–4) 1 (no. 1–4). "The Buddha in Mahayana Buddhism." 1 (no. 2). "The Revelation of a New Truth in Zen Buddhism." 1 (no. 3). "Notes on the Avatamsaka Sutra." 1 (no. 3). "Why do We Fight?" 1 (no. 4).

1922   "Some Aspects of Zen Buddhism." 1 (no. 5–6). "The Meditation Hall and Ideals of the Monkish Discipline" 2 (no. 1–2).

1923   "The Psychological School of Mahayana Buddhism." 2 (no. 3–4). "The Ten Cow-herding Pictures." 2 (no. 3–4). "The Life of Shinran Shonin by Kakunyo Shonin." Translated by D. T. Suzuki. 2 (no. 5). "Zen Buddhism as Chinese Interpretation of the Doctrine of Enlightenment." 2 (no. 6).

1924   "Enlightenment and Ignorance." 3 (no. 1). "Sayings of a Modern Tariki Mystic." 3 (no. 2). "Zen Buddhism on Immorality: Extract from 'The Hekiganshu,' Translated by D. T. Suzuki. 3 (no. 3). (1924–25).

1925   "The Development of the Pure Land Doctrine in Buddhism." 3 (no. 4).

1926   "The Secret Message of Bodhi-Dharma, or the Content of Zen Buddhism." 4 (no. 1).

1927   "Zen and Jodo, Two Types of Buddhist Experience." 4 (no. 2)

"The Lankavatara Sutra, as a Mahayana Text in Especial Relation to the Teaching of Zen Buddhism." 4 (no. 3–4) (1927–28).

1929   "An Introduction to the Study of the Lankavatara Sutra." 5 (no. 1).

1930   "Passivity in the Buddhist Life." 5 (no. 2–3).

1931   "What is Zen?" 5 (no. 4).

1932   "Mahayana and Hinayana Buddhism, or the Bodhisattva-ideal and the Sravaka-ideal, as Distinguished in the Opening Chapter of the Gandavyuha." 6 (no. 1). "Buddhist, Especially Zen, Contributions to Japanese Culture." 6 (no. 2).

1934   "Gensha on Three Invalids." 6 (no. 3).

1935   "Impressions of Chinese Buddhism." 6 (no. 4).

1936   "Zen and the Japanese Love of Nature." 7 (no. 1).

1939   "The Shin Sect of Buddhism." 7 (no. 3–4). "Tract on Steadily Holding to 'the Faith' (執持抄)." Translated by D. T. Suzuki. 7 (no. 3–4).

1949   "Buddhism and Education." 8 (no. 1).

1951   "The Myōkōnin (妙好人)." 8 (no. 2).

NEW SERIES

1965   "On the *Hekigan Roku*" (The Blue Cliff Record). With a translation of Case 1. 1 (no. 1).

1966   "The *Hekigan Roku*—Case 2." 1 (no. 2).

1970   "Self the Unattainable." 3 (no. 2).

1971   "What is the 'I'?" 4 (no. 1). "Infinite Light." 4 (no. 2).

1972   "The Seer and the Seen." 5 (no. 1). "What is Shin Buddhism?" 5 (no. 2).

1973   "A Preface to the *Kyōgyōshinshō*" (Unfinished). 6 (no. 1) "Ummon on Time." 6 (no. 2).

1974   "Zen Buddhism and a Common Sense World." 7 (no. 2). "The Buddhist Conception of Reality." 7 (no. 2).

1975   "Zen and Psychology." 8 (no. 1). "Reality is Art." 8 (no. 2).

1976   "Dōgen, Hakuin, Bankei: Three Types of Thought in Japanese Zen." Part 1, 9 (no. 1); Part 2, 9 (no. 1).

1978   "Zen Hyakudai 'One Hundred Zen Topics'." 11 (no. 1), and "Zen Hyakudai 'One Hundred Zen Topics'." 11 (no. 2).

1980   "Zen Hyakudai 'One Hundred Zen Topics'." 13 (no. 1). "Thoughts on Shin Buddhism." Part 1, 13 (no. 2).

1981   "Thoughts on Shin Buddhism." Part 2, 14 (no. 1). Thoughts on Shin Buddhism." Conclusion, 14 (no. 2).

1982   "What is Zen?" 15 (no. 1). "Talks on Buddhism." Part 1, 15 (no. 2).
1983   "Talks on Buddhism: Buddhism and Christianity." Part 2, 16 (no. 2).
1984   "Transmigration." 17 (no. 2).
1985   "Shin Buddhism." Part 1, 18 (no. 1). "Shin Buddhism." Part 2, 18 (no. 2).

Contributors

Masao Abe 阿部正雄	Margaret Gest Professor of Religion, Haverford College, Pennsylvania. Although a disciple of Shin'-ichi Hisamatsu and Keiji Nishitani, he was closely acquainted with D. T. Suzuki, especially in the last ten years of Dr. Suzuki's life. A leading Japanese Buddhist thinker, he is the author of the recently published *Zen and Western Thought* (1985).
Robert Aitken	A Zen master (*roshi*) of Diamond Sangha, Honolulu, Hawaii, Mr. Aitken was a longtime friend of D. T. Suzuki. He is the author of many books, including *A Zen Wave*, a translation and interpretation of the great Japanese haiku poet Matsuo Basho.
Ernst Benz	Professor of Church History and Historical Theology, University of Marburg, West Germany. He was personally associated with Dr. Suzuki in his later years.
Richard DeMartino	Professor of Religion, Temple University. As a private student of D. T. Suzuki from 1947 until Suzuki's death in 1966, Mr. DeMartino was the Westerner considered to have had the closest personal acquaintance with D.T. Suzuki.

247

Larry A. Fader — Associate Professor of Religious Studies, University of Connecticut. He obtained his Ph.D. in the study of Suzuki at Temple University, and his work has concentrated particularly on Suzuki's early works and his influence on Western thinkers.

Erich Fromm — Psychoanalysist and social philosopher. He taught at several major universities in the United States, although he was teaching at the National University of Mexico when he organized the conference on Zen Buddhism and psychoanalysis in Cuernavaca in 1957. Fromm's writing is very well-known, and includes such famous works as *Psychoanalysis and Religion* (1951) and *The Art of Loving* (1956).

Shōkin Furuta
古田紹欽 — Professor Emeritus of the History of Buddhist Thought, Nihon University, Tokyo. A leading disciple of D. T. Suzuki since his student days, Mr. Furuta was Suzuki's assistant for a time, and much later, editor of Suzuki's *Complete Works* in Japanese (1968–70).

Luis O. Gomez — Professor, Department of Far Eastern Language and Literature, and Director, Collegiate Institute for the Study of Buddhist Literature, University of Michigan.

Wilhelm Gundert — Professor Emeritus, Hamburg University, West Germany. A specialist in Japanese studies at Hamburg University, he translated the *Bi-yan-lu* (*Hekigan Roku*, or Blue Cliff Record) into German, after personal encouragement from D. T. Suzuki.

Shin'ichi Hisamatsu
久松眞一 — Professor of Buddhism at Kyoto University, he was the founder of the FAS Zen Society. A leading disciple of Kitaro Nishida, he was also closely associated with D. T. Suzuki, who appreciated Hisamatsu's Zen thought and character.

Christmas Humphreys — Founder of the Buddhist Society in London. The author of numerous books on Buddhism and a great promoter of Zen Buddhism in the West, Mr. Humphreys championed D. T. Suzuki for many years; he published Suzuki's books in England, and sponsored many lectures on Zen thought.

Philip Kapleau
Chief court reporter for the International Military Tribunal at Nuremburg, he came to Japan for the war-crimes trials in Tokyo. His Buddhist studies began under Suzuki at Columbia University and were followed by a long period of intensive study of Zen Buddhism in Japan. His accomplishments in Zen were formally recognized in 1964, when he was ordained a Zen priest by famous Zen master Yasutani Roshi. Author of *Three Pillars of Zen* (1965) he is now a *roshi* at the Rochester Zen Center, Rochester, New York.

Akihisa Kondō
近藤章久
Psychiatrist, Tokyo. His studies with D. T. Suzuki and Karen Horney in the mid-1950s led him to develop a Zen-oriented psychiatric approach in his work.

Thomas Merton
Member of the Trappist order in Kentucky, Fr. Merton was an influential writer and poet who was deeply interested in Oriental thought, especially Zen. Widely published, his dialogue with D. T. Suzuki appears in *Zen and the Birds of Appetite* (1968).

Keiji Nishitani
西谷啓治
Professor Emeritus of Religion, Kyoto University, and another leading disciple of Kitaro Nishida, his work brought him into the sphere of D. T. Suzuki's influence for many years. A member of the prestigious Japan Academy, he is also the author of *Religion and Nothingness* (1982).

Mihoko Okamura
岡村美穂子
Private secretary and personal assistant to D. T. Suzuki for thirteen years, she was almost indispensable in Suzuki's last years, taking care of his personal welfare and aiding his academic activities. Miss Okamura, now Mihoko Bekku, still gives her time to the activities of *The Eastern Buddhist*.

Torataro Shimomura
下村寅太郎

Professor Emeritus of Philosophy, Gakushuin University, Tokyo. A prominent disciple of Kitaro Nishida and a close friend of Suzuki, he is a well-known scholar in the fields of philosophy of mathematics and Western philosophical history. A prolific author, his books include *Asshishi no Sei Furahshisu* (St. Francis of Assisi) (1965) and *Reonarudo da Vinchi* (Leonardo da Vinci) (1961).

Gary Snyder

Author of many publications, both prose and poetry, Mr. Snyder was closely associated with the Beat Generation and the intellectual movements in San Francisco in the 1950s. As he explains in his essay, reading Suzuki's *Essays in Zen Buddhism (First Series)* changed his life, and he has been involved with Zen ever since.

Alan Watts

Widely acknowledged as one of the most penetrating and readable interpreters of Eastern philosophy for the West, Watts' career was as varied as his interests. An Anglican priest, Watts was also an editor, professor, dean, and freelance author-lecturer. Strongly influenced by D. T. Suzuki, he specialized in Zen Buddhism and Daoism. His many publications include *The Way of Zen* (1955), now considered a classic work in the West.

The "weathermark" identifies this book as a production of John Weatherhill, Inc., publishers of fine books on Asia and the Pacific. Editorial supervision: Darina Williams. Book design and typography: Miriam F. Yamaguchi. Production supervision: Mitsuo Okado. Layout of the photographs: Yutaka Shimoji. Composition, printing, and binding: Korea Textbook Co., Seoul. The typeface used is Monotype Bembo.

Printed in the United States
by Baker & Taylor Publisher Services